LAW OF BANKING SERVICES

THE PRINCIPLES

A. Lewis

M.A. (T.C.D.), Barrister-At-Law

TUDOR

First published in Great Britain by Tudor Business Publishing Limited. Sole distributors worldwide, Hodder and Stoughton (Publishers) Ltd, Mill Road, Dunton Green, Sevenoaks, Kent, TN13 2XX.

British Library Cataloguing in Publication Data

Lewis, Arthur
  Law of banking services : the principles.
  1. Great Britain. Banking. Law
  I. Title
  344.10682

  ISBN 1–872807–20–8

Typeset by Deltatype Ltd, Ellesmere Port
Printed and bound by Billing & Sons Ltd, Worcester.

Cover design by Sharyn Troughton

LAW OF BANKING SERVICES

SERVICES

THE PRINCIPLES

Contents

Introduction

It is my hope that this book will be of assistance to students studying for the examinations of the Chartered Institute of Bankers, also that it may serve to refresh – and bring up to date – the memories of those who have taken and passed the examinations. Indeed the book should be of interest to anyone who is concerned with business law.

I have always believed that whenever possible, and convenient, original sources should be used. Thus I have, from time to time, included extracts from Statutes particularly the Bills of Exchange Act 1882 and the Cheques Act 1957.

Furthermore, and so as to make the book as useful as possible, I have commented on and attempted to explain actual documents currently in use and I have appended some examples in full. I have only been able to do this because of the assistance of the Royal Bank of Scotland plc, Barclays Bank PLC and National Westminster Bank plc, who of course retain the copyright in these documents. I much appreciate the assistance of these Banks in this matter.

To Betty – my wife.

Table of Cases

Table of Statutes

Chapter One

Banker and Customer

It is of the greatest importance to be able to define a banker and a customer because

1. a contract exists between a banker and his customer and it is necessary to know the rights and duties that attach to such a contract.
2. the bank will owe duties to the customer but not necessarily to third parties.
3. the bank may be protected in certain transactions such as collecting the proceeds of a cheque for a customer (S.4 Cheques Act 1957), or when paying a crossed cheque to another bank (Bills of Exchange Act 1882. S.60, S.79 and S.80).

What is a Bank?

There is no single entirely satisfactory definition of a bank but it is generally agreed that a bank:

1. must receive money on current or deposit accounts
2. collects the proceeds of cheques for its customers
3. pays cheques drawn by its customers on itself.

Furthermore a person who lends money as a business must be licensed – *Moneylenders Act 1902*, but this does not apply to a bank.

In *United Dominion Trust Ltd v Kirkwood (1966)* the plaintiff company lent £5,000 to Lonsdale Motors Ltd and in return Lonsdale accepted five bills of exchange, each for £1,000 drawn on it by the plaintiff company. These bills were indorsed by the defendant Mr Kirkwood. On presentation the bills were dishonoured. Lonsdale Motors went into liquidation and U.D.T. brought an action against Mr Kirkwood as indorser of the bills.

The only defence put forward was under the *Moneylenders Act 1900* which requires moneylenders to be licensed. S.6 states "The expression 'moneylender' in the Act shall include every person whose business is that of money lending – but shall not include – (d, any person bone fide carrying on the business of banking".

Mr Kirkwood's defence was that U.D.T. was an unregistered money lender and so could not recover.

Eventually the Court of Appeal, by a majority decision, decided that U.D.T. was a bank.

Lord Denning M.R. stated that although the current accounts were not the usual sort which are characteristic of a banking business there were other characteristics which went to make a banker – stability, soundness, and probity. The reputation of the plaintiff company was undoubted. Four of the big five banks considered the plaintiff company as a banker. They paid crossed cheques presented by the plaintiff company, and gave it clearing house facilities. They answered references regarding customers. On these grounds the Master of the Rolls found for the plaintiff company.

Harman LJ could not accept this view. The plaintiff company had no deposit accounts in the usual sense; it had only so-called "current accounts" of which the court had been shown only one. In his view the documents produced and the evidence given were not enough to show that the plaintiff company was bona fide carrying on the business of banking. Nor was the reputation of the plaintiff company enough, there must be performance behind the reputation. He found against the plaintiff company.

Diplock LJ thought that the relatively small number of current accounts included very few trading customers who used them for payment or collection in the usual sense. However, he accepted the evidence of the reputation which the plaintif company enjoyed in banking and commercial circles, although with considerable doubt.

Thus all three judges considered that United Dominion Trust lacked certain of the requirements that would have brought it within the exemptions stated in the Moneylender's Act as a person carrying on the business of banking. However Denning and Diplock LJJ held that the reputation of the company in banking circles saved it.

The *Banking Act 1979* was passed to provide the Bank of England with supervisory powers over financial institutions. The Bank has power to recognise banking institutions and controls advertisements inviting deposits and provides for the setting up the Deposit Protection Scheme.

An institution may gain recognition as a bank by an application under the Act. It must have assets equal to at least £5 million or £250,000 if it provides a specialised banking service.

Also it must have enjoyed for a responsible period of time a high reputation and standing in the financial community.

An institution, to be recognised as a bank, must provide a wide range of banking services such as

a.   current and deposit account facilities
b.   finance in the form of overdraft or loan facilities
c.   foreign exchange services for domestic or foreign customers
d.   finance through bills of exchange and promissory notes and
e.   financial advice for members of the public and corporate bodies.

If a bank provides specialised services it need only provide current, deposit and overdraft facilities, and one from c, d and e.

The Act of 1979 established a *Deposit Protection Scheme* which is run by a *Deposit Protection Board*. All recognised banks and financial institution must contribute to a fund so that if a bank or licensed institution becomes insolvent the Board will compensate every depositor in those institutions with an amount equal to three quarters of his protected deposit.

In October 1987 a new Act – the *Banking Act 1987* came into force and that Act repealed the 1979 Act. The *Banking Act 1987* provides that there shall be only one category of authorised institutions and that the words "bank", "banker" and "banking" can only be used by authorised institutions that meet the requirements laid down in the Act. The phrase "authorised institutions" includes organisations which are not banks and have never described themselves as such. It also includes organisations which are generally regarded as being concerned with banking transactions but have not described themselves as banks.

The Act provides that the words "bank" and "banker" may only be used if the deposit taking business has a paid-up capital of at least £5 million, unless it is exempt such as the National Savings bank and foreign banks.

What is a Customer?

A customer of a bank is a person who has applied to it to open a current or deposit account and whose application has been accepted.

Duration is not of the essence of the banker-customer relationship. A person whose money has been accepted by the banker on the understanding that he undertakes to honour cheques up to the amount standing to his credit is a customer of the bank irrespective of whether his connection is of short or long duration. In *Commissioners of Taxation v English, Scottish and Australian Bank Ltd (1920)*, the thief of a cheque paid it into the bank and then withdrew the proceeds within a matter of days. The bank claimed protection under the equivalent Australian provision to S.4 of the *Cheques Act 1957*. The court held that the bank had not been negligent and the thief was a customer although only for a few days. A similar English case is *Ladbroke v Todd (1914)*.

The relationship does not arise merely because the bank performs a review on a casual basis.

In *Great Western Railway Co v London and County Banking Co Ltd (1901)* the bank had, for 20 years, cashed cheques across the counter for Mr Huggins who had no account at the bank. The service was presumably as a favour to the local Authority who was the employer of Mr Huggins and who had an account at the bank. One day the bank cashed a cheque for Huggins which he had obtained by fraud from the Railway company. The bank, when sued by G.W.R., tried to claim protection because it had collected for a customer but the House of Lords held Huggins was not a customer as he did not have an account with the bank.

The formation of the banker-customer contract may be before the actual opening of the account and particularly if the service is of a more formal nature. The same reasoning might also apply when a person has a credit card but has not opened an account with the bank which issued it. In *Woods v Martins Bank Ltd (1959)* a person consulted a bank manager for advice as to the investment of certain money which at that time was in a building society. As a result of the advice which he received he authorised the banker to collect the money from the society, to make a certain investment with most of it, and to retain the balance of the proceeds to be dealt with as he should later direct. Unknown to the plaintiff the bank manager was being asked by his Head Office to reduce the size of the debt owed by the company in which he had suggested Mr Woods should make an investment. As a result of the manager's advice Mr Woods incurred a heavy loss and brought this action. Although the bank account was actually opened three weeks after the date when the advice was given, the court held that the relationship of banker and customer arose on the date of the authority to collect the money.

Since this case we now have *Hedley Byrne v Heller and Partners Ltd (1964)* which provides that in similar circumstances the bank would owe a duty of care to a person seeking advice irrespective of whether or not the relationship of banker and customer existed.

Savory (EB) and Co v Lloyds Bank Ltd (1932)
Lawrence LJ was not satisfied that the parties for whose accounts the cheques were collected were customers of the bank because their accounts were at branches of the bank other than those which actually took in the cheques.

This case did establish that there must exist some liaison between the branch which actually receives the credit and the branch where the account is held.

The deposit of a sum of money by a foreign bank with an English bank, with instructions that it be transferred to another foreign bank, does not, without more, make the person at whose request the transfer is made, a customer of the English bank. *Aschkenasy v Midland Bank Ltd (1934)*. Where an English bank acting as agent for a foreign bank habitually collected cheques drawn on other English banks and paid into the foreign bank by that bank's customers, the English bank so collecting a crossed cheque was held by the Court of Appeal to be collecting for a customer within S.4 *Cheques Act 1957*, and not to have been negligent although the cheque was marked "account payee only". Bankes LJ said "In this class of business, if collection of cheques was done between bank and bank it is impossible to contend that the bank for which the respondent was doing business was not in reference to that business the customer. *Importers Co Ltd v Westminster Bank Ltd (1927)*.

Incidents of banker-customer relationship

1.   It is based on contract for general purposes and in addition there may be special contracts such as borrowing or lending. The general contract arises the moment the bank agrees to accept the person as a "customer". It is not in written form and its precise limits are undefined.
2.   The relationship is that of debtor and creditor in relation to deposits with the additional obligation of honouring customers'

cheques when there is sufficient available credit balance. *Foley v Hill (1848)*.

3.   It follows that the banker is entitled to use his customer's money freely as his own. There is no trusteeship or fiduciary relationship between a banker and his customer. There is therefore no duty on the banker not to make secret profits.

4.   Where the customer's account is in credit, the banker is the debtor. But he is no ordinary debtor for he is under no duty to seek out the creditor (i.e. customer) and pay him. Instead, the customer must make a previous demand for payment. In *Joachimson* it was held that the banker's debt is not repayable without a previous demand by the customer. This demand is made when the customer draws a cheque upon his account. However the converse does not apply in the case of an overdraft. It appears from *Parr's Banking Co Ltd v Yates (1898)* that the period of limitation runs from the date of each advance. This ruling does not apply as far as a guarantor is concerned and normal banking practice requires that arrears are repayable on demand.

5.   In *Joachimson v Swiss Bank Corporation (1921)* Atkin LJ summarises the terms of the general contract as follows:

"The bank undertakes to receive money and collect bills for its customer's account. The proceeds so received are not to be held in trust for the customer but the bank borrows the proceeds and undertakes to repay them. The promise to repay is to repay at the branch of the bank where the account is kept, and during banking hours. It includes a promise to repay any part of the amount due, against the written order of the customer, addressed to the bank at the branch, and as such written orders may be outstanding in the ordinary course of business for two or three days, it is a term of the contract that the bank will not cease to do business with the customer except upon reasonable notice. The customer on his part, undertakes to exercise reasonable care in executing his written orders so as not to mislead the bank or to facilitate forgery."

In *Prosperity Ltd v Lloyds Bank Ltd (1923)* the court held that one month's notice to close an account was inadequate. The actual period of notice will depend on the circumstances of the case. It will probably be liberal if the account is in credit.

6.   A banker owes no duty to the public to open at any particular hour. He owes a duty only to his customer to transact business on the days his customers are used to, and at the customary hours.

7. Express terms in banker-customer relationship. There is no specific written or oral notification of the terms of the contract. In *Burnett v Westminster Bank Ltd (1965)* the bank maintained that it was the customer's duty to familiarise himself with any changes in procedure and to carry them out correctly. Mocatta J would have none of this. The banks introduced new systems for their own advantage and could not place the onus on an old customer who had had an account with the bank before the changes were introduced.

Burnett v Westminster Bank Ltd (1965)
Plaintiff had two accounts with the bank at its Borough and Bromley branches. The Borough branch was "computerised" and had issued to plaintiff a book of MICR cheques. Plaintiff used a cheque from his Borough book, but wishing to have the amount debited to his Bromley account, altered the name of the branch in ink. Later he stopped payment of the cheque, advising this to the Bromley branch by telephone and confirming in writing.

Information of this stop was not passed on to the Borough branch, so that when the computer in due course directed the cheque there, it was paid.

The plaintiff's case was the simple assertion that his instructions had not been followed, with the result that his money had been paid away without his authority and contrary to the terms of the banking contract.

The bank claimed that the instructions on the cheque book cover telling customers that no alteration could be made amounted to a sufficient notification that the terms of the contract had been varied.

Held: such a notification did not sufficiently direct the attention of the customer, who had been in account at Borough before the branch went on to the computer, to the change in procedure.

8. *Duty of Confidentiality*
Tournier v National Provincial and Union Bank of England Ltd (1924) established that:
1. The banker is under a duty not to disclose any information about the state of accounts of his customer or any transactions. This duty is a legal one and arises out of contract.
2. The duty of secrecy is, however, subject to the following exceptions.

a.   Disclosure under compulsion of law: e.g., under S.7 of the *Bankers' Books Evidence Act 1879,* bankers can be compelled to produce copies of banking accounts in court. Further, under the *Taxes Management Act 1970* bankers are obliged to disclose to the Inland Revenue all cases where a customer's deposit account has earned a certain amount of interest during the year.

b.   Where there is a duty to the public to disclose. In practice this will seldom happen.

c.   Where the interests of the bank require disclosure. For example, where the bank is suing a guarantor on his liability under a guarantee, the bank must of necessity disclose the customer's overdrawn balance.

d.   If disclosure is made as result of express or implied consent of the customer. For example, an intending guarantor may ask the manager pertinent questions relating to the customer's account, prior to signing the guarantee. In such a case, the bank manager should give clear and succinct replies which are not capable of misinterpretation; and the consent of the customer must be obtained.

In addition to the above exceptions to the rule of confidentiality there are the following cases:

1.   During legal proceedings an order for discovery may be made upon a bank and this means it will be obliged to inform the other party to the proceedings if it has in its possession any relevant documents and if so to allow the other side to see them and copy them.

2.   Also a bank may receive a subpoena which is again an order of the court requiring the bank to appear as a witness and possibly bring into court certain documents and records.

3.   A remedy that may be awarded by the court is that the assets of one party to a legal action be sequestrated. This means that the party in question has refused to obey the court and so the court has ordered some or all of its assets to be taken and held for the period the party is in contempt of the court order.

The *Companies Act 1985*, the *Insolvency Act 1986* and the *Drug Trafficking Offences Act 1986* are statutes which impinge on the bank's duty of confidentiality. By the *Companies Act* the bank may be required to disclose information relating to an investigation of a company's affairs such as insider dealing; the *Insolvency Act* gives an administrator of a company powers to obtain information from a bank; and the *Drug Trafficking Offences Act* gives power to the police and the Customs and Excise to obtain an order prohibiting any person (including a bank) from dealing with the defendant's property when proceedings have been commenced against him and the court believes that he has profited from drug trafficking.

A banker need not inquire into the sources of a customer's money nor concern himself with the claims of third parties that the money is by right theirs. But, in practice where necessary, bankers do make such enquiries.

9. Regarding the care that must be taken by a customer in operating his account *Tai Hing Cotton Ltd v Liu Chong Hing Bank Ltd and others (1985)* is of interest. In this case the plaintiff had lost 5.5 million dollars because of the forgeries perpetrated by an accounts clerk. In Hong Kong the Court of Appeal agreed with the Bank that the plaintiff had been negligent in not checking monthly bank statements.

However, when the case came on appeal to the Privy Council the court held that a customer only has to take reasonable precautions to prevent alteration of his cheques. The customer

1. merely owes a duty to his bank to take care in drawing his cheques as in *London Joint Stock Bank Ltd v Macmillan and Arthur (1918)* in which A, an employee of Macmillan and Arthur, prepared a cheque for his employers to sign. The cheque was made payable to bearer. The cheque showed a figure of £2, but the amount in words did not appear. After the cheque had been signed, A fraudently altered it to show £120 in figures, and added that amount in words. A then cashed the cheque for the altered amount, and Macmillan and Arthur subsequently brought an action for the recovery of £118 from the bank.

    Held: M and A's action failed, because there was an obligation on a customer of a bank to draw cheques with sufficient care to minimise the risk of their being easily altered.

2. to inform the bank as soon as he discovers fraud in connection with his account and those duties are not to be extended. In *Greenwood v Martin's Bank Ltd (1933)*, Greenwood opened an

account with Martin's and his wife kept the pass book and the cheque book. In October 1929 Greenwood asked his wife for a cheque form as he wished to withdraw a sum of money and his wife admitted she had withdrawn the balance on the account in order to help her sister. She begged her husband not to inform the bank and he refrained from doing so. In June 1930 Greenwood discovered that his wife had not been helping her sister and told her that he was going to inform the bank. Soon after, the wife killed herself. Greenwood then sued the bank to recover the money it had paid out on a forged signature. The case went to the House of Lords who held that his failure to disclose the forgeries made it impossible for him to deny that the signature was genuine.

10.   *Mistake by banker in crediting a customer's account*

1.   If a banker credits a customer's account in error and that person alters his position as a result of the overcredit then the bank will not be able to recover the amount overcredited if the customer has acted to his detriment in reliance on the wrong information.

   Lloyds Bank Ltd v Brooks (1950). In that case the bank for a number of years had credited to Miss Brook's account an incorrect amount in respect of the dividends from shares. When the bank claimed repayment Miss Brook's defence that she had altered her position to her detriment was accepted by the court.

2.   If the customer has not acted to his detriment after having been credited in error then the bank will be able to recover the money *United Overseas Bank v Jiwani (1976).*

   In this case Mr Jiwani had opened an account with the bank in Geneva. After he had moved to England the bank received notification from a bank in Zurich stating that 11,000 dollars had been credited to him. The plaintiff bank informed Mr Jiwani who used the money to buy an hotel. Later the plaintiff bank received confirmation of the credit and mistakenly treated it as a new credit and notified Mr Jiwani accordingly. He issued another cheque for 11,000 dollars. When the plaintiff bank sued Mr Jiwani for the recovery of the money the court found in its favour.

   McKenna J held there are three conditions to be satisfied if the defendant were to be allowed to keep the money. He must show

1. The plaintiff bank broke its duty to give him accurate information about his account.
2. That the inaccurate information misled him about the state of the account.
3. Because of his mistaken belief he had changed his position so that it would be unfair to ask him to repay the money.

The judge found that 3 did not apply to Mr Jiwani.

In *Skyring v Greenwood (1825)* the bank had overcredited a customer for five years and the court held it was not entitled to reclaim the money because the customer had altered his position and had spent more than he would have done.

Summary – Banker and Customer

1. It is important to determine whether or not an organisation is a bank and when a person becomes a customer.

    This is primarily because a bank may be protected if it deals with a cheque for a person other than the rightful owner.

2. The main incidents of the banker – customer relationships are stated in *Joachimson v Swiss Bank Corporation (1921)*.

    a. It is based on contract.
    b. The bank must honour its customers' instructions.
    c. The customer must take reasonable care in executing his written orders so as not to facilitate forgery.

    Also the bank must not disclose any information about the customers' account.

    Tournier v National Provincial and Union Bank of England Ltd (1924).

    Exceptions to this are:

    a. under compulsion of law
    b. where there is a public duty
    c. in the interest of the bank
    d. in accordance with the Companies Act 1985, the Insolvency Act 1986, the Drug Trafficking Offence Act 1986

3.   Although a customer has a duty to draw his cheques so as not to facilitate forgery – *Macmillan and Arthur's case (1918)*; he has no duty to read his statement of account – *Tai Hing case (1985)*.

Chapter Two

The Data Protection Act 1984

Nowadays computers are common-place pieces of equipment which are capable of storing, processing and distributing information. It is a possibility that such facilities, in the wrong hands, might pose a threat to individuals and so should be controlled. Furthermore it was decided by the Government that the Council of Europe convention for the protection of individuals with regard to automatic processing of personal data must be ratified. If it had not been ratified, countries who had ratified it might place restrictions on the transfer of personal data to countries which had not ratified it.

The Data Protection Act was passed in 1984. It applies only to automatically processed information and does not cover information which is held and processed manually, for example in ordinary paper files. The Act does not cover all computerised information but only that which relates to living individuals. For example it does not cover information which relates only to a company or organisation and not to an individual. If a person wishes to record and use personal data he will be known as a Data User. It does not matter that the Data User does not have his own computer but uses a bureau or that the computer he has is only a desk top machine and not a mainframe. In each case he is still a Data User and has his responsibilities under the Act. The Act requires that every Data User who keeps personal data on a computer must register with the Data Protection Registrar. However there are exceptions. These exceptions apply where the Data User makes a limited use of information for one purpose, for example:

1. Personal data held by an individual in connection with personal, family or household affairs or for recreational purposes.
2. Personal data used only for calculating and paying wages and pensions, keeping accounts or keeping records of purchases and sales in order to ensure that the appropriate payments are made.

3.   Personal data used for distributing articles or information to the data subjects.
4.   Personal data held by an unincorporated members' Club e.g. a sports or recreational club which is not a registered company.
5.   Personal data which the Law requires the user to make public such as personal data in the Electoral Register kept by an Electoral Registration Officer.
6.   Personal data which is required to be exempt in order to safeguard National Security.

Also information which is processed only for preparing the text of documents is also outside the scope of the Act. This rule is sometimes referred to as the "Word Processor Exemption". Its effect is that the Act does not apply to information entered on to a computer with the sole purpose of editing the text and printing out a document.

In all the above examples where an exemption exists the effect is that the Registrar cannot take enforcement action and neither can an individual exercise his rights of access under the Act.

The Register

The Act creates a register of Data Users and every Data User who holds personal data must be registered unless the data are exempt. The Data User's register entry is compiled by the Registrar from the information given in the application. It contains the Data User's name and address together with broad descriptions of the type of data which the Data User holds, the purposes for which the data are used, the sources from which the Data User intends to obtain the information, the people to whom the Data User may wish to disclose the information and any oversea countries to which the Data User may wish to transfer the personal data. The register is open to public inspection at the Registrar's office in Wilmslow in Cheshire and an index to the register may be inspected in major public libraries throughout the country.

Data Protection Principles

The Act provides that in addition to registering with the Data Protection Registrar a Data User must abide by the eight Data Protection Principles. These state that personal data shall:

1.   be obtained and processed fairly and lawfully
2.   be held only for the lawful purposes described in the register entry

3.   be used only for those purposes and only be disclosed to those people described in the register entry
4.   be adequate, relevant and not excessive in relation to the purpose for which they are held
5.   be accurate and where necessary kept up to date
6.   be held no longer than is necessary for the registered purpose
7.   an individual shall be entitled to have access to data held about himself and if appropriate to have such data corrected or deleted
8.   the data must be surrounded by proper security.

In order to enforce compliance with the principles the Registrar can serve three types of notice. They are:

a.   An *Enforcement Notice* requiring the Data User to take specified action to comply with a particular principle. Failure to comply with the notice would be a criminal offence.
b.   A *Deregistration Notice* cancelling the whole or part of the Data User's register entry.
c.   A *Transfer Prohibition Notice*, preventing the Data User from transferring personal data overseas if the Registrar is satisfied that the transfer is likely to lead to a principle being broken. Again failure to comply with such a notice is a criminal offence

A person on whom a notice is served is entitled to appeal against the Registrar's decision to the Data Protection Tribunal.

Rights of the individual whose personal data are held on file

Such a person is called a Data Subject and he is entitled to seek compensation through the courts if he has suffered damage caused by the loss, unauthorised destruction or unauthorised disclosure of his personal data. He may also seek compensation through the courts for damage caused by inaccurate data. If personal data are inaccurate then the Data Subject may complain to the Registrar or apply to the courts for correction or deletion of the data.

Every Data Subject is entitled on written request to be supplied by any Data User with a copy of any personal data held about him or her. This right is called "Subject Access Right".

If the Data Subject considers there has been a breach of one of the principles of data protection then he is entitled to complain to the Data Protection Registrar. If the complaint is justified and cannot be resolved informally then the Registrar may use his powers to prosecute or to serve one of the notices already mentioned.

Disclosure of personal data
The Act does not prevent a Data User from disclosing information about an individual and such disclosure may be made if either:

a.   the person to whom the disclosure is made is described in the disclosure section of the Data User's register entry or
b.   the disclosure is covered by one of the "non disclosure exemptions". These would include, for example, disclosures required by law or made with the Data Subject's consent.

The Data Protection Registrar

The Data Protection Registrar is an independent officer who reports directly to Parliament. His duties include establishing the register of Data Users, spreading information on the Act, promoting compliance with the Data Protection Principles, encouraging the development of Codes of Practice to help Data Users comply with the principles and finally to consider complaints about breaches of the principles of the Act and where appropriate to prosecute offenders or serve notices on registered Data Users who are breaking the principles.

If the Registrar is satisfied that a Data User has breached a principle he can serve an Enforcement Notice directing that person to take specific steps to comply with the principle within a specified time. If the Registrar considers that compliance with the principle cannot be secured by the service of an Enforcement Notice he can issue a Deregistration Notice. This cancels from the register the whole or part of any register entry.

Finally the Registrar can also issue a Transfer Prohibition Notice to prevent the transfer of personal data overseas. A Data User who receives one of these notices can appeal to the independent Data Protection Tribunal. The tribunal has the power to substitute its own decision in place of the Registrar's.

Breach of an Enforcement or Transfer Prohibition Notice is a criminal offence. The Registrar employs teams of regional investigators who check whether Data Users are properly registered and investigate complaints of breaches of principle.

Summary – The Data Protection Act 1984
1.   The Act is intended to regulate information kept on computers relating to living individuals.
2.   It does this by requiring the users of such information to apply for permission to collect it and to collect it in a fair and lawful manner.
3.   It gives the individual whose information is recorded the right of access to it and to have it corrected or deleted.
4.   The Act creates the office of the Data Protection Registrar and gives him power over the data user and the manner in which he uses the information.

Chapter Three

Lien Appropriation and Combination.

A lien is a right, the word "right" must be stressed, to retain possession of property belonging to another until a debt due from the owner of the property to the person who is in possession of it has been paid. One should remember that possession of goods is a matter of fact – ownership is a matter of law. Thus a person may have goods in his possession but may not be the owner of them (he might have stolen them or borrowed them). Thus a lien is a right a person may have to retain possession of goods even though another person has the right of ownership in them.

It may arise in a number of situations for example, when one person has sold goods to another and the purchaser has become insolvent, then the seller may keep possession of the goods. Or when a person has left his car with a garage for repairs and when he comes to collect it he is dissatisfied with the amount he is being charged and refuses to pay. The garage may then keep possession of the car until the debt has been paid.

In normal circumstances of course, one person will not have any right to interfere with the goods of another. Where a lien exists then a person does have this right and consequently the circumstances surrounding a lien have to be carefully examined.

In the case of bankers there is what is called a banker's lien and this may exist over bills and securities left with the banker by a customer who owes a debt to the banker. In *Brandao v Barnett (1846)* it was held "Bankers most undoubtedly have a general lien on all securities deposited with them as bankers by a customer unless there be an express contract or circumstances that show an implied contract, inconsistent with lien". Also a lien may be excluded by express contract or when the circumstances show an implied contract inconsistent with a lien e.g. safe custody of valuables.

Notice that if a banker has a lien, it has not been given expressly to him by the other party as in the case of a charge but has arisen because of circumstances. It is in fact said to be "non-consensual". If a banker has taken a charge of another persons personal property then that right will have been given to the banker with the consent of the other.

What sort of securities?

The lien that a banker may be able to exercise will be over such securities that come into the banker's hands in his capacity as banker, in the course of banking business. A lien normally attaches to such securities as a banker ordinarily deals with for his customer, otherwise than for safe custody.

In some cases, when a banker is collecting the proceeds of a bill of exchange for a customer, he may become a holder for value of that instrument. These cases are:

a.   Section 2 of the *Cheques Act 1957* provides that

A banker who gives value for, or has a lien on, a cheque payable to order which the holder delivers to him for collection without indorsing it has such (if any) rights as he would have had if, upon delivery, the holder had indorsed it in blank.

In other words, the unindorsed cheque is treated as if it had been indorsed in blank, thereby making it a bearer cheque. We know that the person in possession of a bearer cheque is the holder (*S.2 of the Bills of Exchange Act 1882*).

2.   As section 2 of the *Cheques Act 1957* insists on the banker giving value, it means that where it applies, the banker will become a holder for value. Consequently, if the cheque is dishonoured he may sue the drawer.

3.   A banker may give value for a cheque in these ways:

a.   If he lends further sums to the holder on the strength of the cheque.

b.   If he pays over the amount of the cheque or part of it in cash or on account before it is cleared: *Midland Bank Ltd v Charles Simpson Motors Ltd (1961)*.

c.   If he agrees either then or earlier, or as a course of

business, that the customer may draw against the cheque immediately, before it is cleared.

d.   If the cheque is paid in specifically to reduce an existing overdraft.

e.   If he gives cash over the counter for the cheque at the time it is paid in for collection.

f.   If he has a lien on the cheque.

Note: *Section 2 of the Cheques Act 1957* covers only cheques. Furthermore, it can be invoked even if the cheque was not indorsed at all. But it has no application if the cheque bears a forged or irregular indorsement.

Westminster Bank v Zang (1965)

The application of section 2 of the *Cheques Act* is exemplified by this case, the facts of which are: Zang lost money gambling with Tilley. He asked Tilley if he could let him have £1,000 in return for a cheque. Tilley gave Zang the money in return for the cheque. Tilley had taken the £1,000 from the company, Tilley Autos Ltd. He was the company's managing director and controlling shareholder. Consequently he paid it in for the company's account but as the cheque had been made payable to himself he should have indorsed it before paying it in. This he did not do and this omission was not noticed by the collecting branch cashier. On presentation the cheque was dishonoured and Tilley borrowed it to sue Zang on it but abandoned his action. The bank later sued Zang themselves because Tilley Autos' account was overdrawn. To do so successfully they had to establish that they were holders for value.

The bank lost its action because even though section 2 of the *Cheques Act* could be satisfied, the bank was held not to have given value for the cheque. The bank's argument, that by crediting the cheque to the account of Tilley Autos Ltd and reducing the company's overdraft by £1,000 they had given value, was dismissed on the ground that the bank's paying-in-slip had a note to the effect that the bank reserved the right to refuse to pay against uncleared effects. This prevented any implied agreement from arising in the circumstances. The bank lost its lien when it lent the cheque to Tilley.

It was further held that the words "for collection", which appear in section 2 of the *Cheques Act 1957*, are not to be confined to cases where the bank is to collect for a customer's account. It applies if the cheque is being collected for *any account*.

In *Barclays Bank Ltd v Astley Industrial Trust Ltd (1970)*

The bank honoured cheques drawn by a customer after being assured that five cheques drawn by the defendants and payable to the customer would be lodged. The cheques were paid in as promised, but the defendants stopped payment of them. The court held that the bank had a lien on the five cheques and as a result of the combined effects of sections 27(3) and 29(1) of the *Bills of Exchange Act 1882* was entitled to recover in respect of the cheques to the extent of their lien from the defendants.

In *Davis v Bowsher (1794)* the class of securities that may be subject to a lien was described as "all the paper securities which come into the hands of the banker".

In *Re United Service Co. Johnstone's Claims (1870)*, the securities were share certificates and in *Misa v Currie (1876)* an order to pay money to a particular person. In *Wylde v Radford (1863)* it was held that a conveyance of land was not subject to a general lien.

In *Misa v Currie (1876)* the House of Lords expressly stated that money paid to a banker could be subject to the banker's lien. However there is some doubt as to the particular application of this statement because the money paid in is not identifiable and the banker can do what he likes with it. Of course the banker owes a debt of similar amount to the customer but a debt cannot be the subject of a lien.

Appropriation of Payments

When a debtor owes several debts to the same creditor and a payment is made, it maybe of importance as to which debt the payment should be appropriated. The reason is that a debt may become statute barred if it is in existence for more than six years. This is provided for in the *Limitation Act 1939* which prescribes certain periods of time within which actions must be brought otherwise they will become "statute barred".

If an action becomes "statute barred" because it hs not reached the court within the period of time laid down by the Act, then all rights to bring the action have ceased to exist.

An action for breach of contract or to recover a debt must be brought within six years of the right of action arising (twelve years if contained in a deed).

However a debt may be appropriated or linked to a debt on which no action to recover it may be brought because it is over six years old. See (2) below.

The rules are:

1. The debtor can appropriate, expressly or by implication, provided he does so at the time of payments. For example, if the debtor owes £100 and £75, and sends a cheque for £75, there will be an implied appropriation, in the absence of anything to the contrary, to the second debt. A cheque for £50 would be unappropriated by the debtor and would bring into operation the next rule.

2. In the absence of an appropriation by the debtor, the creditor can appropriate at any time. A creditor can appropriate the debtor's payment to a debt which the creditor cannot enforce by action because it is statute-barred, or if it is a guarantee, which he cannot prove in the form required by the *Statute of Frauds 1677*, but the creditor cannot appropriate the debtor's payment to a debt which is illegal.

    In *Seymour v Pickett (1905)* S. was an unregistered dentist who could not recover any fee for performing a dental operation, but could sue for the price of materials supplied. S's bill against P ws £45 – £20 for services and £25 for materials supplied. P paid £20 without appropriating it. In an action by S the court held:

    a. S could appropriate the £20 to the payment of his professional fees
    b. the appropriation could be made by S for the first time in the witness box

3. In the case of a current account there is "no room for any other appropriation than that which arises from the order in which the receipts and payments take place and are carried into the account. Presumably, it is the sum first paid in that is first drawn out. It is the first item on the debit side of the account that is discharged or reduced by the first item on the credit side; the appropriation is made by the very act of setting the two items against each other" Sir William Grant in *Clayton's case (1816)*.

Example – X guarantees Y's account with the bank. When Y is overdrawn up to £1,000, X revokes his guarantee as to future transactions. The bank keeps the old account going and Y pays in various sums amounting to £1,000, but draws out sums equal to that amount. As soon as Y has paid in £1,000, the liability of X to the bank will be extinguished, because these payments in will be appropriated by the rule in Clayton's case to the satisfaction of the overdraft existing when they were paid in. See *Deeley v Lloyds Bank (1912)*.

This rule only applies to current accounts, but it is not confined to banking accounts. It includes "current accounts for goods supplied and work done rendered periodically with a balance carried forward" (per Scrutton LJ in *Albermale Supply Co Ltd v Hind & Co (1928)*. It does not mean that when an account containing several items is rendered by the creditor, a payment by the debtor "on account" is appropriated to the first item on the account. In such a case the creditor can appropriate as stated in the second rule (*The Mecca (1897)*).

Operation of the Rule in Clayton's case

The rule in Clayton's case is not obligatory. The bank must decide whether to allow the rule to apply and not break the account, or whether to prevent the rule from applying by ruling off the account and opening a new one.

In some cases the rule will not apply especially between a trustee and a beneficiary (the rule in Hallett's case). This case concerned a trustee who paid trust money into his own account and the court presumed that any money drawn out was taken from his personal funds and not from the trust moneys.

Let us take a partnership account in the name of

Brown, Jones and Roberts.

DATE	PARTICULARS	DEBIT	CREDIT	BALANCE
June 30	Balance	–	–	£500DR
July 2	La Boutique	£25	–	£525DR
July 6	Smith Bros.	£120	–	£645DR
July 7	Cheque	–	£200	£445DR
July 10	Cash	£10	–	£455DR
July 16	British Rail	£50	–	£505DR

If during the operation of an account which is overdrawn some right against the debtor is established, then any credit subsequently paid into the account will be appropriated to reduce the debt then outstanding whilst all further payments out will constitute fresh advances not covered by the security.

BROWN dies ————— July 18th —————————————————				
July 19	Cheque	–	£500	£5DR
July 20	Robson	£450	–	£455DR
July 21	Davies	£30	–	£485DR

Assume that joint and several liability exists and that Brown dies on the 18th July his estate will thus have to contribute towards repayment of the debt outstanding at that date i.e. £505. However the account is continued and so the £500 credit of 19th July repays almost the whole of this sum and Brown's estate cannot be held liable for the amount of disbursements made after his death. His estate would be liable therefore for £5 only. As a consequence, of the balance of £485DR shown £480 is the liability of Jones and Roberts only – Brown, who may have been the stronger financially, is released.

In order to preserve the liability of Brown's estate the precaution of "breaking the account" or "ruling off the account" should have been taken at the time of Brown's death. The account *Brown, Jones & Roberts* would then have shown a debt of £505 for which Brown's estate and the two survivors would have been jointly and severally liable. The subsequent entries should have been placed through a new account upon which the liability if any would be that of Jones & Roberts and this could be restricted if desirable.

Thus the rule in *Clayton's case* may affect the banker to his detriment

a.   in the case of an overdrawn account if he fails to break the account on death.

b.   in the case of joint accounts with joint and several liability i.e. partnership accounts.

c.   on death or bankruptcy of a guarantor

d.   on notice of appointment of a receiver for a company's account.

There is one case where the rule in Clayton's case is to a banker's advantage and this is where the bank takes a debenture from a company incorporating a floating charge as security for an advance.

If the company goes into liquidation within 12 months of the creation of the charge and when the charge was given the company was insolvent, the floating charge will be invalid save in respect of new monies advanced subsequent to the creation of the charge. If sufficient money has been paid into the account to cover the debt outstanding when the charge was taken, the Rule in Clayton's Case will operate in favour of the bank because all moneys paid into the account after the charge was executed will be deemed to have been appropriated to reduce the debt outstanding at the time of the execution of the charge and all subsequent drawings will amount to new lendings secured by the charge.

Combination

This is sometimes called consolidation or set off of accounts and may arise when the debit balance of one account and the credit balance of another are combined so that the result will be the partial or full repayment of a debt.

A banker has a right to combine different accounts in the name of the same customer provided he has not agreed to keep them separate and provided the accounts are in the same right.

In *Greenhalgh v Union Bank of Manchester (1924)* the court held that when a banker has more than one account, in the same right, of the same customer, no right of set-off exists between the two accounts, without notice.

In that case Swift J said "a banker has no right, without the assent of the customer to move either assets or liabilities from the one account to the other. The very basis of his agreement with the customer is that the accounts shall be kept separate".

The Institute of Bankers seemed to favour this view at the time but it was contrary to the judgment in *Garnett v McKewan (1872)* which was approved by the Privy Council.

In Garnett's case the customer had a credit balance at one branch of the bank upon which he drew cheques. The bank having ascertained that the customer had an overdraft at another branch of the bank, set off the two accounts without notice to the customer and dishonoured his cheques. The court upheld the bank's right to act in this way.

A customer is not entitled to expect his cheques to be honoured at one branch where he has a credit balance, if at the same time he has a debit balance at another branch of the same bank and there is no duty on the part of the bank to keep the accounts separate.

It is also clear that a bank has a right to combine balances without notice to the customer especially when the balances are on active running accounts. However some bankers take a letter of set-off from their customers.

Barclays Bank Ltd v Okenarhe (1966) followed *Garnett v McKewan (1872)* and held that a bank is entitled to combine several accounts of a customer, even if kept at different branches, and to set off credits in one branch against debts in another branch. This right of combination is similar to the general lien of a banker but it may be excluded by agreement.

It is not necessary to give notice to the customer since he is considered to know his net position with the bank.

In *National Westminster Bank Ltd v Halesowen Presswork and Assemblies Ltd (1972)*

Halesowen kept a No 1 account with the bank which became overdrawn. It opened a No 2 account in April 1968 as a trading account, the No 1 account then becoming frozen. It was agreed between the company and the bank, on the opening of the No 2 account, that *in the absence of materially changed circumstances*, the bank would allow these arrangements to run on unchanged for four months.

On 12 June 1968 a cheque for £8,611 in favour of the company's No 2 account was paid into a branch of the bank in another town. The credit was passed to the account on 13 June and cleared on the 14 June.

On 12 June 1968 the company went into voluntary liquidation. The final balances of the two accounts were No 1 account overdrawn £11,339; No 2 account credit £8,634.

The bank proposed to combine the accounts and prove for the net balance. The liquidator challenged the bank's right to do so.

Roskill J found for the bank. In his judgment he analysed the legal rules governing a banker's right of lien, or right of set-off. "The right arose whenever a customer owed money to a banker, as a banker, on the general balance of his account. The right to exercise the lien could be modified or excluded by express or implied contract between the parties. No exercise of his lien could be made by the banker in breach of any agreement with his customer. The lien was exercisable on all securities which came into the possession of the banker as a *banker*. They must belong to the customer in the same right as that in which the customer was indebted to the banker. Such securities include cheques and their proceeds."

In the Halesowen case the bank was bound by the four months' agreement, but this was brought to an end by the liquidation. From 12 June therefore the bank was free to set-off the balances. The cheque for £8,611 had by that date passed into the bank's possession and therefore the bank's right of lien extended to that cheque and subsequently, to its proceeds.

The liquidator appealed and the Court of Appeal reversed the decision by a majority of two to one. The court first considered the effect of the resolution to wind up on the agreement between the bank and the company. They thought that the calling of the creditors to a meeting to consider the resolution to wind up amounted to "materially changed circumstances"; but Lord Denning MR thought that the agreement was to be interpreted that the accounts were to be kept separate for four months unless the bank gave notice to determine it by reason of a material change in circumstances. The bank had not done so.

The court then considered the effect of S.31 of the *Bankruptcy Act 1914* (now replaced by S.323 of the *Insolvency Act 1986*) which provided that where there have been mutual credits, mutual debts and other mutual dealings between a debtor and his creditors, an account shall be taken of what is due from one to the other, and the balanace of this account, and no more, shall be claimed or paid. This avoids a creditor from having to pay in full any sum he owes to the bankrupt, whilst receiving only a dividend in respect of the debts owed to him by the bankrupt.

Eventually the case was taken to the House of Lords, which reversed the decision of the Court of Appeal and found in favour of the bank. It was held that the parties could not contract to exclude the operation of the *Bankruptcy Act*. Therefore section 31 would apply, and the customer's balances could be set-off against the other.

Summary – Lien, Appropriation and Combination

1. A lien is a right to retain possession of property belonging to another.

2. A banker may exercise a banker's lien over bills and securities left with him by a customer who owes a debt to the banker. *Brandao v Barnett (1846).*

3. A banker may exercise a lien over a cheque which the holder delivers to him for collection, provided he has given value for it. *Section 2 Cheques Act 1957.*

4. Appropriation means linking a payment to a bank to some outstanding debt. Debts usually only may be sued upon provided the action is commenced within six years from the date when the debt was created. However a payment in may be linked (and thereby cancel) a debt which is more than six years old.

5. The rule in Clayton's case is of importance to bankers because it provides that the first payment in may be linked with the earliest outstanding debt. This may be significant if some security has disappeared between the date of the creation of the debt and the payment in.

6. In *Barclays Bank Ltd v Okenarhe (1966)* it was held that a bank is entitled to combine several accounts of a customer even if they are kept at different branches. It is not necessary to notify the customer.

Chapter Four

Consumer Credit Act 1974

Credit, in the sense of payment being deferred for goods or services, has become a feature of our modern life. For many years attempts have been made to control the credit industry and to protect the consumer. This has been done by regulating the supply of credit and by the advertisement of credit by the *Pawnbrokers Act 1872–1960*, the *Moneylenders Acts 1900–1927*, the *Hire Purchase Act 1965* and the *Advertisements (Hire Purchase) Act 1967*.

These Acts gradually became less and less effective and it was evident that some of the legislation was being bypassed. For example the Moneylenders Acts applied only to moneylenders, and to loans made by moneylenders. They did not apply to other forms of credit and certain types of business e.g. banking, in the course of which loans of money were made, were exempted from the operation of the Acts.

The *Consumer Credit act 1974* now regulates many different forms of credit. It is comprehensive in its scope and it controls the business of giving credit by the issue of licenses. It restricts advertising and canvassing and gives wide supervisory powers to the Director General of Fair Trading. It also controls agreements made by individuals by stating the formalities required and it deals with the matters of termination, cancellation and default of agreements.

What sort of transaction is affected by the Act?

The two transactions regulated by the Act are:

1.   a consumer credit agreement
2.   a consumer hire agreement

The titles given to these agreements bring up a number of new concepts which must now be examined in some detail.

Sections 8–20 deal with the various types of credit and hire agreements and linked transactions.

Credit is defined as a cash loan and any form of financial accommodation.

All types of loan are covered and examples are given in Schedule 2 Part II of the Act e.g.

1.   moneylenders loans
2.   bank loans
3.   overdrafts
4.   pawnbrokers loans
5.   advances on mortgage
6.   the sale of goods on instalment credit terms (e.g. credit sales, conditional sales, budget accounts, option accounts, subscription accounts)
7.   the supply of services on credit, check and voucher trading
8.   credit cards
9.   check cards

In all of these cases in return for goods or services payment is deferred whether the payment is to be made in one amount or by instalments.

A Consumer Credit Agreement

A consumer credit agreement is defined as a personal credit agreement by which the creditor provides the debtor wth credit not exceeding (at present, 1991) £15,000.

A personal credit agreement is an agreement between an individual called "the debtor" and any other person called "the creditor" by which the creditor provides the debtor with credit. The term individual includes a partnership or other unincorporated body of persons not consisting entirely of bodies corporate. Therefore an agreement to provide credit for a company will not be a personal credit agreement and so will not be affected by the Act. An agreement with a partnership can be a personal credit agreement even though the partnership is in business and the loan is for business purposes. Whether or not the Act applies to the transaction will be determined by the status of the debtor and not by the purpose for which the loan has been made and by the amount advanced.

A Regulated Consumer Credit Agreement

This is a consumer credit agreement which is not an exempt agreement.

Exempt Agreements

These are specified in section 16 and include:

1. Consumer credit agreements secured by a mortgage over land where the creditor is a local authority or a building society.
2. Agreements secured by mortgage over land where the creditor is one of a number of Insurance Companies, Friendly Societies and Land Improvement Companies specified by the Secretary of State or is a Trade Union of employers or workers.
3. Fixed sum debtor-creditor-supplier agreements (other than hire purchase or conditional sale agreements) when the number of payments to be made by the debtor does not exceed four.
4. A running-account credit agreement where the debtor is required to repay the debt in one single payment. Examples of this type of agreement would be a credit card issued by American Express or Diners Club.
5. Low cost debtor-creditor agreements when the rate of interest does not exceed 13% or 1% above the base rate determined by the Bank of England.
6. Any agreement made in connection with trade in goods or services between the United Kingdom and an overseas country.

The above agreements are exempt agreements and so are not affected by the provisions of the Act. However the fact that an agreement is exempt does not exclude the power of the Court to investigate a bargain which it considers to be extortionate in regard to the rates of interest required and other factors (Sections 137–140). Thus the Court has power to re-open any agreement regulated or not, whether it is below £15,000 or not.

If the debtor convinces the Court that the credit bargain is extortionate then the Court may make one of the orders listed in Section 139(2) of the Act, viz:

1. direct accounts to be taken between any persons

2.   set aside the whole or part of any obligation imposed on the debtor or a surety by the credit bargain or any related agreement

3.   require the creditor to repay the whole or part of any sum paid under the credit bargain or any related agreement by the debtor or a surety whether paid to the creditor or any other person

4.   direct the return to the surety of any property provided for the purposes of the security or

5.   alter the terms of the credit agreement or any security instrument.

Any application to have a credit agreement set aside must be made by the debtor or any surety to the High Court or County Court. In England and Wales application in respect of a regulated agreement or any other agreement, not being a regulated agreement under which the creditor provides the debtor with a fixed sum credit or running-account credit, must be made in the County Court.

Fixed-Sum and Running-Account Credit

Section 10 describes the two types of credit. A *fixed sum credit* is a once and for all credit. The amount of the credit is fixed and agreed between the parties. It may be paid by the creditor to the debtor as a lump sum or by instalments. Examples would be moneylenders and bank loans, pawnbrokers loans, hire purchase, a credit sale and conditional sale agreements and check and voucher trading.

In determining whether the amount of credit comes within the £15,000 limit a distinction must be made between credit and the total charge for credit. Thus the important figure is the amount of the loan or the capital sum not including the interest.

A *running-account credit* is sometimes named as a revolving credit. In this case the debtor does not have to apply for further credit but by his agreement with the creditor he has a right to further credit – usually subject to a credit limit. In order to decide whether or not a running-account credit falls within the definition of a consumer credit agreement the credit limit must not exceed £15,000. However this limit may be exceeded merely temporarily (Section 10(2)). Furthermore there are three situations where the agreement will still be subject to the Act even though there is no credit limit or that it exceeds the specified amount (£15,000 at present).

1. If the debtor is not allowed to draw at any time an amount that exceeds £15,000 as credit but excluding any charge for credit. This situation could arise if a bank has allowed a customer overdraft facilities of say £60,000 (or even without limit) but stipulates that he can only draw say £10,000 in any one month.

2. The agreement provides that if the debt exceeds a sum not exceeding £15,000 then the rate of interest will increase.

3. If at the time the agreement was entered into, it is probable that the debit balance will not rise above the specified amount (£15,000).

In each of these cases the agreement would be within the financial limit (£15,000). These exceptions have been made so as to avoid the situation where a creditor might agree to provide credit in excess of the specified amount, knowing that the debtor will not require more than the specified amount (e.g. £15,000) but so as to take the agreement outside the provisions of the Act.

Consumer Hire Agreements

So far we have considered consumer credit agreements. A consumer hire agreement is an agreement made by a person called the owner with an individual (not a company) called the hirer. The agreement must be capable of lasting more than three months and must not require the hirer to pay more than £15,000. Also Section 15 makes it clear that a consumer hire agreement is not a hire purchase agreement.

All consumer hire agreements will be regulated agreements if they are not exempt agreements. Such exempt agreements are those exempted by order of the Secretary of State where the owner is a company authorised to supply electricity, gas or water or where the subject of the agreement is a meter or metering equipment owned by the Post Office.

A hire purchase agreement differs from a consumer hire agreement in that in the former case the hirer who has possession of the goods will become the owner of them if the agreement is complied with and he opts to purchase the goods. In a consumer hire agreement there is no question of the hirer becoming the owner of the goods.

Small Agreements

These are regulated consumer credit agreements for credit not exceeding £50 other than a hire purchase or a conditional sale agreement or a regulated consumer hire agreement which does not require the hirer to make payments exceeding £50 provided that in either case the agreement is an agreement which is either unsecured or secured by a guarantee or indemnity only.

In the case of a running-account credit the credit limit must not exceed £50.

The provision relating to small agreements is included in the Act so that such small agreements may be excluded by other sections in the Act from certain technical requirements of those sections. Therefore Section 17 makes provision to prevent the splitting up of agreements into two or more agreements below the £50 limit, so as to circumvent the provisions of the Act.

Non-Commercial Agreements

Such an agreement is a consumer credit agreement or a consumer hire agreement not made by the creditor or owner in the course of a business carried on by him. Such private agreements are excluded from some of the provisions of the Act.

Multiple Agreements

Section 18 provides that an agreement that falls within more than one type of agreement, such as a running-account credit and a fixed-sum credit, shall be called a multiple agreement. Where there is a multiple agreement each part is to be treated as a separate agreement (Section 18(2)).

A credit card agreement will be multiple if the card can be used to obtain goods or services (a debtor-creditor-supplier agreement) or cash (a debtor-creditor agreement).

It should be noted that Section 18(5) provides that in the case of a running-account credit, a term of the agreement that allows the credit limit to be exceeded only temporarily, shall not be treated as a separate agreement or as a separate agreement providing fixed-sum credit in respect of the excess. This will permit a bank to honour cheques drawn on it in the case of a temporary excess of an agreed overdraft.

Linked Transactions

When a person enters into an agreement to obtain goods on credit or to hire goods it is quite usual for an additional agreement to be entered into such as one for installation, insurance or maintenance. Such agreements will be linked to the regulated agreement if:

1. It is entered into in compliance with a term of the principal agreement.

2. The principal agreement finances the linked transaction. This may occur if the debtor obtains a loan from a finance company to finance his purchase from a dealer. This is known as a debtor-creditor-supplier agreement. The contract between the debtor and the dealer is a linked transaction.

    It will also arise where a debtor uses a credit card or check or voucher in order to obtain goods from a supplier. The contract for the goods or services is a linked transaction.

3. If the creditor, owner, negotiator or credit broker suggests to the debtor or hirer that he should enter into an agreement so as to induce him to enter into a principal agreement. Such as when it is suggested by dealer or broker arranging a loan that an insurance policy be entered into with a particular company. That transaction would be linked with the principal agreement.

Control of Credit Agreements

The foregoing is concerned with the various types of credit agreements and the nomenclature used in the *Consumer Credit Act 1974*. The important point to be borne in mind is that certain agreements are regulated by the Act and whether or not an agreement is regulated must be established.

The Director General of Fair Trading has been given powers to issue licences to bodies involved with various activities of the credit industry. Basically a person requires a licence if he carries on a business in the course of which regulated agreements are made with customers (debtors or hirers) (Section 21).

A licence is not required if the business:

1. provides credit only in excess of £15,000 or which rents goods where the hirer must pay more than £15,000.

2.   provides credit or hire only to companies.

3.   provides credit or hire only under exempt agreements.

Unlicensed Trading

Section 39 provides that a person who trades when unlicensed has committed an offence and will be liable to criminal sanctions. Furthermore Section 40 provides that the agreement itself may not be enforced against the debtor or hirer unless the Director General of Fair Trading authorises it. In deciding whether or not to allow the agreement to be enforced the Director must consider to what extent other debtors or hirers have been prejudiced, whether or not he would have been likely to grant a licence and the creditor's degree of culpability in failing to obtain a licence.

Seeking Business

This may be done by advertising, by canvassing or by giving quotations.

Advertising

The provisions related to advertising and quotations apply not only to persons who are carrying on a consumer credit business or a consumer hire business but also to those who carry on a business in the course of which they provide credit to individuals secured on land and that the advertisement or quotation need not relate to a regulated agreement.

The provisions extend to any form of advertising – by television, radio, distribution of samples, catalogues, exhibition of models or in any other way.

The Secretary of State is empowered to make regulations concerning the form and content of advertisements. The charge for credit must be expressed as an annual percentage rate (A.P.R).

Quotation

A quotation is a document in which prospective customers are given information about the terms on which the person who carries out a consumer credit or hire business is prepared to do business. These are all subject to controls.

Canvassing

This occurs where the canvasser solicits the entry of a consumer into a regulated agreement by making oral representations during a visit not previously arranged. The canvassing is said to be "off trade premises" if it takes place somewhere other than the place of business of the creditor or owner, the supplier, the canvasser or the consumer. Such off trade premises canvassing is an offence unless it is in response to a written invitation from the person making the invitation.

It is also an offence to send a document to a minor inviting him to borrow money, obtain services, goods or hire on credit.

Finally it is an offence to give a person a credit-token if he has not asked for it in writing. Such a credit-token may be given, without request, if it is given under a credit-token agreement already made or in renewal or replacement of a credit-token previously accepted by the debtor.

Making a Regulated Agreement

The agreement between the creditor and the debtor or the owner and the hirer will be made when it has been signed or executed by both parties. Section 61(1)(a).

The document must contain all the terms of the agreement and these shall be legible.

The form and content of the agreement are laid down by the Secretary of State. In any case the debtor or hirer must be made aware of

1. his rights and duties
2. the amount and rate for the total charge for credit
3. the protections available to him.

If the agreement is
1. a non-commercial agreement
2. a debtor-creditor agreement enabling the debtor to overdraw on a current account or
3. a debtor-creditor agreement to finance the making of payments, arising on or connected with the death of a person, then, the above provisions will not apply (Section 74)

Mortgage of Land

If the security for the loan or hire is land then Section 58 will apply. This provides that the creditor/owner must give to the debtor/hirer a copy of the unexecuted agreement not less than seven days before the unexecuted agreement is sent for signature. This is called the consideration period and during it no approach must be made by the creditor/owner to the debtor/hirer. This provision will not apply if:

1.   the loan is a restricted-use loan to finance the purchase of mortgaged land. This would apply if a person borrows money from a bank or building society to buy the land which is to be used as security for the loan.
2.   the agreement is for a bridging loan in connection with the purchase of the mortgaged land or other land.

Restricted-use Credit

Under a credit agreement the credit may be restricted-use or unrestricted-use credit. If the credit is granted by a regulated consumer credit agreement and can only be used in a particular way, e.g.

1.   to finance a transaction between the debtor and the creditor
2.   to finance a transaction between the debtor and a person (the supplier) other than the creditor or
3.   to refinance any existing indebtedness of the debtor whether to a creditor or to another person.

then in these cases the credit is said to be "restricted-use credit".

   If it is possible for the credit to be used in any way the debtor chooses even though that might be contrary to an agreement between the creditor and debtor, the credit will be said to be "unrestricted-use credit".

Copies of the Agreement

Not Signed by Creditor/Owner

If, when the unexecuted agreement is presented personally to the debtor/hirer for his signature but it has not become an executed agreement (because the creditor has not signed) then the debtor/hirer must be given a copy of it. If the unexecuted agreement is sent to the debtor/hirer for his signature then a copy of it must also be sent together with any supporting documents. Later when the creditor/ owner signs, a second copy of the agreement must be sent within seven days of the creditor/owner signing unless it is a credit-token agreement.

Signed by creditor/owner
If the unexecuted agreement is presented personally to the debtor/ hirer for signature and when he signs it becomes an executed agreement, then a copy of the executed agreement and any supporting documents must be then and there delivered to him, but no further copy is required.

If the unexecuted agreement is sent to the debtor-hirer for him to sign a copy must be sent at the same time. No further copy is required if the debtor/hirer signs because the creditor/owner has already signed it before sending it.

Cancellation

The normal rule for making a contract requires that a valid offer is made which is accepted unconditionally. So long as the parties really are in agreement i.e. there is no mistake or deception, then an agreement has been entered into which cannot be set aside easily. However as regards regulated agreements it may be possible for an individual to change his mind after entering into an agreement provided certain rules are complied with.

Section 67 of the Act provides that a regulated agreement may be cancelled by debtor or hirer if the antecedent negotiations included oral representations made in the presence of the debtor or hirer unless the agreement is signed by the debtor or hirer on trade premises. Also the agreement may not be cancelled if, although signed off trade premises, the debtor has not been subject to face to face persuasion.

This provision is intended to protect individuals who are subject to persuasion by door to door salesmen and sign the agreement on the doorstep. This would also apply if the negotiations are conducted at a dealer's place of business and the debtor takes home the agreement to sign. On the other hand if there has been no face to face persuasion, such as in a Mail Order transaction, contracts made in this way cannot be cancelled. Neither can the following agreements be cancelled:

1.   a non-commercial agreement
2.   an agreement enabling the debtor to overdraw on a current account if the Director General of Fair Trading so determines.
3.   a debtor-creditor agreement to finance the making of payments arising on the death of a person provided the Director General so determines.
4.   a small debtor-creditor-supplier agreement for restricted use.

A Cooling-Off Period
The period in which the debtor/hirer is permitted to serve notice of cancellation (the cooling-off period) is a period ending on the fifth day following the day on which he received the second copy of the agreement or if no second copy is required the notice informing the debtor of his cancellation rights.

Effect of Notice of Cancellation
The notice of cancellation is effective at the time of posting whether or not it is actually received.

The notice of cancellation must be served on the creditor/owner, the credit-broker or supplier who took part in the antecedent negotiations or any agent of the debtor/hirer or creditor/owner.

The notice of cancellation will cancel the agreement and any linked transaction. Any payments made are recoverable. If however the creditor has advanced a sum of money during the cooling-off period this does not become immediately repayable (Section 71).

Connected Lender Liability

A credit card transaction may be two-party or three-party. If the supplier of the goods issues his own credit card this will be a two-party credit agreement.

A three-party transaction is where the issuer of the credit card is not the supplier of the goods. Section 75 of the *Consumer Credit Act 1974* is of importance in this case because that section makes liable the issuer of the credit card jointly and severally with the supplier in respect of any claim of the debtor for misrepresentation or breach of contract in relation to the transaction financed by the agreement.

In the case of a two-party transaction then the supplier and the issuer of the card are one person and of course the supplier will be liable directly to the debtor. This provision whereby the creditor may be made liable together with the supplier is intended to ensure that creditors will take care to associate only with reputable suppliers. Of course Section 75 is of particular value if the supplier himself should become insolvent and then the debtor will still be able to enforce his rights against the creditor. This has occurred quite frequently when Tour Operators have gone into liquidation and their customers have been able to recover against the credit card company.

Section 75, at present, only applies to a transaction where the cash price exceeds £100 and does not exceed £30,000.

Also remember that Section 75 does not apply to exempt agreements and so does not apply to American Express or Diners Club credit card agreements.

Extortionate Credit Bargains

An important provision of the *Consumer Credit Act 1974* is contained in sections 137 to 140. These are concerned with extortionate credit bargains and Section 137 gives the Court power to re-open a credit agreement. This power may be exercised by the High Court, the County Court or the Sheriff's Court in Scotland, if the Court considers that an agreement is extortionate. All credit agreements are subject to this power not only regulated ones and exempt, small and non-commercial agreements are affected.

Section 138 states the factors to be taken into account in deciding whether or not an agreement is extortionate. In deciding whether a bargain is extortionate the following matters shall be considered:

1. interest rates prevailing at the time the agreement was made
2. the debtor's age, experience, business capacity and state of health
3. the degree to which the debtor was under financial pressure *cf divers* when he made the bargain
4. the degree of risk accepted by the creditor
5. the creditor's relationship with the debtor
6. whether or not the cash price was quoted for any goods or services
7. in relation to a linked transaction factors applicable include how far the transaction was required for the protection of the debtor or the creditor or was in the interest of the creditor
8. any other relevant consideration.

If the Court decides that a credit bargain is extortionate then it may relieve the debtor from any sum in excess of what is fair and reasonable or it may alter the terms of the agreement or even require the creditor to repay any sums already paid.

Matters Arising During the Currency of an Agreement

The creditor has a duty to supply unrequested periodic statements of account in the case of an overdraft or credit card agreement (a running-account credit agreement).

In the case of a fixed-sum credit agreement the creditor, if so requested by the debtor, must give him a copy of the agreement and inform him of the total sum paid, the sum which has become payable and the dates when payment must be made.

If a debtor is liable to make payments to the same creditor in respect of two or more regulated agreements then he has a choice as to which debt a payment he makes may be linked or appropriated. This is the normal rule relating to appropriation.

In the case of credit-tokens which include credit cards the general rule is that the debtor is not liable to the creditor for any loss arising from the use of the credit card by another person who is not the agent of the debtor. In any case Section 66 provides that a debtor shall not be liable under a credit-token agreement unless he has accepted it

1.   by signing it
2.   by giving a receipt for it
3.   by using it.

If, after accepting the credit card the debtor permits its use by another person then he will be liable to the creditor.

Termination of the Consumer Credit Agreement

Section 94 provides that a debtor may repay his debt at any time by notice to the creditor and payment of the debt to him. The debtor may then be entitled to a rebate for early settlement (Section 95). He is also entitled to a statement from the creditor of the amount he owes and if the creditor fails to provide this information the agreement cannot be enforced and if the information is not given within one month an offence will have been committed.

Summary – Consumer Credit Act 1974

1. This Act applies to credit transactions which may be consumer credit agreements or consumer hire agreements.
2. A licence is required by any person proposing to give credit under a regulated credit agreement.
   This requirement does not exist if:

   a. the credit is in excess of £15,000
   b. the other party is a company
   c. the agreement is an exempt agreement.

3. Seeking business includes quotations, canvassing, advertising and such matters of gaining business are regulated.
4. As regards the mortgage of land, Section 58, requires that the creditor/owner must give to the debtor/hirer a copy of the unexecuted agreement not less than seven days before the unexecuted agreement is sent for signature.
5. Section 137 to 140 are important because they are concerned with extortionate credit bargains.

Chapter Five

The Financial Services Act 1986

The FSA received the Royal Assent on 7 November 1986 and came fully into force on 29 April 1988.

The act came about as a result of the appreciation that it was necessary to have the means of regulating investment business and that investors required protection.

Prior to the Act there were some methods of protection contained in the *Prevention of Fraud (Investments) Act 1939* which was re-enacted by the *Prevention of Fraud (Investments) Act 1958*.

Professor L. C. B. Gower was appointed in 1981 to head a committee charged with the review of the protection required by investors and the need for some control of dealers in securities, investment consultants and managers.

The Financial Services Act itself has effected a complete overhaul of the legal framework for the regulation of investment business. The Act is divided into 10 parts:

Part 1. This creates a framework for the regulation of investment business.

Part 2. Extends the investment control to Life Assurance when it is used as a form of investment.

Part 3. Establishes a framework for the regulation of Friendly Societies.

Part 4. Introduces a new regime for the official listing of securities on the Stock Exchange.

Part 5. Deals with offers of unlisted securities.

Part 6. Provides new rules relating to take-over offers.

Part 7. Makes a number of changes to the law on Insider dealing contained in the *Company Securities (Insider Dealings) Act 1985*.

Part 8–10. Deal with disclosure of information, reciprocity of access for financial business in foreign markets and miscellaneous matters.

It will be apparent that Part 1 is the most important part as far as bankers are concerned and we must now consider that section in some detail.

Definition of Investments

An investment is defined very widely and includes any right, asset or interest which falls within the following categories.

1. Shares and stock in the share capital of a company
2. Debentures, including debenture stock, loan stock, bonds, certificates of deposit and any other instrument creating or acknowledging indebtedness. A cheque or other bill of exchange, a bankers' draft and letter of credit; bank notes; current, deposit or savings accounts are excluded.
3. Government, local authority or other public authority securities.
4. Warrants or other instruments entitling the holder to subscribe for investments in the above categories.
5. Certificates or other instruments conferring rights to acquire, dispose of, underwrite or convert any investments falling within the above categories.
6. Units in collective investment schemes. This includes units in unit trusts.
7. Options to acquire or dispose of investments as defined.
8. Futures for investment purposes.

A definition of investments excludes by implication, land and physical commodities such as works of art, antiques and old coins. Similarly gold and silver will not be regarded as investments unless they are expressed in the form of options.

Investment business

This is defined as dealing in investments: buying, selling, subscribing for or underwriting investments or offering or agreeing to offer investments, either as principal or as agent.

Arranging deals in investments: making, offering, or agreeing to make arrangements with a view to another person buying, selling, subscribing for or underwriting the particular investment.

Managing investments: managing, offering or agreeing to manage assets belonging to another person if these assets consist of or include investments.

Advising on investments: giving or offering or agreeing to give advice to investors on the merits of the purchase, sale, subscription for or underwriting of investments or on the exercise of rights conferred by investments to acquire, dispose of, underwrite or convert an investment.

Certain activities which might be considered to constitute investment business are specifically excluded. These include dealing as a principal as where a person buys securities on his own account. Such a person will not be regarded as carrying an investment business unless he is making a market or is soliciting the public to buy or sell investments. Also it will not be regarded as investment business where a financial package is linked with the sale of goods or supply of services; where a company operates a "share shop" for its employees; a trustee manages investments for his beneficiary or advice is given in the course of a profession, provided the investment dealing is not predominant. Also many daily newspapers contain financial columns which contain investment advice. Even so newspaper proprietors and financial journalists are not required to seek authorisation provided that their primary purpose is not to lead persons to invest in any particular investment.

The Framework for Regulation

The Secretary of State for Trade and Industry is authorised under the Act to regulate the investment industry so as to protect investors. He may delegate his tasks to a designated agency which is, in the first instance, the Securities and Investments Board (SIB).

The Securities and Investments Board

This is a private company limited by guarantee and financed by a levy on certain organisations. It may exercise its powers flexibly and quickly but is subject to the control of the Secretary of State. He may remove Board members, he may withdraw in whole or in part the powers given to the SIB or he may direct the SIB to alter its rules or practices. In addition the SIB must also submit an annual report to parliament which will be debated. The SIB will delegate its powers to other bodies, the main categories being Self Regulating Organisations (SRO) and recognised professional bodies (RPB). In addition the SIB may recognise a recognised investment exchange (RIE) and a recognised clearing house (RCH).

So the structure will be as follows:

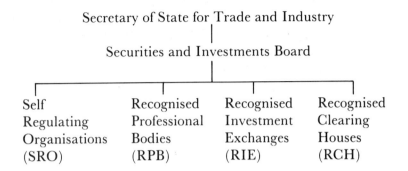

Secretary of State for Trade and Industry

Securities and Investments Board

| Self Regulating Organisations (SRO) | Recognised Professional Bodies (RPB) | Recognised Investment Exchanges (RIE) | Recognised Clearing Houses (RCH) |

Self Regulating Organisations

The SIB has recognised the following as SROs.

The Securities Association (TSA) – these are firms dealing and broking in securities, international money market instruments, forward agreements and related futures and options. They also are concerned with investment management and advice incidental to this business.

Association of Futures Brokers and Dealers (AFBD) – these firms deal in broking in futures and options also they are concerned with investment management and advice incidental to their business.

Financial Intermediaries, Managers and Brokers Regulatory Association (FIMBRA) – these are firms dealing and broking in securities and giving professional advice and management.

Investment Management Regulatory Organisation (IMRO) – these are investment managers and advisors including managers and trustees of collective investment schemes and in-house pension fund managers.

Life Assurance and Unit trust Regulatory Organisation (LAUTRO) – these are life companies and unit trust managers and trustees for the management and selling of insurance linked investments or units in a collective investment scheme by themselves and their sales forces.

Recognised Professional Bodies

In their practice professionals such as accountants, solicitors etc provide an important source of investment advice and other investment services such as insurance broking. These professional bodies will only be involved in investment business to an insignificant degree within the main body of their professional activities. However they may be authorised by the SIB provided:

1. the professional body regulates the practice of a profession which is not, wholly or mainly, the carrying on of an investment business.

2. it regulates the practice of a profession recognised for a statutory purpose or in the exercise of statutory powers.

The SIB has identified twelve professional bodies that are possible candidates for recognition. These are:

1.   The Law Society of England and Wales
2.   The Law Society of Scotland
3.   The Law Society of Northern Ireland
4.   The Institute of Chartered Accountants of England and Wales
5.   The Institute of Chartered Accountants of Scotland
6.   The Institute of Chartered Accountants in Ireland
7.   The Chartered Association of Certified Accountants
8.   The Institute of Cost and Management Accountants
9.   The Institute of Consulting Actuaries
10. The Faculty of Actuaries
11. The Royal Institute of Chartered Surveyors
12. The Institute of Chartered Secretaries and Administrators

Whether or not any of the above bodies will apply for recognition by the SIB will probably depend upon the amount to which the membership of the profession is involved in public practice. When deciding to recognise a professional body the SIB must be satisfied that the rules of the profession will provide equivalent investor protection to that provided by its own rules. Also the professional body must have adequate arrangements and resources for the effective monitoring and enforcement of compliance to its rules. The enforcement arrangements must provide for the withdrawal or suspension of certification. Also the arrangements must provide a proper balance between the interests of persons certified by the body and the interests of the public. Furthermore arrangements must be made for the investigation of complaints against its members or its regulation of investment business.

Recognised Investment Exchanges and Clearing Houses

Persons running a market or exchange will normally be carrying on investment business and will therefore need to be authorised, unless that market or exchange obtains exemption by becoming recognised by the SIB.

Any body corporate or unincorporated association may apply for recognition as an RIE. The procedure is the same as for recognition as an SRO. The criteria for recognition include the following:

1. The exchange must have sufficient, financial resources to enable it to perform its functions in a proper manner.
2. Its rules and practices must ensure the orderly conduct of business and afford proper protection to investors.
3. It must limit dealings to investments to which there is a proper market.
4. It must impose information requirements on issues of investments so that people dealing in these can ascertain their current value.
5. It must have arrangements for ensuring the performance of transactions effected on it.
6. It must provide satisfactory arrangements for recording transactions effected on the exchange.
7. It must have adequate arrangements for monitoring and enforcing compliance with its rules.
8. It must have effective arrangements for the investigation of complaints.

The SIB will consider a number of candidates for recognition and these include:

1. The International Stock Exchange
2. London Commodities Exchange
3. London International Financial Futures Exchange (LIFFE)
4. London Metal Exchange
5. An Exchange for Unlisted Securities
6. An Association of International Bond Dealers
7. Certain Overseas Exchanges.

Authorisation

Anyone who carries on an investment business in the United Kingdom must be authorised subject to certain exemptions.

Exempt Persons
1. Bank of England
2. Lloyds
3. Listed Money Market Institutions
4. President of the Family Division of the High Court
5. Accountant General of the Supreme Court
6. The Public Trustee
7. The Central Board of Finance of the Church of England etc.

In this connection it should be noted that many financial conglomerates will be supervised under other regulatory systems – for example, by the Bank of England in the case of banks and by the Department of Trade and Industry in the case of Insurance Companies.

1. Members of Self Regulatory Organisation (SRO's) are entitled to operate an investment business, i.e.:
   a. to deal in investments
   b. to arrange investment deals for others
   c. to manage investments
   d. to advise on investments
   e. to operate a collective investment scheme such as a unit trust.

   The SRO's will have satisfied the requirements of the Securities and Investments Board (SIB).
2. Certain professional bodies will be recognised by the SIB and will be able to authorise persons applying to it to engage in investment business. Authorisation will be granted by means of the issue of an Investment Business Certificate. This may only be granted to persons whose main business is the practice of a profession rather than an investment business.
3. Direct authorisation by the SIB will be granted if the applicant is a fit and proper person to carry on the investment business.
4. Overseas persons will require authorisation if they conduct investment business in the United Kingdom, whether or not they have a place of business in this country.

   Nationals of other EEC Member States will automatically be authorised provided they have no permanent place of business in the United Kingdom and are authorised to conduct investment business in their own State.

Conduct of Investment Business

The Financial Services Act contains powers to enforce compliance with the statutory rules and other regulations. These powers may be exercised by:

1.   Criminal prosecution brought by the Secretary of State or the Director of Public Prosecutions
2.   Civil action by any person who has suffered loss as a result of a transaction. Such a person may bring an action for damages against any person who has broken the rules and regulations (other than the financial resources rules) of the SIB, an SRO or a recognised professional body, as the case may be.
3.   Other procedures. In this connection the Act provides for the establishment of a Financial Services Tribunal to serve as a forum to hear appeals against certain decisions made by the Secretary of State or the SIB. The tribunal will consist of three persons nominated from a panel of ten. They must be legally qualified and at least one member must have had recent business experience.

The persons who may refer a matter to the Tribunal will be those who have received from the SIB:

1.   Notice that the SIB intends to refuse to grant authorisation or to withdraw or suspend authorisation.
2.   Notice that the SIB intends to terminate or suspend authorisation by virtue of authorisation in another EEC member state.
3.   Notice of intention to disqualify a person from employment in an investment business.
4.   Notice of a proposed public statement relating to an authorised person's misconduct.
5.   Notice of the imposition, rescission or variation of a prohibition or of a refusal to impose, rescind or vary one.

Any person affected has twenty eight days from the date on which the notice was served to require the SIB to refer the matter to the Tribunal.

From the above it will be apparent that the power to bring a criminal prosecution is the most effective sanction.

Misleading Statements and Practices

The Act (Section 47) creates two offences, the first of which is contained in Section 47 (1). This section provides that a person who:

1. makes a statement, promise or forecast which he knows to be misleading, false or deceptive
2. conceals any material facts or
3. recklessly makes a statement, promise or forecast which is misleading, false or deceptive shall be guilty of an offence.

The second offence is contained in Section 47 (2). This provides that any person who intentionally does any act or engages in any course of conduct which creates a false or misleading impression as to the market in or price or value of any investments shall be guilty of an offence.

For each offence the punishment for a person convicted on indictment is imprisonment for a term not exceeding seven years or to a fine or to both. If convicted before the magistrates the punishment is imprisonment not exceeding six months or a fine or both.

Rules for the Conduct of Business

Section 48 empowers the SIB to make rules relating to the conduct of business. The principles are set out in Schedule 8 of the Act.

1. Investment business should be carried on honestly and fairly.
2. Operators should carry out their responsibilities capably, carefully and to the best of their abilities.
3. They should be fair to their customers, which implies avoiding conflicts of interest.

There are also certain general requirements such as:

1. *Know your customer*. This means that the authorised person must take steps to find out about his customers' personal and financial situation so that he may be given the "best advice".
2. *Cold calling*. Unsolicited calls are forbidden by Section 56 except in relation to life assurance and unit trusts. When a sale results from an unsolicited call in relation to these two matters the investor must be informed that he has a fourteen day cooling off

period in which he can change his mind and cancel the agreement.

3.   *Customer agreements.* The rules relating to customer agreements will apply to all firms except registered life offices and trustees of regulated collective investment schemes.

Two types of investor need not be asked to sign a full customer agreement i.e.

1.   Occasional customers who may be offered "occasional customer agreements" and
2.   Business, experienced or professional customers who may be offered a "terms of business letter".

Apart from these all customer agreements must include the following information:

1.   Basic details about the investment business.
2.   The type of services offered.
3.   If the services include recommending purchases of single premium life policies or units in regulated collective schemes, a warning that the purchases cannot be cancelled, other than by mutual agreement.
4.   A statement of whether the customer agrees to the firm making uninvited calls on the customer and if so the circumstances in which such calls may be made.
5.   Where non business and non professional investors agree to unsolicited calls a warning that the investor will forfeit his right under the cancellation rules to treat any agreement entered into in consequence of such a call as unenforcable.
6.   The basic method and frequency of remuneration payable by the customer to the firm and a statement of whether the firm will earn any commissions other than from the customer and whether these will be passed on to the customer.
7.   The customers' investment objectives e.g. Capital growth, income etc.
8.   Restrictions or guidelines on what the business should put the investor in to.
9.   Statement of particular exchanges or markets which the customer doesn't want to get involved with.
10.   If the types of investment in which the investors funds are to

be sunk are not readily realisable, a warning of the risks involved.

11.   Arrangements by which a customer can terminate his contract without incurring any penalty charges.

12.   Arrangements for receiving instructions and reporting any advice to the customer.

13.   The accounting arrangements for the customer and arrangements for holding money or investments for the customer.

14.   In the case of a managed portfolio, its initial composition and the periods of account for which statements are to be provided.

Where the customer agreement concerns futures, options and contracts for differences, the agreement, in addition to the matters noted above, must also include:

1.   a warning of the risky nature of the investment
2.   a statement of the circumstances in which an investor will have to apply a deposit or a margin in support of a transaction or supplement that payment
3.   a statement of the circumstances in which the firm may close out existing contracts without reference to the customer.

A relationship with a customer for which a full agreement is required can be commenced only after the agreement has been received by the customer and he has signed and returned it.

An occasional customer agreement must outline the advice which the firm has given to the customer and any instructions that the customer has given to the firm. The agreement must be received and agreed by the customer before any transactions are conducted under it.

A "Terms of Business" letter must identify the investments and services for which the customer is to be treated as a business, professional or experienced investor.

Summary – Financial Services Act 1986

1.   The Act seeks to establish some controls over the business of dealing with investments.

2. Investment business is defined as buying, selling, arranging deals, managing and advising on investments.
3. A regulatory framework is set up under the DTI.
4. The SIB (Securities and Investments Board) may recognise and authorise SRO's, RPB's, RIE's, and RCH's.
5. All these organisations have to comply with certain standards and must give evidence of financial probity.
6. The Act creates two offences.

   a. It is an offence for any person to knowingly or recklessly make a misleading statement or to conceal any material fact. Section 47(1).
   b. It is an offence for any person to intentionally create a false impression as to the market in or price of any investments. Section 47(2).

Chapter Six

The Law of Agency

The examples of agencies that exist are commonplace and everyone probably appreciates their purpose. An estate agent is someone who acts on behalf of another to sell or buy his house or land. Theatrical artistes have agents who negotiate terms with producers of theatrical or TV shows. The agents are people who bring their principals into contractual relationship with third parties. In other words they make contracts with people; but these contracts will be binding not on themselves but on the people they are representing. In a typical agency relationship the agent makes the contract and then disappears, leaving the contract proper between the principal and the third party.

Principal

Of course there may probably be a contract between the principal and the agent but this is not the main contract – the important one is that between the principal and the third party.

The purpose of the law of Agency is to establish whether or not the agency relationship exists. Depending on the answer to that question the rights and duties of the parties can be determined.

As always the law seeks to determine the rights and liabilities of the parties. Is the agent himself to be liable, may the third party sue the principal or may the principal sue the third party?

Liability of the Agent

From a practical point of view I think one should consider the matter from the point of view of the third party. Does he know that he is dealing with an agent? That depends on whether or not he is informed on this point. Quite obviously an agent does not go round wearing a cap bearing the word "Agent" on it. So only if the agent notifies the person he is dealing with that he is an agent will the third party know this fact.

The normal agency situation is when the agent informs the third party that he is an agent acting for a certain principal. In that case the third party knows the position and the contract will be between the principal and the third party.

Looking at the agency relationship from the point of view of the principal – as a general rule it all depends on whether or not he has authorised the agent as to whether he will be liable or not. Thus if the agent is authorised to enter into a contract and the third party knows that he is dealing with an agent and maybe knows the identity of the principal then the contract when made will lie between the principal and the third party. The agent will have neither rights nor duties under the contract.

If the third party does not know he is dealing with an agent, because the agent has not informed him of the fact, then the third party will naturally conclude that he is dealing with the person who is the agent in his own right. Consequently the third party may only sue the agent, if the need arises. However if he later does discover the existence of the principal and his identity then he may sue him. He cannot of course sue both agent and principal. In this case the third party will believe he is dealing with the agent in his own right because he has not been informed that he is an agent. This is sometimes referred to as the doctrine of the undisclosed principal.

Another situation may arise when the agent informs the third party that he is an agent but does not identify his principal. This may occur when a large important company is wishing to buy certain property and if it became known that such a wealthy client had an interest in acquiring the property the price might become inflated. In this case the third party knows he is dealing with an agent and so it is up to him whether he continues to deal with a principal whose identity he does not know. At any rate the agent will have no liability in the matter.

Signatures

An agent may be liable if he signs a document, but it depends on the manner in which he signs it.

1.   The agent may sign in his own name. In that case it is propably true to say that the agent has accepted liability unless of course he makes it clear that he is signing as agent. However he must be careful to make sure that he is not merely describing his relationship to his principal e.g. A signs in his own name and adds "Chartered Civil Engineer". *Sika Contracts Ltd v B L Gill and Closeglen Properties Ltd (1978)*. It was held that A was liable as he had merely described his occupation.

   However in *Universal Steam Navigation Co Ltd v Mckelvie and Co (1923)* A was not liable when he signed in his own name "as agents".

   Section 26 of the Bills of Exchange Act 1882 provides:

   a.   Where a person signs a bill as a drawer, indorser or acceptor, and adds words to his signature, indicating that he signs for or on behalf of a principal or in a representative character, he is not personally liable thereon; but the mere addition to his signature of words describing him as an agent, or as filling a representative character, does not exempt him from personal liability.

   b.   In determining whether a signature on a bill is that of the principal or that of the agent by whose hand it is written, the construction most favourable to the validity of the instrument shall be adopted.

   The effect of this is that where an agent signs, in his own name, a deed or a bill of exchange then he will be liable on these documents. P will not be liable if his name does not appear on these documents. An exception would be if A signed a deed and was authorised by a power of attorney.

2.   If a person signs "per procurationem" then it indicates that he has only a limited authority. Often a person will sign in this way on behalf of a company. The principal therefore will only be liable if the agent is acting within his actual authority.

3.   The principal may of course authorise the agent to sign using his (the principal's) name. This is in order.

4.   No one has a proprietary right to any name, unless it is subject

to the trade mark rules. Therefore a person may use any name that he wishes so long as there is no dishonest intent.

In *Chapman v Smethurst (1909)* a promissory note was signed by the managing director who signed it "S Ltd. – S. M.D." The court held that this showed that the company S Ltd was to be bound and not S.

In *Elliott v Bax-Ironside (1925)* two directors signed a cheque as "I and M directors F Ltd" and on the back they indorsed it by signing "F Ltd." "I and M – directors". The two directors were held liable for the second signatures because they had merely indicated their occupations and the company was already liable because of the signatures on the front.

In *Bondina Ltd v Rollaway Shower Blinds Ltd (1986)*

The printed cheque form of a company contained its name, the branch of the bank and the number of the cheque. It was signed by two directors who added their names (W,M). It was held that the directors had adopted all the printing on the cheque including the name of the company and so the directors were not liable.

Liability of Principal

From the principal's point of view he will usually only be liable if he has authorised the agent to enter into his contract. This is known as the express appointment of an agent.

However an agency relationship may arise in other ways e.g.

1. If the principal holds out the agent as having his authority. That means the principal gives the third party the impression that the agent has the authority of the principal to make the contract he is making with the third party.

    A case in point here is *Watteau v Fenwick (1893)* where a firm of brewers forbade the manager of a public house to buy cigars for the business. The manager did in fact buy cigars in disoebedience of this order and the court held that the brewers were nevertheless still liable. They had held out the manager as having the normal authority of a manager of a public house which was to buy cigars for the business and had not communicated their restriction on his authority to the seller of the cigars.

2. The agent may have exceeded his authority but nevertheless the principal decides to adopt his contract. This is called

ratificat^n

"ratification" and is only possible if the agent notified the third party that he was an agent.

In *Keighley, Maxsted & Co v Durant (1901)* no ratification was possible because the agent had contracted in his own name.

Also in order for the principal to ratify an unauthorised contract of his agent, he must have had contractual capacity both at the time the contract was made and when it was ratified. Finally if the principal was a company then it must have been in existence when the contract was made. Thus a pre-incorporation contract will not bind a company when it is later incorporated – *Kelner v Baxter (1866)*.

3.   The agent is a carrier and is carrying perishable goods belonging to the principal. Something occurs to prevent their delivery and so the carrier must do something immediately otherwise the goods are going to become worthless. He sells the goods in order to minimise the principal's loss. On the face of it he will be liable to the principal, however if he can show that he tried to get in touch with him and failed and it was an emergency then he will be declared to be an "agent of necessity".

Selling perishable goods to limit principal's loss

In *Springer v G W Railway (1921)* the delivery of a consignment of tomatoes was delayed and so the carrier sold the perishable goods and the question arose – was he liable for interfering with the goods of another and did the purchasers get a good title to the goods which they bought? The court held that an agency of necessity had arisen and so the carrier was not liable to the owner, and the purchasers of the goods acquired good title to them.

Thus it can be seen that sometimes it can be said that an agent has been appointed expressly. In other cases the agency relationship merely arises because of circumstances – a relationship e.g. husband and wife; a situation e.g. perishable goods prevented from being delivered and the carrier sells them; or the holding out of a person as having the authority of another as in *Watteau v Fenwick (1893)*.

Where a man and a woman are living together (not necessarily as man and wife) then the woman has the right to pledge the man's credit for the purchase of necessaries i.e. food and certain articles for the home. This is the common law position and it is interesting to consider how this position may be affected by the modern approach to sexual equality.

There is one case when an agent must be appointed by a deed and that is when his principal expects him to execute a deed. The deed appointing the agent is called a power of attorney and often old people incapable of acting for themselves appoint some other person to deal with their affairs.

Power of Attorney

A power of attorney is required by the agent if it may become necessary for him to make a transaction by deed. In this case the attorney or agent must himself be appointed by deed. The law has always treated a transaction by deed in a special way. A deed was quite simply a document to which had been affixed a seal. At one time a seal was a large piece of wax on which a person's coat of arms would be impressed when the wax was in a molten state. It was necessary for the person executing the deed to state, with his finger on the seal, "I deliver this as my act and deed". Since the *Law of Property (Miscellaneous Provisions) Act 1989* a seal is not necessary but it must be made clear in the document that it is intended to be a deed. Nevertheless certain transactions will have no legal effect unless contained in a deed e.g. conveyance of the legal estate in land, or a legal mortgage of property.

Mtg of Land must be a deed

Powers of Attorney Act 1971

Signature and sealing may be by a person other than the donor if in his presence and by his direction – in this case 2 witnesses are necessary. The power of attorney must be stamped within 30 days of its execution.

The advantage of taking a power of attorney from the point of view of a bank is that the power can be made irrevocable and if it is given to secure a proprietary interest of the donee or the performance of an obligation owed to him, then so long as the obligation or interest continues the power will not be revoked by death, bankruptcy or mental incapacity of the donor. Such a situation could arise when a bank takes an equitable mortgage of a legal estate by receiving the title deeds. The deposit will be accompanied by a memorandum authorising the bank to sell the property in certain circumstances. Here the bank will have a proprietary interest in the land and so the power cannot be revoked.

if irrevocable power not revoked by death or bankruptcy

Eg mtge Bank has title deeds + memorandum authorising bank to sell property in certain circs

Bank has proprietary interest in land so can't revoke power

Powers which have not been given by way of security will be revoked by the death or mental incapacity of the donor.

This situation has been improved by the *Enduring Powers of Attorney Act 1985*. This provides that where an "enduring power" has been created it will not be revoked by the mental incapacity of the donor. The *Enduring Powers of Attorney (Prescribed Forms) Regulations 1986* specify the form that must be completed by the donor and the attorney.

If the attorney believes that the donor is becoming incapable he must apply for registration of the instrument creating the power to the Court of Protection. Before applying for registration he must give notice to certain relatives of the donor.

If the donor does eventually become incapable, the attorney may only act in accordance with the directions of the court until the instrument has been registered as mentioned above.

The timing of the creation of the enduring powers is of the greatest importance because a sane person may not be willing to execute the document and once he has become insane it is too late as the instrument could then be declared invalid.

In two cases *Re K* and *Re F* the court decided that it was sufficient if the donor understood the nature and effect of the power of attorney he or she was signing. It will not be necessary for the donor of the power to be able to manage his own affairs.

Duties of an Agent

The relationship between the principal and the agent, no matter how the relationship arose, is essentially one of trust (a fiduciary relationship).

1. The agent must obey the instructions given to him by his principal even if he thinks the instructions are wrong. Sometimes of course the principal may expect the agent to advise him and indeed this may be the reason he is employing an agent viz. to use his skill and care. The agent must not delegate his duty to another person unless such delegation has been agreed with the principal, is the custom of the trade or the delegation merely takes place in relation to purely administrative matters.

2. An agent must not allow his personal interests to come into conflict with those of the principal.

3. The agent must not make a secret profit or take a bribe from a third party. In *Reading v Att. Gen. (1951)* it was held that a sergeant in the British Army had misused his position by sitting on a lorry thereby giving the impression that it was a military convoy and so it was not inspected. He was ordered to repay the money he had received to the State.

4. If the agent accepts a secret commission or a bribe the following consequences may ensue:

    Salford Corporation v Lever (1891) Lever agreed to pay the Corporation's agent 1 shilling per ton if his tender for the supply of coal was accepted. When the bribe was discovered it was held that both the giver and the taker of the bribe could be sued and prosecuted under the *Prevention of Corruption Act 1906*. Also the agent could be dismissed without receiving his commission and the contract with the third party could be set aside. In that case it was held:

    a. The principal may dismiss him.
    b. He can recover the secret commission from the agent. If the commission has not been paid over to the agent, the principal may recover it from the person who promised the agent.
    c. Whether he has recovered the secret commission or not, the principal may still bring an action for damages against the person who gave the agent the bribe.
    d. He may refuse to pay the agent any commission or remuneration. If he has already paid it, he may recover it from the agent.
    e. The principal may repudiate the whole contract entered into by the agent whether the offer of a bribe did influence the agent's course of action or not.

5. The agent must not disclose any confidential information he has obtained through acting as agent. He must inform the principal of all matters relating to the agency when they come to his notice.

6. No delegation. This duty is often expressed by the latin maxim "delegatus non potest delegare." This is because the relationship between a principal and agent is a personal one. Where the agent's authority is coupled with a discretion

(e.g. to inspect a picture, and if it is genuine, to buy it), delegation of such authority will be a breach of the confidence reposed in the agent.

Delegation is permissible in the following cases:

a.   Where delegation was in the contemplation of the parties at the commencement of the agency.

b.   Where the appointment of a sub-agent is necessary for the proper execution of his work.

c.   If delegation becomes necessary as a result of a sudden emergency.

d.   Where delegation is sanctioned by trade, custom or usage.

e.   Where the work will not call for the exercise of any discretion by the sub-agent.

f.   Delegation is also possible where part of the work requires special skill (e.g. solicitor to draft a conveyance of a house) and the agent does not have that skill.

Care and Skill

A paid agent is liable to the principal if he fails to do the work and as a result the principal suffers damage, as held in *Turpin v Bilton* (1843). A gratuitous agent is not liable for non-feasance.

However, once he commences the work he will be liable if he does not exercise appropriate care and skill: *Coggs v Bernard.* (1703).

A gratuitous agent must use the care and skill he will give to his own affairs. This means he must use such skill as he possesses. A paid agent must use the skill he claims to possess, or may be implied from his profession.

Rights of the Principal

The duties of the agent give corresponding rights to the principal. He may sue the agent for damages if he commits a breach of any of these duties.

Rights of the Agent

1.   *Right of Re-imbursement.*   Any reasonable expenses necessarily incurred by the agent in performing his duties must be repaid to him by his principal. This obligation may be enforced even where no amount has been fixed, by a quantum meruit.

2.   *Set-off.*   If the principal brings an action against the agent for breach of duty, the agent may exercise his right of setoff for any sums due to him either as commission or as indemnity for expenses incurred.

3.   *Lien.*   If the principal has failed to pay the agreed commission or an indemnity to the agent and the agent has any goods of the principal in his possession, then subject to certain conditions, the agent may exercise a lien on such goods and retain possession until the principal has honoured his obligation.

4.   *Action for the Agreed Commission or Remuneration.*   The agent is entitled to his commission after he has performed his agency.

Duties of the Principal

The rights of the agent impose corresponding duties on the principal: e.g., a duty to pay the agent the agreed commission and to indemnify the agent for any expenses incurred by him.

Termination of the agency

As the agency relationship is usually based upon agreement between the principal and agent then it follows that it may be terminated by mutual agreement. Apart from that however the principal may withdraw or revoke the authority of his agent; but if he does that he must remember to notify any third party with whom the agent may have had dealings, otherwise the principal might be liable if the agent contracts with them. Where the agent's authority is coupled with an interest then revocation is not possible, e.g. where the principal owes a debt to a person and authorises him to collect rents from houses he owns.

Furthermore the agency relationship may be terminated by operation of law. This means if a certain event occurs, such as the death or insanity of either principal or agent, or the bankruptcy of the principal then the agent's authority will be terminated. The point about this means of terminating the agency contract that should be borne in mind by the agent is that any of these events will take away the agent's authority whether or not he knows that the event has occurred. Consequently if the event occurs unknown to the agent he may be acting without authority and this will result in his

[margin handwritten note: P to notify 3rd parties if agents authority terminated]

[margin handwritten note: As Authy taken away whether or not known P dead, mad or bankrupt]

being made liable for any contract he makes after the event has occurred.

In *Yonge v Toynbee (1910)* the principal became insane, unknown to his solicitors, who were acting for him in litigation. Because the solicitors took steps which resulted in the other party incurring expenses the court held that they were liable to reimburse the other party. The solicitors had acted without authority, although innocently, and thus were liable for breach of implied warranty of authority. This action is interesting because it means that when an agent notifies a party that he is an agent then the other party is entitled to assume that he has the authority he professes to have. If that turns out not to be so then the agent will be liable for breach of his warranty of authority.

Bankers as Agents

The relationship between a banker and his customer is discussed elsewhere. The general relationship is that of debtor and creditor. In addition the banker is the agent of his customer for the purpose of honouring his cheques when he is referred to as a "paying banker" and for collecting the proceeds of cheques for his customer when he is known as a "collecting banker".

In addition to the general contract which is described in *Joachimson v Swiss Bank Corporation (1921)* there may be special contracts such as the following:

Advising on investments
The principles here are similar to those applicable to the giving of information as to the credit and standing of third parties.

The law is not settled whether this forms part of a banker's normal business. In *Banbury v Bank of Montreal (1918)* it was pointed out that the limits of a banker's business cannot be laid down as a matter of law. He is under no obligation to offer advice as to investments.

In *Woods v Martins Bank Ltd (1958)*, it was established that where a banker does advise on investments as part of his normal business, he is then under a duty to do so without negligence.

If the banker does not advise as part of his normal banking business, he may nevertheless offer to advise in a particular case without responsibility. In such a case, the reservation must be made in the clearest terms.

Many banks now offer such advice as part of their normal banking business.

Keeping valuables in safe custody

1. Where a banker assumes charge of a customer's valuables for "safe custody" he may do so with or without payment.

2. If it is done without any payment for the accommodation, the banker's position is that of a gratuitous bailee: *Leese v Martin (1873)*. In such a case the bank is bound to take "the same care of the property entrusted to him as a reasonably prudent and careful man may fairly be expected to take of his own property."

3. If the banker is a paid bailee he must safeguard the property entrusted to his care by every means in his power. The employment of facilities at the banker's disposal, such as safes, strong-rooms, etc, will be included in the care he must take of his customer's valuables.

4. Apart from negligence, a banker is not liable for the loss of a customer's goods even if the loss was caused by the fraud or felony of members of his own staff. *Foster v Essex Bank* (17 Massachusetts Reports) ? *Doubtful*

5. A paid bailee is liable for ordinary negligence but a gratuitous bailee is only liable for gross negligence. Hence as a banker holds himself out as a person skilled in taking care of valuable articles, he must use that skill even if he is only a gratuitous bailee for otherwise he would be guilty of gross negligence.

Status Inquiries

This is not a term of the banking contract. Nevertheless bankers are often requested to give information as to the credit and standing of a customer. The following points are relevant:

Under *Lord Tenterden's Act (Statute of Frauds Amendment Act 1828)*, S.6, a bank is liable for a false and fraudulent misrepresentation as to the credit of a third party. This Act does not apply in the case of innocent misrepresentation.

A banker does not owe an inquirer any duty of care as such. The duty, if any, is one of common honesty, which however produces no cause of action. But in *Hedley Byrne & Co Ltd v Heller & Partners Ltd* the House of Lords pointed out that in certain circumstances there may be a special relationship between two people, based neither on contract nor on a fiduciary relationship, but from a relationship of proximity, which will give rise to a duty to take care in giving references. This may happen, for example, where the inquirer relied upon the banker's special knowledge of the customer.

This duty may be excluded by a properly worded disclaimer of liability incorporated into the reference.

Summary – Law of Agency

1.   The Agency relationship arises when one person authorises another to make a contract on his behalf.

2.   A bank may be involved because sometimes, when dealing with a customer, e.g. a company, it will be dealing with a director who will be the agent of the company. Sometimes the bank itself may act as agent for a customer e.g. collecting the proceeds of a cheque from the paying bank.

3.   The Agency contract need not be in writing. However if the agent is given a power of attorney then he must be appointed by deed. The *Enduring Powers of Attorney Act 1985* is important in this respect because in certain circumstances the agent will not lose his authority merely because the person who authorised him has died or become insane.

4.   The agent owes certain duties to his principal, principally that of acting in good faith.

Chapter Seven

The Law of Partnership

Both partnerships and companies are business associations and if a sole trader decides to give up trading on his own then he can either form a partnership or a company. This would necessitate his joining with other people but that would be a normal step in the progression of a sole trader. Having started on his own he finds that, if his business is prospering, he will soon need more money. He can of course borrow money but there must be a limit to how much can be borrowed. However people may be prepared to supply the money if they, personally, can have some control over how the money is being used and for that situation to arise then a legal bond must be established. Both partnerships and companies are therefore different forms of legal relationships established for the purpose of running a business.

The *Partnership Act 1890* states that a partnership is "the relation which subsists between persons carrying on business in common with a view of profit". The legal term for a partnership is a "firm".

Notice that the *Partnership Act* speaks of "a relation which subsists". In other words if some people are carrying on business in common it may be that they are in partnership and do not realise that fact and accordingly the rules relating to such associations are contained in the Act of 1890.

From the definition above, three elements must exist before there can be a partnership:

1. there must be a business;
2. the business must be carried on in common;
3. it must be carried on with a view of profit.

The following relationships are therefore not partnerships;

1. Joint or part ownership of property does not of itself create a partnership.
2. Clubs and trade associations.

3.   Companies registered under any of the *Companies Acts*, are not partnerships.
4.   Barristers are not allowed to enter into partnerships.

No formalities are needed to form a partnership although there must be an agreement between the persons concerned to work in common. It may be that a number of persons are working together in a business with a view of profit and they know nothing of partnerships. Nevertheless a court may decide that they are legally in partnership and so the provisions of the *Partnership Act 1890* will apply. In particular Section 24 provides that:

1.   all partners will share equally in the profits even though they have contributed different amounts;
2.   no partner may receive any remuneration;
3.   every general partner may take part in the management of the firm;
4.   a partner is entitled to be indemnified by the firm in respect of payments made and liabilities incurred by him:

   a.   In the ordinary and proper conduct of the business of the firm; or
   b.   In or about anything necessarily done for the preservation of the business or partnership property.

Section 24 further provides that

1.   No person may be introduced as a partner without the consent of all existing partners.
2.   Any difference arising as to ordinary matters connected with the partnership may be decided by a majority of the partners.
3.   No change may be made in the nature of the partnership business without the consent of all the existing partners.
4.   Subject to any agreement between the partners, the partnership will be dissolved by the death of any partner.

It will be apparent that if these provisions were to apply then the partners would not always be particularly satisfied. Therefore it is more usual for a partnership agreement to be entered into called "Articles of Partnership" or if by deed, a "Deed of Partnership". In such an agreement the partnerss may agree anything they like and so it is usual, taking some of the previous points,

1.   for the partners to agree that if one were to die his share of the partnership would be purchased by the surviving members;
2.   the profits will be distributed pro rata to the amount of capital contributed by each of the partners;
3.   the partners to receive an annual remuneration like any other employee.

The Firm Name

It sometimes happens that the partners carry on business under a name which is different from the names of the partners. This is known as the *firm name*.

Before the *Companies Act 1981*, it was necessary for the firm name to be registered under the *Registration of Business Names Act 1916*, however that Act was repealed and the provisions relating to business names have been consolidated in the *Business Names Act 1985*. The business name does not now need to be registered, but S.4 of that Act requires that publicity be given regarding the partners who are trading under a business name.

The methods of publicity are:

1.   The name of each partner must be disclosed on all business letters, invoices and receipts.
2.   The name and address of each partner must be displayed in any premises where the business is being carried on.
3.   There must be disclosed, in relation to each partner, an address within Great Britain at which service of any document would be effective.

Failure to comply with the disclosure requirements is an offence punishable with a fine. Furthermore, if a firm using a business name has failed to comply with the disclosure requirements, and sues for breach of contract, the claim may be dismissed if the defendant can show:

1.   That he has a claim against the firm arising out of the contract, which he is unable to pursue because of the plaintiff's non-compliance, or:
2.   That he the defendant has suffered financial loss in connection with the contract, because of the plaintiff's non-compliance.
     The court may however in such circumstances permit the

[handwritten margin note: Business Name does not have to be reg'd but publicity must be given]

proceedings to continue if satisfied that it would be "just and equitable" to do so.

Relationship of partners to third parties

An important feature of a partnership is that each partner is considered, in law, to be the agent of his fellow partner as regards the making of contracts which are made in the course of the partnership business (S.5). Thus every partner has authority to buy and sell goods commonly used in the partnership business; he can hire and fire staff; if it is a trading partnership (which is one which buys and sells goods as opposed to merely giving a service) then each partner has authority to issue negotiable instruments, to borrow money and pledge goods in the firm's name. Thus if a person is in a partnership (and remember he may not fully appreciate this fact) then he can be made liable for certain contracts made by a fellow partner. As far as the third party is concerned who has been dealing with the partnership it may well be important to have it established that a number of people are in partnership because then the list of defendants is extended and the plaintiff will have a better chance of getting his money.

So much for contracts, but the same reasoning applies as far as wrongful acts committed by a partner are concerned; his fellow partners will be held liable for these, provided of course they are committed in the course of the partnership business.

Relationship of partners between themselves

Between themselves the partners have rights and owe duties and these are set down in the articles of partnership as mentioned earlier, but also the contract of partnership is a contract of good faith in its operation. This means that there need not be the fullest disclosure when the contract is entered into, and so it is up to each partner to satisfy himself that he is doing the right thing by entering into partnership with his fellow partners (rather like marriage). However once the contract is made then there must be the fullest disclosure of all relevant matters concerning the partnership business. A partner may not make a secret profit and must render total account of his dealings. In the same vein a partner must not set himself up in competition with the partnership business.

At all times therefore every partner must conduct himself with good faith towards his fellow partners.

Section 25 provides that a majority of the partners cannot expel any partner without authority expressed in the Articles of Partnership.

Joint and Joint and several liability

In joint liability there is a single liability for the firm's contracts. Thus a creditor will have only one action – he may sue one partner or he may sue all the partners together – but he cannot do both. However under the *Civil Liability (Contribution) Act 1978* a creditor may sue the firm or each of the partners in the firm. This has always been the case where liability is joint and several. For that reason banks have always preferred joint and several liability. Even though the distinction between joint and joint and several liability has disappeared by virtue of the 1978 Act, banks still require liability to be joint and several because:

1. when a partner is bankrupt or dies the bank may proceed against his estate equally with his personal creditors.
2. if there is a debit balance on the partnership account the bank will obtain a right of combination in respect of a credit balance on the partner's personal account, since the partner is personally liable for the debt.

Retiring and New Partners' Liability

In the absence of any contrary agreement, a partner's liability for contracts or debts contracted while he was a partner does not cease upon his retirement. He remains liable for debts incurred whilst he was a member of the firm. The creditors may, however, agree to discharge him from his liabilities and agree to look to the new firm for payment by making a contract of novation which is a "new contract".

A valid contract of novation is usually effected by the introduction of an incoming partner who agrees to be liable together with the remaining partners for the retired partner's share of the debts.

Where the surviving partners do not intend to take on a new partner, the retiring partner's release by the creditors must be by deed.

An incoming partner is not liable for debts of the firm before he joined unless he is a party to a contract of novation.

Retiring Partner's Liability for Post-Retirement Debts

Section 36 of the *Partnership Act 1890* provides that a retiring partner may be liable for debts incurred after his retirement.

Creditors are divided into two classes:

1. Those who had dealt with the partnership before the retirement.
2. Those who did not deal with the partnership before the retirement.

The retiring partner is liable for new debts contracted with any creditor in group 1 unless the latter has received individual notice of his retirement.

If a creditor is aware of the retirement, the retiring partner will not be liable for post-retirement debts even if he has not given notice to the creditor.

With creditors in group 2 notice in the *London Gazette* is sufficient notice of retirement to the creditors.

If no Gazette notice is given a retiring partner will still not be liable for post-retirement debts to a creditor who did not know that he was a partner: *Tower Cabinet Co v Ingram (1949)*.

However if a partner has died and the firm's business is continued under the old name the continued use of that name or of the deceased partner's name shall not of itself make the deceased's personal representatives liable to partnership debts after his death. (S.14, S.36).

Dissolution of a Partnership

As we have seen, a partnership will usually come into existence because of the agreement of the persons who wish to join in partnership with one another. Thus it is quite logical for such a relationship, which came into being because of an agreement, to be terminated by agreement. On the other hand a partnership may be formed for a particular length of time or to perform some purpose. Obviously when the period of time has expired or the purpose has been achieved the partnership will be at an end. In addition the *Partnership Act* provides that a partnership will automatically be dissolved if one of the partners dies or becomes bankrupt. However the old partnership will not be dissolved if the partnership agreement provides for alternative arrangements to be made (e.g. the remaining partners to buy the share of the deceased or bankrupt partner). Thus any agreement with A, B and C will continue notwithstanding the death etc of A, if this has been agreed.

In the case of the death of a partner the deceased's estate will not normally be liable for debts incurred by the firm after his death and so it is essential that the account with the partnership is broken when the bank is notified of a partner's death etc.

Apart from the above ways in which a partnership may be dissolved, it may be that the partners cannot agree between themselves. In that case an application may be made to the court to issue an order dissolving the partnership. This application must be based on one of the following grounds:

1. The insanity of one of the partners, under the *Mental Health Act 1983*.
2. Where a partner has become permanently incapable of carrying out his share of the partnership business.
3. When a partner wilfully and persistently commits a breach of the partnership agreement.
4. On the ground that the partnership can be carried on only at a loss, and there is no prospect of the firm making a profit.
5. When a partner has committed some act which will prejudicially affect the carrying on of the business. In *Carmichael v Evans (1904)* it was held that a conviction for dishonesty was sufficient reason for the dissolution of a firm of solicitors.
6. In circumstances that the court thinks just and equitable.

Public Notice of Dissolution
On dissolution every partner may publish a notice to this effect in the *London Gazette* and may compel the other partners to sign the notice. S.37.

Dissolution rescinds the power of the partners to act as agents for the firm, except in respect of:

1. transactions started but not completed; and
2. acts which are necessary to wind up the partnership affairs e.g., employing an accountant to prepare the final acounts. S.38

Partnership Property

This includes property originally brought into the partnership or was later acquired in the course of the partnership business or was bought with money belonging to the firm.

Naturally, upon the dissolution of the partnership it will be necessary to collect in the partnership property, liquidate it and distribute it. This will be done in the following order:

1.   Creditors of the firm will be paid.
2.   Partners will receive their loans to the firm if any.
3.   Partners will receive their capital contributions.
4.   Any surplus to be divided amongst the partners in the proportion in which profits are divisible.

If there are insufficient partnership assets to cover items 1, 2 and 3 then each partner must pay towards the deficiency in the proportion in which they shared profits.

If a partner, due to insolvency, is unable to contribute his equal share of the lost capital then the solvent partners are not liable to contribute it for him. In *Garner v Murray 1904* it was decided that each partner must contribute his share of the deficiency ingoring the share of the insolvent partner. Then the assets are distributed according to the rules mentioned earlier.

Bankruptcy of the Partnership
This must be distinguished from the bankruptcy of a partner which will result in the dissolution of the partnership unless the partners have agreed otherwise.

The *Insolvent Partnerships Order 1986* permits partnerships to be wound up as if they were unregistered companies and does not necessarily involve the bankruptcy of the partners.

Instead a creditor may present a bankruptcy petition against one of more of the partners; or petition for the winding up of the firm and the bankruptcy of the partners. *The Insolvent Partnerships Order 1986* provides that a creditor has three choices:

1.   to wind up the partnership alone as if it were an unregistered company.
2.   to make bankrupt the partners alone.
3.   wind up the partnership and make bankrupt all the partners.

A petition for winding-up may be presented by a creditor or a partner on the following grounds:

1. the partnership has ceased to carry on its business.
2. the partnership is dissolved
3. the partnership is unable to pay its debts
4. it is just and equitable that the partnership be wound up.

A partnership is deemed unable to pay its debts if

1. a creditor who is owed £750 or more has demanded payment in writing and no payment has been made within three weeks or no security has been given.
2. notice of an action for debt has been served against a partner for a partnership debt and he has not paid within three weeks.
3. an execution against the partnership is unsatisfied.
4. the firm's liabilities exceed its assets.

The partnership and the bank

As regards the relationship between the bank and a partnership when opening an account the same criteria apply and have to be examined as when opening an account for a single person viz the identity of the customer – who are the partners? What is their business? and are they the sort of customers the bank would want to do business with?

The question for consideration is the authority for opening the account. One partner does have implied authority to open an account in the name of the partnership but does not have the authority to open an account for the partnership in his own name.

Alliance Bank Ltd v Kearsley (1871)
The defendant was William Kearsley and he and his brother James were in partnership. In 1864 James opened an account for the partnership but in his own name in Manchester. The reason was that he was the only resident partner.

When the account became overdrawn the bank tried to recover the money from the other partner. The claim failed because the court held that one partner has no authority to open a partnership account in his own name so as to bind the other partners.

In practice therefore a bank will get all the partners to sign the mandate and then the difficulty regarding the authority of any partner and the name of the account will be avoided.

Mandate for partnership accounts

A typical mandate form for a partnership account will:

1. state the name of the firm
2. specify the names of the partners who are authorised to sign cheques and orders or instructions authorising payment on behalf of the firm.
3. authorise the bank to deliver up any items held in safe custody and to act on the instructions of the named signatory.
4. In particular the partners will agree that they will be jointly and severally liable for any debts owing to the bank.

Summary – The Law of Partnership

1. A partnership consists of a number (not more than 20, unless authorised) of persons working in a business together for profit.
2. Each partner will bind his fellow partners by any contract he makes which he has authority to make.
3. A partnership is based on agreement between the partners and so they can agree anything between themselves and these agreements may be written down and are called Articles of Partnership.
4. A bank when conducting business with a partnership will usually get all partners to sign the mandate so there can be no possibility of any partner trying to avoid his liabilities.

Chapter Eight

Law of Companies

In addition to a partnership there is another form of business organisation called the registered company or limited company. It is called by these names because such a company is formed by registering certain documents with the Registrar of Companies and it is a limited company because the liability of its shareholders is limited.

A company is an artificial legal person. In other words it is a person in the eyes of the law and has rights and duties like any human person. This point was established in the famous case: *Salomon v Salomon & Co (1897)*

In that case Mr Salomon formed a company to take over his business of manufacturing shoes. The company paid Mr Salomon for his business partly in cash, partly in shares and partly by a charge over the company's assets. The company was wound up and its debts to creditors were in excess of its assets. Therefore the creditors claimed the assets of the company arguing that a person cannot owe money to himself and as Mr Salomon owned the company he and it were the same person. The court held that the company was a separate person from Mr Salomon who owned it.

However being artificial a company cannot be seen – it exists on paper. One can look at a factory manufacturing soap but one is not looking at Unilever plc or Lever Bros. plc but at a factory which happens to be owned by a person whose name is Unilever plc. One says one is going to do some shopping in Marks and Spencer. The shopping is being done in a shop owned by a single person called Marks and Spencer plc. How does one know that a company exists then? As a company exists only on paper – the Certificate of Incorporation is the document that brings a company into existence and this is proof of the company's existence. It is issued by the Registrar of Companies when he has examined the documents filed in his office by the promoters of the company.

The concept that a company exists as a single person on its own is the basis of company law. Together with the principle that the liability of the shareholders is limited to the amount due to be paid (if any) for their shares, they are the two main differences between a company and a partnership. As we have seen the partners contribute money to the assets of the partnership but if this is insufficient to pay the debts of the partnership then the partners must continue to provide more money, even if that means they are bankrupting themselves. In the case of a company the shareholders have contributed to the assets of the company but if this proves to be insufficient to pay the creditors of the company then the shareholders will lose their money in the company, but will not have to provide more money. The other difference is that the company is a person separate from the persons (the shareholders) who own it. A partnership is not a separate person but consists of the partners. As an illustration, it is often said that if all the partners of a partnership are in a room and a bomb explodes killing them all, that would be the end of the firm. But if all the shareholders of a company were killed in the same circumstances that would not be the end of the company. It would continue its existence, but with different shareholders of course.

The law relating to companies is contained mainly in the *Companies Act 1985*. This is the last in a long line of Companies Acts and in the main is a consolidating Act.

Formation of a Company

The people who wish to form a company as a vehicle for running their business are called promoters. It is possible to buy a ready-made company or it may be decided to form a company from scratch. The procedure for this is to file with the Registrar of Companies certain documents – the most important being the Memorandum of Association and the Articles of Association.

The Memorandum of Association

By section 2 of the *Companies Act 1985* the memorandum of every company must state

1.   the name of the company
2.   whether the registered office of the company is to be situated in England and Wales or Scotland.

3. the objects of the company
4. in the case of a company having a share capital the memorandum must also state the amount of the share capital which the company proposes to be registered and the division of that capital into shares of a fixed amount.
5. also in the case of a company limited by shares there must be a statement that the liability of its members or shareholders is limited.

This document was of the greatest importance to outsiders dealing with the company because it contained the objects clause which stated the purposes for which the company had been formed and in so doing it established the powers of the company to enter into contracts. The rule was that a company could only enter into a valid and enforceable contract if it had power to do so. If any contract it made was outside its powers (ultra vires) then the contract was null and void. This principle was known as the "ultra vires doctrine" and was intended to protect investors in the company and those who were considering lending money to it. By consulting the objects clause then such people would know the permitted activities of the company.

However in practice this was not particularly helpful because the lawyers who drew up a company's documents usually made the objects so wide as to cover every possible activity that the company might have wished to enter into in the future. Nevertheless if a company entered into a contract and it was discovered that it lacked the power to enter into that particular contract then the contract would be void and the company could not be sued successfully. Since our entry into the European Economic Community we have had to modify our company law in certain areas to accord with Common Market practices.

The latest position is that the Companies Act 1989 has amended the Companies Act 1985. Section 108-112 of the 1989 Act has effectively abolished the "ultra vires" rule. These changes came into force on 4th February 1991. Section 35 of the 1985 Act (as amended) does away with the "ultra vires" rule.

Section 35 A of the 1985 Act (as amended) relates to the power of directors to binds the company to acts within the power of the company.

Section 35 B of the 1985 Act (as amended) provides that a party to a transaction with a company is not bound to enquire into the terms of the company's memorandum nor as to any limitation in the directors' powers.

Section 110 of the *Companies Act 1989* inserts a new *section 3A* into the *1985 Act* which allows a company to state that its objects are,'To carry on business as a general commercial company.' A company which chooses this option in preference to a traditional objects clause will have power to carry on any trade or business and to do all things incidental or conducive thereto.

The Department of Trade and Industry has issued the following note:-

"Ultra Vires" reform – Companies Act 1989 (Sections 108–112)

The provisions of the 1985 Act which deal with the ultra vires doctrine and the authority of the board of directors are amended (the ultra vires doctrine is a common law rule which, in the absence of statutory provision, renders void acts by a company which are beyond its stated objects). The main features of the amended provisions are

1. the validity of a completed act of a company is not to be called into question on the grounds of lack of capacity by reason of anything in the company's memorandum of association;

2. in favour of a person dealing with the company in good faith, the power of the board of directors to bind the company or authorise others to do so is to be free of any limitation in the company's constitution;

3. a third party is to have no duty to enquire as to the capacity of a company or the authority of directors to bind the company;

4. transactions which are beyond the authority of the board of directors and to which directors or connected persons are a party are to be voidable in certain circumstances at the instance of the company;

5. if a company states that its object is to carry on business as a "general commercial company" it will have the object of carrying on any business or trade whatsoever, and will have the power to do whatever is incidental or conclusive to that object;

6. the provisions on capacity and authority are qualified in the case of charitable companies, so as to maintain current controls on charitable companies and to assist in the recovery of misappropriated charitable property. In order to prevent those provisions on charitable companies undermining the provisions affecting companies generally, charitable companies are required to disclose their charitable status in their official documents if the status is not apparent from their name.

Alteration of the Objects

A company may alter its objects by the passing of a special resolution to that effect.

After the resolution has been passed the company must wait for twenty-one days (before implementing the alteration) to see whether any members who oppose the alteration may apply to the court to have it set aside. An application to cancel the alteration will not be entertained by the court unless it is made by

1. at least 15 per cent of the members; or
2. the holders of at least 15 per cent of any debentures issued by the company.

The court may on such an application make an order confirming the alteration or may provide for the purchase by the company of the shares of any members of the company.

If the alteration is confirmed (i.e. the dissentients are over-ruled) the company must deliver to the Registrar a printed copy of the memorandum as altered.

Section 110 of the *Companies Act 1989* inserts a new *section 4* into the *Companies Act 1985.*This allows a company to alter its objects for any reason.

The Name of the Company

The name chosen must not be undesirable in the opinion of the Secretary of State for Trade and Industry. A name is undesirable if it is either:

1. too similar to the name of another company, or
2. misleading; e.g., the name suggests that the company has connections with a government department, a member of the royal family, a district or a country.

Once the Secretary of State has approved a name for the company, it must be painted or affixed on the business premises of the company, engraved on its seal, and mentioned on all business documents and negotiable instruments.

A company limited by guarantee may be allowed to dispense with the word "Limited" by the Secretary of State if the following conditions are satisfied: S.30

1.   the company is formed for promoting commerce, art, science, religion, charity or any other useful object;
2.   its profits are to be devoted to the promotion of those objects; and
3.   no part of its profits is to be distributed to the members in the form of dividends.

A company may alter its name provided the following procedure is adopted;

1.   The company must pass a special resolution to effect the change, and,
2.   obtain the written consent of the Secretary of State.

Once the alteration of the name has been made, the Registrar of Companies will issue an altered certificate of incorporation.

If a company has a trading name different from its registered name, the *Business names Act 1985* will apply. The effect of this Act has been noted in the chapter on Partnerships.

Articles of Association

The other important document is the *Articles of Association*. This is of importance to the shareholders of the company because it contains their rights as to transfer of shares and payment of dividends. It also contains information regarding the holding of meetings, the appointment of the directors and their powers. Thus the articles are of importance to insiders. If a company does not wish to draw up its own articles then it may adopt the ready made set of articles known as Table A which is to be found in a statutory instrument called *The Companies (Tables A to F) Regulations 1985.* (S.1 1985 No 805 as amended by S.1 1985 No 1052)

In the case of a company limited by shares, its articles are not registered, Table A automatically applies to it.

The following are some of the matters which are provided for in a company's articles:

1.   Calls on its shares.
2.   The company's lien on its shares.
3.   The transfer of shares.
4.   The exercise of the borrowing powers of the company.

5. The delegation of the management of the company to the board of directors.
6. The voting rights of members.
7. The payment of dividends.
8. Variation of the members' rights.
9. The conduct of meetings.
10. The capitalisation of profits.
11. The use of the company's seal.

Effect of the Articles

When registered, the articles constitute a contract between the members and the company. This contract binds the members to the company but only in their capacity as members. Hence if the articles confer on a member or any other person a right not shared by all the other members of the company, this cannot be enforced against the company.

In *Eley v Positive Assurance Co (1876)* a member was made a solicitor for life of a company by the articles of the company. When he was dismissed he sued the company but it was held that the contract in the articles should not be enforced by him as the right he sought to enforce was not a "membership right".

The members in their capacity as members are bound to the company: *Companies Act S.14.*

Alteration of the Articles

By Section 9 of the *Companies Act 1985* a company may alter its articles of association by a special resolution. Any alteration is as valid as if it was originally contained in the articles.

Directors

Mention has been made of the fact that the company is an artificial person and cannot be seen but only exists on paper. So the question will no doubt occur as to how can a company operate. The answer is through human agents called directors. The directors' powers are contained in the articles and so they operate and decide matters on behalf of the company, provided they have the necessary authority to act. Thus when one says, "The company has decided to buy X Co. plc" what that really means is that the directors have so decided.

However when one considers who appoints the directors, then the answer is the shareholders in general meeting. Thus the shareholders own the company and they appoint the directors to run the company on their behalf. The directors are given certain powers to act without recourse to the shareholders but of course such powers may be curtailed or extended as the shareholders wish. The directors may only act on behalf of the company within the powers of the company and also within their own powers. These powers are set out in the Articles of Association. Certain matters may need the authority of the shareholders in general meeting e.g. the fixing of a dividend, the passing of the accounts or the appointment of the auditors.

As an agent is in a position of trust as regards his principal, so is a director as regards the company. A director must exercise his powers for the purpose for which they are conferred and for the benefit of the company and must not put himself in a position in which his duties to the company and his personal interests may conflict.

Some directors (called non executive directors) are appointed because of the contacts they can bring to the company. They might have been Cabinet Ministers, Trade Union leaders etc. Other directors perform some particular function within the company, such as Financial Director, Production Director etc. These latter are known as Managing directors or executive directors.

Article 70 of Table A states that "Subject to the provisions of the Act, the memorandum and the articles and to any directions given by special resolution, the business of the company shall be managed by the directors who may exercise all the powers of the company."

If a company has as its object "to carry on business as a general commercial company" then it will have the power to do whatever is incidental or conclusive to that object.

A person dealing with a company must ensure

1.   The directors must have the necessary power to enter into any particular transaction on behalf of the company.
2.   If any particular procedure has to be followed then the transaction must have been made according to that.

If a bank is contemplating lending money to a company it must ascertain the directors' powers to borrow money on behalf of the company by consulting the articles. In some cases the shareholders may desire to restrict the directors' borrowing powers.

It can happen that an act is intra vires the company but ultra vires the directors. In that case the unauthorised act of the directors may be ratified by the company.

However it may be that a bank should not consult the Articles because once it does, it will have actual notice of any limitation on the powers of the directors. If the bank does not have actual notice then it may be protected by *Section 35 A of the Companies Act 1985* (amended).

As regards any particular procedure that needs to be followed, the *rule in Turquand's case* may be of assistance.

The Rule in Turquand's Case

This rule reiterates the rule of agency that a person who deals with an agent will be able to bind the agent's principal provided the agent acted within the scope of his actual or apparent authority.

The rule merely extends it to the special circumstances of companies when the directors act as its agents.

Every person dealing with a company is deemed to know the contents of its public documents – i.e. the memorandum, articles and presumably copies of any special or extraordinary resolutions it may have passed. This is because copies of these documents must be filed with the Registrar of Companies and are therefore accessible and open to members of the public to inspect.

An outsider is, however, not entitled to insist on proof by the directors that the rules and procedures for the internal management of the company have been complied with before he contracts with them.

The rule in *Royal British Bank v Turquand* therefore states that a third party dealing with the agents of the company is entitled to assume that the agents have authority to bind the company with reference to the part of their authority which derives from the "indoor management" of the company. Hence if the directors need an ordinary resolution before they can do a certain act and they do it without the resolution being passed, since the third party cannot know whether it was passed or not, he is entitled to assume that it was passed.

The rule is subject to certain limitations such as if the third party knew or should have known of the irregularity.

Now that the ultra vires rule has been abolished then a company will be able to do anything that the directors wish. It will be unnecessary for an outsider to consult the memorandum. However, presumably the powers of the directors may be restricted by the articles but so long as the outsider has no actual notice of the contents of the articles then presumably he will be able to rely on the word of the directors and will be protected if he does so.

Although directors are agents of the company, they do have a greater number of restrictions placed upon them.

Personal Liability of Directors

It is the main purpose of forming a company to avoid liability attaching to its members of managers.

However there are exceptions to this rule.

1. *Guarantee*. A loan to a company (usually a small one) may be supported by a guarantee from a director.
2. A director may be liable for breach of warranty of authority.
3. *Promoters*. A person who contracts on behalf of a company before it is formed is liable on the contract.
4. *Bills of Exchange*. Where a director has failed to disclose that he was acting as agent of the company. He may be personally liable if he signs in his own name unless he uses "For" or "per pro" or "for and on behalf of" or he signs "as agent for the company".

    If he signs a cheque in his own name but the company's name is printed on the cheque and there is an account number this may indicate that liability is attached to the holder of that account, so that if it is the company's account, the company alone is liable. *Bondina Ltd v Rollaway Shower Blinds Ltd (1986)*.
5. If the membership of a company falls below two and the company continues in business for more than six months after that, the remaining member is jointly and severally liable with the company for its debts *(S.24 Companies Act 1985)*.
6. *Fraudulent and wrongful trading*. A feature of the new insolvency legislation has been the attempt to ensure that any liability for fraud or wrongful transactions may be placed upon the

directors of a company and that they should not be allowed to shelter behind the corporate façade. Directors may be civilly or criminally liable for fraudulent trading (*Section 213 Insolvency Act 1986*) if it can be shown, in a winding up of a company, that the business of the company was carried on with intent to defraud the creditors of the company.

In *Re William C Leitch Brothers Ltd (1932)* it was held to be fraudulent to continue to trade when the directors must have known there was no reasonable prospect of the company being able to pay its debts.

It is sometimes difficult to prove the necessary 'fraudulent intent' on the part of the directors.

Therefore S.214 of the *Involvency Act 1986* makes a director liable where a company is in insolvent liquidation and the directors should have realised that the company had no prospect of avoiding liquidation. This is known as wrongful trading.

Note that liability for wrongful trading (not fraudulent trading) may attach to "shadow directors". These are persons in accordance with whose directions the company is accustomed to act. A bank therefore could on occasions, be classified as a shadow director. It must be careful to give advice only and not instructions.

Section 212 of the Insolvency Act 1986 makes a director liable for misfeasance and breach of duty to the company.

Apart from the *Insolvency Act*, eight months earlier the *Company Directors Disqualification Act 1986* was passed. This Act consolidated the law relating to disqualification orders contained in the *Companies Act 1985* and the *Insolvency Act 1985*.

Under this Act a director may be disqualified if

1. he has been convicted of an indictable offence in connection with the management or liquidation of a company.
2. he has persistently been in default in delivering any document to the Registrar.
3. he has failed to comply with any provision of the Act and in the 5 years up to that conviction has been convicted of 3 or more similar offences. The director may be disqualified for up to 15 years.

A register of disqualified orders will be kept by the Secretary of State.

Meetings

The business of the company is transacted by means of passing resolutions at meetings. The meeting must be properly called and constituted according to the rules contained in the Articles of Association and according to the general law relating to meetings. For example, all persons who have a right to attend a meeting must be notified that one is to take place. Such persons may have to be given a minimum length of notice to attend. Also there must be a quorum present at the meeting, which means there must be a minimum number present in order for a valid resolution to be passed. Sometimes it is also necessary that the members constituting a quorum must have no personal interest in the matters being discussed or at least must have disclosed any interests they might have.

When a bank lends money to a company and takes security from it, it will require a certified copy of the resolution which authorises the charge. If a quorum was not present or if it was an invalid quorum because one of its number was an interested party then it would follow that any resolution passed would itself be invalid.

A bank therefore must be on its guard and if it knows that the meeting was invalid then it must reject any resolution made by such a meeting. This situation arose in *Victors Ltd v Lingard (1927)* in which the directors of the company personally guaranteed the company's overdraft with the bank. Later the directors in meeting resolved that the company should issue debentures to the bank as additional security. The articles of the company provided that no director should vote in connection with any matter in which he was personally interested.

In the subsequent case Romer J held that by agreeing to the issue of debentures by the company the directors were thereby relieving themselves of their personal liability for the overdraft and so were interested parties.

To avoid any difficulty which might arise as a result of a similar situation the bank should examine the articles to see how many directors must form a quorum and whether it must be a disinterested quorum. The bank may also rely on the Rule of Turquand's case and Section 35 of the *Companies Act 1985*.

If the ultra vires doctrine is abolished in the near future then a bank will be safe so long as it does not have actual notice that a director is exceeding his ostensible authority.

Every company must hold once a year a General Meeting of shareholders at which the accounts of the company are presented by the directors, who may have to submit to questioning from the shareholders. At this Annual General Meeting, of which the shareholders must receive 21 days notice, they appoint or re-appoint the directors and the auditors. They also confirm, or not as the case may be, the dividend proposed by the directors to be distributed. Every company must hold its first General Meeting – the statutory meeting – within six weeks of its formation.

Apart from the annual Meeting, the directors may, either of their own accord or because they have been so required by members of the company holding not less than one-tenth of the paid-up capital of the company – call on Extraordinary General Meeting of shareholders who must be given 14 days notice. At these meetings proposals are made and if accepted resolutions are passed. If the subject matter of the resolution is not particularly important, then it may be passed by an ordinary majority. However, if the matter is important, e.g., changing the name of the company or modifying the details of the objects clause of the Memorandum – then such a resolution must be a special resolution. Therefore it must be passed by a majority of 75% of those who attend and vote at the meeting. The same majority is required to pass an extraordinary resolution. If it is desired to propose a special resolution then 21 days notice must be given to those persons entitled to attend.

Capital

The share capital of a company goes under a number of different names. First there is the *Authorised Capital* or *Nominal Capital*. This is the capital stated in the Memorandum of Association and which the company is authorised to issue. It may not, at least initially, issue all its authorised capital and so the capital that has been issued is quite reasonably called *Issued Capital* or *Allotted Capital*. If some shares are issued only partly paid then the amount the shareholders have actually paid for their shares is called the *Paid Up Capital*. It is not so common nowadays for a company to issue partly paid shares.

Preference Shares

The capital is divided usually into two main classes, preference shares and ordinary shares. The preference shares, as their name implies, give the holder of such shares preference over other shareholders in the payment of dividends and also in the re-payment of capital in the event of the company being wound up. Preference shareholders receive a fixed dividend from any profits set aside by the directors for distribution. The dividend never varies and so such shares are usually considered solid and dependable and suitable for trustee investments. Preference shareholders are also usually given a preference as to return of capital in a winding-up. When the company is a going concern, the following presumptions apply to preference shares:

1.   They confer a right to a cumulative dividend, this means that if no dividend is declared in any particular year, the arrears of dividend must be carried forward from year to year until they are all paid, before the ordinary shareholders can receive any dividends.

2.   They are non-participating. This means they do not confer any right to participate in the profits of the company after the ordinary shareholders have been paid a dividend.

Redeemable Preference Shares

A company may, however, issue preference shares which from their inception are redeemable, either at a fixed date or after a certain period of time at the option of the company.

Sections 159 and 160 of the *Companies Act 1985* lay down conditions to be fulfilled before a company may redeem redeemable preference shares. Basically these conditions seek to maintain the capital of the company. For example, the redemption must be made out of profits, and only shares which are fully paid may be redeemed.

Ordinary Shares

These normally carry the residue of profits available for distribution as dividend after the preference shareholders, if any, have been paid their fixed dividend. *Ordinary Shares* are sometimes called the risk capital. This is because the dividend paid to the ordinary shareholders varies according to how well or badly the company has performed during the year. After the preference dividend has been paid then the residue is distributed to the ordinary shareholders and of course the amount will depend on the performance of the company.

In a winding up, if preference shares have priority as to return of capital, the ordinary shares will be entitled to the surplus assets, unless there are deferred shares. Hence ordinary shares are sometimes called the equity share capital of the company because they take what is left (the equity). Also the ordinary shareholders have a vote at the Annual General Meeting of the company and so the power to control the company rests with them.

These are the two main types of capital, preference or ordinary. There are other types of shares but these are not so common.

By issuing shares a company acquires money for its activities. However by issuing shares to the people who contribute money the company is acquiring more shareholders and consequently the control of its existing shareholders is being weakened. An alternative method of acquiring money is for the company to borrow it and in that case it will issue debentures to those people who lend it money. A debenture is a document which is evidence of a debt. The point about debentures is that the holders of these are not members of the company and do not have the same control over the company as do the shareholders. Instead of dividends, debenture holders receive interest on their holdings. However, like shares, debentures may be transferred on the Stock Exchange.

Running a Company's account

If the customer is a company there are certain matters which must be considered.

1. The bank must see the certificate of incorporation because this document establishes the existence of the company.
2. The bank must examine the company's memorandum of association in order to ascertain the powers of the company. In addition the articles of association must be examined to ascertain the power of the directors to borrow money for the company.

Once the ultra vires rule has been abolished then presumably it will no longer be necessary for a bank to examine the above mentioned documents. A bank will be able to assume that the company has power to do anything it wants so long as it is not aware of any restriction on the company's authority, or on the authority of the directors.

3.   If a company wishes to borrow money the bank must ensure

1.   the company has power to borrow. This will be implied in the case of a trading company but is usually stated in the objects clause of the memorandum.

2.   the loan is to be used for an intra vires purpose. *Re Introductions Ltd (1969)*

3.   the directors have the authority to borrow the money on behalf of the company.

4.   The bank will wish to see a resolution of the board of directors appointing the bank as the bankers of the company. At this time the persons with signing powers will be designated in the mandate given to the bank.

5.   If the company is a public company the bank will require to see the certificate to commence business.

6.   When the account has been opened a bank must take the same care in paying company cheques as it does in the case of an individual. In collecting the proceeds of a cheque the amount must only be credited to the account of the company. Collecting the proceeds of a cheque payable to a company for the account of a third party is an unusual transaction and inquiries should be made. If the practice is likely to become commonplace then an authority authorising such collections should be taken from the company concerned.

7.   In the same way that a loan to a company will be void if it is to be used for an ultra vires purpose a bank may also be in difficulties if it lends money to a company which is to be used for an illegal purpose and this purpose was known or should have been known to the bank. It may be that the bank could be held liable as a constructive trustee if it knowingly pays out money for the purpose of the loan.

An example would be when the company proposes to lend money to a director. The rules relating to loans to directors were strengthened following major scandals in the 1970s. *Sections 330–342* of the *Companies Act 1985* govern such a transaction and make such a loan illegal if made to a director or to a "connected person", i.e.

1.   directors' families

2. companies in which the director owns over one fifth of the equity.
3. the trustee of a trust whose beneficiaries include the director or members of the classes referred to above.
4. a partner of the director or any person in 1, 2, or 3 above.

In addition to loans purely and simply, other transactions, are also caught by the prohibitive section such as

– a quasi loan which includes the provision of credit card facilities as where the company is the cardholder and the card is used by the director
– a credit transaction where goods or services are provided on the undertaking that payment will be made later e.g. hire purchase terms.
– and back to back arrangements where company X lends to the directors of company Y on the understanding that company Y will lend to the directors of company X.

Sections 332–338 provide certain exceptions to the above prohibitions. The overall effect is: To allow all loans up to £2,500 for each director. To allow credit transactions if they are on normal commercial terms. To exempt loans to cover expenses incurred by a director if the transaction has the approval of the general meeting, subject to a maximum of £10,000 for directors of public companies. To allow quasi loans up to £1,000 if the terms require payment within 2 months. To allow credit transactions or the making of guarantees up to £5,000.

Money lending companies may make loans or quasi loans to directors on normal commercial terms subject to a maximum of £50,000. The terms may be more favourable if intended for house purchase or improvement.

Recognised banks can lend to their directors without limit provided the loans are on normal commercial terms. However the £50,000 limit applies if the loan is for house purchase or improvement.

8. A public company is not permitted to give financial assistance to anyone for the purpose of purchasing shares in the company. *Section 151.*

Exceptions would be if the loan is part of a larger transaction and not merely to purchase shares e.g.

S151

1.   the distribution of lawful dividends.
2.   the allotment of bonus shares.
3.   reductions of capital confirmed by the Court.
4.   provision of money to allow employees to buy shares.
5.   lending money is part of the company's business.

The importance to a bank of the points mentioned in 7 and 8 is that the bank may become involved if it lends money to the company for either of these purposes. If may become involved because it may be that the bank will be considered a constructive trustee if it knows or should have known that the company's funds held by the bank were being used for an illegal purpose. If that is so the bank may have to compensate the company for the illegal payments the directors have ordered it to make.

9.   *Shadow Directors*

Section 251 of the *Insolvency Act 1986* defines a shadow director as "a person in accordance with whose directions or instructions the company is accustomed to act".

Thus the definition could apply to a number of persons such as

1.   an Administrative Receiver under a bank debenture who continues to trade with the company during the receivership.
2.   a parent company which exercises control over a subsidiary.
3.   also it may be that in a liquidation of a company a bank could be held to have been giving instructions. It will be up to the manager concerned to ensure that he is merely advising and not directing or instructing.

Summary – Law of Companies
1.   A Company is an artificial legal person. This means it cannot be seen but exists only on paper.
2.   It acts through human agents called directors.
3.   The two main documents of a company are:

    a.   the Memorandum of Association
    b.   the Articles of Association

4.   After November 1990 it is likely that the Articles will be the

most important of these documents because that will determine whether the power of the directors is to be restricted.

5. Even so such restriction will not affect third parties dealing with
the company provided they did not know of the existence of
any restriction.

Chapter Nine

Negotiable Instruments – Generally

This subject seems to hold many terrors for large number of students but in fact if a small number of concepts are understood there should be no difficulties in understanding and learning the subject except for the amount of detail involved.

Firstly we should consider property generally. Property comprises anything that a person may own and remember that the word "own" means "has a right to". As always law is concerned with the rights of persons. Now what a person may own is either land or anything which is not land called personal property.

The law relating to land is a complex subject on its own so we can ignore that for our present purposes.

Let us consider personal property. This is a wide division of property and in itself it may be sub-divided into tangible things and intangible things.

Tangible things are designated by the old Norman French words of "choses in possession". Such things can be seen, touched and counted.

Intangible things are called "choses in action". This is because, as they cannot be seen and touched, then ownership of them can only be evidenced by a piece of paper (an instrument). So oranges can be seen and counted – they are choses in possession. The same applies to coins in my pocket. Instead of the oranges it may be that a cargo of oranges is being transported to this country and before they arrive they may be sold. The buyer can be given a document called a bill of lading which is evidence of his right to the oranges when they arrive. Instead of the coins in my pocket, I can have a postal order or a cheque entitling me to the amount of the coins. The bill of lading, the postal order and the cheque all entitle the owner of these instruments to something – either the oranges or the money, but of course they are worthless themselves. It is only because of the form of the documents and what they contain that they entitle the owner to something of value. Admittedly, to say that a chose in action is a piece of paper is not entirely accurate because the goodwill of a business or the copyright of an author are choses in action but they are not evidenced by pieces of paper. One other principle of law must be observed here – that is that ownership is a right to something. When one buys goods one is hoping to acquire a right of ownership in the goods. It follows that if A has stolen something from B and then sells it to C, C will not become the owner, because A did not have the right of ownership and so is not in the position of being able to pass a right of ownership on to C. This principle applies to the transfer of choses in possession, and also to the transfer of choses in action generally.

The transfer of a chose in action
A piece of land may only be transferred by means of a document called "a conveyance" or one should write more correctly even though pedantically the legal ownership of a piece of land is transferred by a conveyance.

A chose in possession is transferred by delivery. Indeed, ownership is usually presumed to reside in the person who has possession of the chose in possession. This is sometimes described by the phrase "possession is nine tenths of the law".

A chose in action however must usually be transferred in a particular manner laid down by law. Thus to transfer a share certificate it is necessary to use a share transfer form and complete it with the details of the transferee. Also the company whose shares they are must be notified of the transfer. Finally, the principle regarding the right of ownership also applies; and so if a person transfers a chose in action to which he does not have the right of ownership then the transferee will likewise not get a good title.

Now some choses in action entitle the holder to goods but a number of them entitle the holder to a sum of money. As money is so vitally important in commercial transactions it gradually became desirable to have some rather less formal system of transferring a right to a sum of money. Thus it was that certain choses in action began to be treated differently from others – the need for a formal method of transfer was abolished, it was no longer necessary to notify the person who ultimately would be called upon to make payment, of the transfer. Most importantly of all, the transferee of these special choses in action would get a good title to it, in certain cases, even though the transferor did not have a good title. This last point was of particular importance and in fact is the basis of negotiability. These choses in action which received this special treatment became known as negotiable instruments. They include:

Bills of Exchange including cheques
Promissory notes
Dividend Warrants
Bearer Bonds
Bearer Scrip
Debentures payable to bearer
Share warrants
Treasury bills

The attributes common to these documents are

1.   They are transferable merely by delivery if payable to bearer or by indorsement if payable to order.
2.   The party who will be called upon to pay on the document need not be notified of the transfer.
3.   The transferee who takes in good faith and for value will get a good title notwithstanding any defect in the title of the transferor.

This last point requires some clarification. The transferee is known as the holder of the negotiable instrument. In order to get a good title to it he must have given value for it and the document itself must have been in order. If the document contains a forged indorsement for example, the person to whom it was transferred will not become the owner of it.

Example 1 A draws a cheque payable to bearer and gives it to B. X steals the cheque and gives it to C, to whom he owes money for goods he has purchased. C is the owner of the cheque, provided he took it in good faith.

Example 2 A draws an order cheque payable to B. X steals the cheque and gives it to C to whom he owes money for goods he has purchased. X will of course have to forge B's indorsement and so even though C took the cheque in good faith he will not be the owner of it because of the forgery.

This then is the essence of negotiability. Of the instruments which are negotiable we shall only be concerned with bills of exchange, including cheques. Finally it should be remembered that in this context negotiable does not mean transferable. It refers to the fact that in certain cases a person may become the legal owner of an instrument even though he received it from someone who was not the owner.

Example 3 A cheque marked "not negotiable" may still be transferred. However the person who receives it will get no better title than that of the person from whom he received it.

Bills of Exchange

Let us now consider the operation of a bill of exchange. Say a manufacturer sold goods to a wholesaler for £1,000 and he in turn sold them to the retailer for £1,000. For the sake of simplicity let us ignore any profit margin. So W owes £1,000 to M and R owes £1,000 to W.

Assuming M and W had no more money and also, as is quite likely, W has given R the retailer 3 months credit. The situation is that W cannot pay M until he is paid by R and R does not have to pay for three months. Thus all the parties are at a standstll for 3 months.

```
           £1,000                    £1,000
    R————————————————W————————————————M
```

However a bill of exchange could be used to break the impasse. W could draw a bill on R for £1,000 payable in 3 months time. He could do this because R owes him the money. Also as W owes M £1,000 it would be convenient if R were ordered to pay M. So the bill is drawn by W (the drawer) on R (the drawee) by which R is ordered to pay M (the payee) £1,000 in 3 months time. The bill is then given to M; so how much better off is he with the bill than without it? He can do any of three things.

1. He can do nothing and wait for payment from the drawee for 3 months. Even here he is better off with the bill than without it because if he has difficulty in getting payment at least he has a signed acknowledgement by W (who has signed the bill as drawer) that he owes M £1,000.

2. M can sell the bill or discount it as it is called. If he does this he will receive £1,000 less the interest on that sum for 3 months plus handling charges.

3. M can use the bill as cash and transfer it to some person to whom he owes £1,000. In this way the bill may be passed from hand to hand until the time when the 3 months have expired

(the bill is said to have matured) when the person who is the holder at that time can obtain his money from the drawee.

Points to note from the definition of a Bill of Exchange are:

1. It must be an unconditional order in writing. Usually the word "Pay" is used. It must not be a mere request.

    However an order may still be unconditional if it is coupled with

    a. an indication of the particular fund out of which the drawer is to reimburse himself or a particular account to be debited with the amount.

    b. a statement of the transaction which gives rise to the bill.

    Where a cheque bears a receipt form on the back the test to determine whether it is a valid bill is whether the direction is addressed to the drawee or the payee. If it is addressed to the drawee the bill is invalid.

2. The order must be for a sum certain in money. However the money can be paid with interest at a stated rate, by instalments or in foreign currency according to a rate of exchange.

3. There must be a certain or determinable time of payment. Thus the bill may be payable:-
    a. on demand or at sight or on presentation
    b. at a fixed period after date or sight
    c. on or at a fixed period after a person's death.

4. The bill must be payable to a payee who can be identified or to the order of that person or to bearer.

At this point one must remember that law is concerned with the rights of people and relating this to bills of exchange it is concerned with the rights of persons to the bill. If a person is the lawful owner of a bill then he can enforce his rights on it against anyone who has signed it. Initially only the drawer's signature will appear on the bill, it is then given to the payee. It is only natural that if it is a time bill (one payable at some future date) then it would be advisable to ask the person who eventually will be called upon to pay up to promise that he will make payment on that future date. This person is the drawee and so usually a bill will be presented to him for acceptance.

Acceptance When the drawee signifies that he has accepted the bill he must write "accepted" on the bill and sign it. His acceptance may be general or qualified. If it is qualified in any way then the payee may treat the bill as dishonoured by non acceptance.

General Acceptance
In this case the drawee agrees to fulfil all the terms of the order of the drawer without qualification.

Qualified Acceptance
This expressly varies the effect of the bill as drawn. In other words, the drawee states by his acceptance that he does not propose to honour all the terms of the order in the bill. It must be emphasised that a qualified acceptance does not make the order in the bill conditional. It is still unconditional and so the bill remains valid. This is because the drawee is not giving any order.

There are five types of qualified acceptance:

1. *Conditional*: This makes the payment by the acceptor dependent on the fulfilment of a condition stated in the acceptance. E.g. "Accepted, payable on giving up a bill of lading for seventy-six bags of seed."
2. *Partial*: An acceptance to pay part only of the amount for which the bill is drawn. E.g. bill drawn for £500 and accepted as to £300.
3. *Local*: Acceptance to pay only at a particular place. E.g. "Accepted payable at Barclays Bank, only." If the word "only" is omitted, the acceptance is general.
4. *Qualified as to time*: E.g. a bill drawn payable thirty days after date, accepted payable forty days after date.
5. *Acceptance by one or more of the drawees but not all*: E.g. where a bill is drawn on X, Y, Z is accepted by X and Y but not Z.

    Effect of a qualified acceptance:
    1. A holder may refuse to take a qualified acceptance and if he does not obtain an unqualified acceptance he may treat the bill as dishonoured (S.41(1)).
    2. If a qualified acceptance is taken and the drawer or indorser has not expressly or impliedly authorised the holder to take a qualified acceptance, or does not subsequently assent to it, such drawer or indorser is discharged from his liability on the bill.
    3. In the case of a partial acceptance, the holder may take it and subsequently notify the drawer and indorsers without discharging them from liability.

4.   A foreign bill which has been partially accepted must be protested as to the balance (S.44(2)).

Presentment for acceptance: Presentation for acceptance is essential only in three cases: (section 39)

1.   Where a bill is payable after sight then presentation for acceptance is necessary in order to fix maturity date of the bill.
2.   Where a bill is drawn payable elsewhere than at the residence or place of business of the drawee.
3.   Where the bill expressly stipulates that it shall be presented for acceptance.

a.   Apart from section 39, bills should be presented for the following two reasons:

i.   Once the drawee accepts, he becomes liable on it.
ii.   If he refuses to accept, the holder has an immediate right to sue all prior parties without having to wait until the date of maturity.

b.   Where a drawee accepts a bill payable elsewhere than at this residence or place of business, the bill is said to be "domiciled" at the place of payment. Unless a banker has expressly or impliedly agreed to pay bills domiciled with him, he is under no legal obligation to do so even though the customer has a balance sufficient to cover the bills. If the banker pays, the relationship between him and the customer then is not debtor and creditor, but principal and agent.

Presentment for payment

By section 52(1) a general acceptance by the drawee to pay at maturity makes him liable and presentment to him for payment is not necessary. Presentment for payment is necessary where the acceptance is qualified.

The rules concerning presentment for payment are similar to those for acceptance but in this case emphasis is placed upon presentment at the proper place. This is defined in section 45(4) as the place of payment specified in the bill; if no place is specified then at the address of the drawee or acceptor given in the bill or his last known place of business or ordinary residence.

The time for presentment for payment is the last day of the time for payment or if that is not a business day then the succeeding business day. If the bill is payable after a period of time after date, after sight or after the happening of a specified event, the time for payment is determined by excluding the day from which the time is to begin to run and by including the day of payment.

Dishonour

A bill may be dishonoured by non acceptance or by non payment. If a bill is drawn payable on demand then the drawee must pay when it is presented to him, if he does not, then the payee may treat the bill as dishonoured by non payment. If the bill is payable at some future time then it may have been accepted but when the holder comes to present the bill for payment it may again be dishonoured by non payment. If a bill is dishonoured for whatever reason, the holder may enforce his rights against anyone who has signed the bill. In order to do this he must notify the drawer and each indorsee of the fact that the bill has been dishonoured. In practice the holder notifies his previous indorser, who notifies his previous indorser and so on. Thus in this way everyone who is liable on the bill is informed of his liability.

By section 52(3), notice of dishonour is not necessary to render the acceptor/drawee liable.

By section 48(1) if a bill is dishonoured for non-acceptance and notice of dishonour is not given, the rights of a subsequent holder in due course are not affected by the failure to give notice, e.g., A draws on B in favour of C (payee) who indorses it to D. D presents the bill to B who refuses to accept. The bill is dishonoured by non-acceptance (S.43(1)). D, the holder, must give notice of dishonour to A (drawer) and C (indorser) before he can enforce his rights against them. If he fails to do so A and C will be discharged. However, if he subsequently negotiates it to a holder in due course (say E), E can sue A and C and is not prejudiced by D's failure to give notice.

1. To be a holder in due course, E must take the bill without notice that it had been previously dishonoured.
2. If the bill had been dishonoured by non-payment there cannot be a subsequent holder in due course because the bill is then overdue. (See S.29).

The rules as to the giving of notice of dishonour are set out in section 49.

These require that the holder of the bill must give notice of dishonour, verbally or in writing or by the return of the bill, to anyone whom he intends to make liable on the bill. In practice he will merely notify his previous transferor. The notice of dishonour may be given as soon as the bill is dishonoured and must be given within a reasonable time. That means:-

(a)   where the person giving and the person to receive notice reside in the same place the notice must be given or sent off in time to reach the latter on the day after dishonour of the bill.

(b)   where the person giving and the person to receive notice reside in different places, the notice must be sent off on the day after the dishonour of the bill, and if there be no such post on that day then by the next post thereafter.

Notice is deemed to have been given if it was duly addressed and posted, even if it was lost in the post.

The rules as to delay and excuses in giving notice of dishonour are contained in section 50.

Noting and Protesting

When a bill is dishonoured a distinction is made between an inland bill which is one which is drawn and payable in the British Isles, or which is drawn in the British Isles on a British resident; in any other case the bill is a foreign bill. When a foreign bill is dishonoured then it must be "noted and protested".

1.   *NOTING*: Where a bill has been dishonoured the holder takes it to a notary public who then represents the bill. If it is again dishonoured, he notes on it:

    a.   the date;
    b.   a reference to his register;
    c.   the noting changes; and
    d.   his initials.

    He will also attach a ticket stating the answer given when the presentment was made.

2.   *PROTEST*: This consists of the obtaining of a certificate from a notary public attesting the dishonour of the bill. The certificate is a formal declaration signed by the notary public. It must contain a copy of the bill. The details of a protest are given in section 51(7).

    Where a bill requires to be protested and a notary public is not available, any householder or substantial resident of the place may in the presence of two witnesses, give a certificate, signed by them attesting the dishonour of the bill. A specimen form of "householder's protest" is given in the First Schedule to the Act.

A protest must be made by the day following the day of dishonour. In order to extend this period of time the dishonour of the bill may be noted and then a protest may be made at any time after the noting.

Noting and protesting are essential in the case of a foreign bill because the procedure provides evidence of the dishonour which will be acceptable to foreign courts. In addition an inland bill must be protested if payment from a referee in case of need is requested. A referee in case of need is a person whose name is inserted on the bill by the drawer to whom the holder may turn for acceptance or payment should the drawee refuse to accept it or pay upon it. In the same way a person may intervene if a bill is dishonoured, and accept the bill or pay it for the honour of a person who is liable. Legal proof of payment for honour should always be obtained, this is "a notarial act of honour".

Transfer of a Bill
When a bill has been issued it may then be transferred from one person to another and of course what is actually being transferred is the right to the sum of money that the bill will entitle the holder to receive.

If the bill is made payable to bearer then it may be transferred by simple delivery and the holder of such a bill will be the person who has possession of it.

If the bill is made payable to a named payee or order, then it is an order bill. It may be transferred by the payee indorsing the bill, designating the indorsee and giving delivery to him. The indorsee will then become the holder.

Holder in due course

As was mentioned earlier, a feature of bills of exchange is that a person can be the legal owner of a bill even though he received it from a person who was not the legal owner of it. Thus a thief may steal a bearer bill and pass it to X and X will become the legal owner of it, provided of course that X did not know he was receiving the bill from a thief and also provided X had given something of value for the bill.

However if the thief has stolen an order bill and because an order bill requires indorsing before it can be transferred, the thief had forged the indorsement of the person from whom he had stolen the bill and then passed it to X. X will now not become the legal owner of the bill because of the forged indorsement. Now this is rather hard on X who may have given something of value for the bill and may have received it not knowing he was taking it from a thief. The forged indorsement makes all the difference.

To summarise the position – the holder in due course, as he is called, is a holder who has a right to enforce payment on the bill against all parties who are liable on it. Also he will get a good title (become the legal owner) to the bill notwithstanding the fact that he takes it from a person who had no title to it. However in order to establish himself as a holder in due course he must have taken the bill in good faith not knowing of the lack of title of the person from whom he received it, and he must have given value for it – the bill itself must be complete and regular and especially must not contain a forged indorsement if it is an order bill. S.29(1).

Discharge of a bill
Finally, a bill is said to have been discharged, which means all rights of action on it are extinguished, in the following ways:

1.   Payment by the drawee/acceptor to the holder. Payment to any other person such as one claiming under a forged indorsement will not discharge the drawee's liabilities.
2.   By express waiver.
3.   By cancellation.
4.   By material alteration.

Summary – Negotiable instruments generally
1.   Negotiable instruments are those documents, the ownership of which can be transferred quite informally by delivery. The effect is that the transferee may get a good title to such a

document even though he receives it from a person who is not the rightful owner. This will only happen if the document is in bearer form.

2. Bills of Exchange need not be studied in detail but a knowledge of them is necessary because a cheque is a bill of exchange.

Chapter Ten

Cheques – in Particular

A cheque is defined as a bill of exchange drawn on a bank and payable on demand.

Thus the drawee of a cheque is always a banker. A cheque does not need to be accepted and the drawer is never discharged by the holder's failure to present the cheque for payment within a reasonable time.

The relationship between the drawer and the drawee, in the case of a cheque, is important because it is the relationship between a bank and its customer. This relationship is a contractual one that creates a debtor-creditor relationship and has been examined in Chapter 1.

By reason of the contract between bank and customer there are duties placed on each party. The main duty of the bank is to pay its customer's cheques up to the amount of the credit balance of their accounts provided the following conditions are complied with:

1. The cheque must be in writing, it must demand payment and be signed by the drawer (or customer).
2. The cheque must be drawn on the branch which holds a credit balance and the request for payment must be made during banking hours.
3. The cheque must be in unambiguous form. This means that as a cheque is a mandate from the customer to the banker then "the banker has a right to insist on having his mandate in a form which does not leave room for misgiving as to what he is called upon to do." Lord Haldane in *London Joint Stock Bank Ltd v Macmillan and Arthur (1918)*.
4. If any modifications to the contract between bank and customer are to be made then they must be communicated expressly to the customer and it probably would not be sufficient for the banker to place a notice in the cheque book especially if there had been a course of dealing between the

customer and the banker before the changes were made. *Burnett v Westminster Bank Ltd (1965)*.

5. There must be sufficient funds in the account on which the cheque is drawn. In this connection one should remember that a banker may be able to consolidate two accounts of a customer even if these accounts are at different branches – *Garnett v McKewan (1872)*. This facility applies to a bank but not to a customer. He has no right to insist on payment of a cheque at one branch where he has no funds merely because he has funds at another branch. Also, in England, a cheque is not an assignment of funds and so the holder of the cheque has no claim against the banker if he refuses, for whatever reason, to pay on the cheque. In Scotland, a cheque operates as an assignment to the payee of the amount for which it was drawn out of the credit balance of the customer's account. If therefore in Scotland a customer draws a cheque for an amount in excess of the credit balance on his account the practice is for the banker to transfer the balance to a separate account to be held for the holder of the cheque. In England a banker is not bound to pay part of a cheque if he has insufficient funds to pay the whole amount.

6. *Cheques out of date*. Sometimes called stale cheques, it is the custom of bankers not to pay cheques if six months or sometimes twelve months have elapsed after their issue.

7. *Postdated cheques*. Such cheques are not invalid but should not be paid by a banker because the customer may countermand payment before the due date of the cheque. Also if a banker pays a postdated cheque he may have to dishonour other cheques which he would otherwise have been able to pay.

Crossings

A particular feature of cheques is the crossing. This consists of two parallel transverse lines drawn across the face of the cheque. The effect of this is to ensure that the cheque cannot be cashed across the counter of the paying (drawer's) bank but must instead be paid into another bank and that bank will collect the proceeds for its customer. The purpose of crossing a cheque is obviously to make it more difficult for the wrong person to get his hands on the proceeds.

In addition to the general crossing just referred to there are also the following crossings:

A special crossing – where the name of a banker is written across the face of the cheque and the cheque is only payable to that named bank.

Account payee – this is an instruction to the collecting banker to pay the proceeds only into the account of the person named on the face of the cheque as payee. If any other account is credited the collecting banker will lose his protection under Section 4 of the *Cheques Act 1957* unless the bank can show that it has made reasonable enquiries. *Bevan v National Bank Ltd (1906)*.

However, the words "account payee" do not prevent the cheque being transferred, and so if a cheque bearing these words is indorsed in blank and then stolen, a holder in due course would get a good title. Therefore it is essential that the words "not negotiable" are added.

Not negotiable – these words may be added to a general or a special crossing and they have the effect of destroying the cheque's negotiability. This means that although it may still be transferred, the person who receives it will get no better title than that of the person from whom he received it. *Universal Guarantee Property Ltd v National Bank of Australasia (1965)*.

In the case of a bill of exchange other than a cheque the words "not negotiable" prevent the bill being transferred. *Hibernian Bank v Gysin and Hanson (1939)*.

Revocation of a banker's authority

Section 75 of the *Bills of Exchange Act 1882* provides that "The duty and authority of a banker to pay a cheque drawn on him by his customer are determined by (1) countermand of payment, (2) notice of the customer's death".

1. A banker will require the written and signed authority of his customer, accompanied by the date, number, amount and name of the payee of the cheque. If a verbal request to stop payment is received the bank may merely suspend payment pending the receipt of written confirmation. If the account is joint and the bank's mandate does not require all parties to draw a cheque then a countermand of a cheque drawn by one party may be lodged by another party. *Gaunt v Taylor (1843)*.

The conditions for a countermand to be effective are:

a. The countermand must actually come to the notice of the banker. In *Curtice v London City and Midland Bank Ltd (1908)* a customer sent a telegram to his bank countermanding payment of a cheque but the telegram was left in the bank's letter box until 2 November. On 1 November a cheque had been paid and so the customer claimed against the bank. The Court of Appeal held that the claim must fail as the cheque had not been effectively countermanded.

b. The stop notice must be sent to the branch of the bank where the account is held. *London Provincial and South-Western Bank Ltd v Buszard (1918)*.

c. If the customer fails to adequately identify the cheque he wishes to be stopped he cannot blame the bank if it pays on that cheque *Westminister Bank Ltd v Hilton (1926)*.

d. The countermand must be given to the bank before payment of the cheque and the question may arise as to what moment of time payment takes place.

   The customer must not have agreed not to countermand payment, which would be the case if a cheque card were used. Also it is only the drawer who can stop a cheque, not the payee. If the payee notifies the bank that he has lost the cheque then the bank should get in touch with the customer.

2. *Notice of customer's death or insanity*
   Note that it is the notice of the death or insanity and not the event itself that terminates a banker's authority to pay cheques. In general any credit balance of a customer must be held by a banker and only paid to an executor, administrator or Committee in Lunacy after the appropriate legal formalities have been complied with.

Other events that determine a bankers authority

1. Insolvency of the customer.
2. Garnishee proceedings. This is an order of the Court which a judgment creditor may obtain to restrain a bank from paying funds it owes to a judgment debtor, the service of a garnishee

order on a bank will suspend its duty to honour its customer's cheques. So if A has obtained judgment against B for a sum of money but B has omitted to pay up, A can get a garnishee order from the court directed at any person who owes money to B, such as his bank. This person is called the garnishee.

3.   An injunction restraining a bank from paying out money from a customer's account (e.g. a Mareva injunction).

4.   Outbreak of war between the country where the bank is situated and the country of which the customer is a national.

Breach of contract

If a bank fails to pay its customer's cheque when there are adequate funds in his account then the bank would be in *breach of contract* and would be liable to the customer. If the customer is a trader he may claim substantial damages without proof of actual loss. If he is not a trader he can only claim nominal damages unless he can establish actual loss.

Defamation

In addition the banker runs the risk of a libel action on the grounds that by not honouring his customer's cheques (incorrectly) he has given the payee and others the impression that the customer is the sort of person who issues "dud" cheques.

A bank therefore should make every effort to avoid a libel action if possible, by taking care as to the comments it makes on the cheque. Answers such as "Requires confirmation", "Words and figures differ", or "Indorsement irregular" would not be libellous. If such phrases cannot be used then "Refer to drawer" would be in order.

In *Evans v London and Provincial Bank (1917)* the wife of a naval officer, who sued for the dishonour of a cheque, received only one shilling in damages.

In *Cox v Cox and Co (1921)* when a cheque has been returned marked "N.S. Present again in a few days" the plaintiff sued for dishonour of the cheque and for libel. The bank paid £50 into court in respect of the breach of contract which the plaintiff accepted and continued the action for alleged libel. The jury found in favour of the defendants and Darling J stated that he considered the plaintiff would not have recovered the amount of £50 if it had not been paid in.

The customer for his part owes the bank a duty to take care in drawing his cheques and a duty to disclose to the bank any forgeries of which he is aware.

Bearer cheques and other cheques

In order for an instrument to be a valid cheque it must be made payable to a specified person or his order or to bearer.

Bearer Cheques

These do not require indorsement and so a person who receives a bearer cheque from a thief who has stolen it from the rightful owner will nevertheless become the rightful owner of it provided he took it without the knowledge that he was receiving it from a thief. An order cheque will be treated as a bearer cheque in the following circumstances

1. if it is indorsed in blank. In other words if the rightful owner of the cheque indorses it merely by signing his name without naming the indoresee. In that case the order cheque will require no further indorsement.

2. Section 7(3) of the Bills of Exchange Act 1882 provides

"Where the payee is a fictitious or non existing person the bill may be treated as payable to bearer."

If therefore a clerk issues a cheque of his employer payable to a fictitious person and then the clerk indorses the cheque to an innocent person for value, the innocent person will get a good title to the proceeds of the cheque because of S.7. The person who receives the cheque will be able to enforce it against the drawer and the fact that it is not a genuine indorsement will be irrelevant because the cheque/bill has become a bearer cheque/bill by virtue of section S.7(3).

The question that remains is what is a fictitious person? The courts have decided that depends on whether the drawer intended the payee to receive the money. This is a good reason for making the bill not negotiable.

Bank of England v Vagliano Brothers (1891)

Glyka, an employee of Vagliano Brothers, forged a signature of a person named Vucina as drawer of a bill in favour of Petridi and Co, with whom Vagliano did business. Vagliano accepted the bill which had been drawn on him, and Glyka then forged Petridi's indorsement before presenting it to Vagliano's bank for payment. The bank, having paid Glyka, then debited Vagliano's account but Vagliano, on learning of the fraud, claimed that his account should not have been charged by the bank.

Held: Although Petridi was an actual person, the drawer of the bill (i.e. Glyka) never intended that he should receive payment under the bill. Petridi, as payee, was therefore in effect a fictitious person so far as the bill was concerned; consequently the bill was payable to bearer. As the bank had paid the bearer of the bill (namely, Glyka), Vagliano's claim failed, and the bank was in order in charging his account with the amount of the bill.

Vinden v Hughes (1905)

X, an employee of Vinden, persuaded V to draw cheques in favour of certain persons who were actual customers of V, by telling V untruthfully that the amounts of the cheques were owing to the persons concerned. X then forged the indorsements of the payees and obtained payment of the cheques by purporting to negotiate them to Hughes.

Held: As the payees were existing persons, and the drawer of the cheques (Vinden) intended payment to be made to those payees, the forgeries by X prevented Hughes from obtaining a good title. Vinden was therefore able to recover from Hughes the amount paid to Hughes by Vinden's banker.

In *North and South Wales Bank v Macbeth (1908)* Macbeth was induced by the fraud of White to draw a cheque in favour of Kerr who was an existing person. Macbeth intended him to receive the money.

White obtained the cheque, forged Kerr's indorsement and paid the proceeds into his account with the appellant bank.

Macbeth sued the bank, claiming it had converted his money. The bank replied that the cheque was drawn in favour of a fictitious person and so it became a bearer cheque.

The House of Lords decided the section did not apply as the drawer intended the payer to receive the money. The bank was therefore liable.

Order cheques

Cheques are usually made payable to the payee or to his order. Thus the payee may receive the proceeds of the cheque or he may indorse the cheque in favour of an indorsee so that person may receive payment. Sometimes a cheque is made payable to "wages or order" or to "cash". Such an instrument is not a cheque but is a mandate to pay money. The collecting banker has the same statutory protection as he has in relation to cheques.

Orbit Mining and Trading Co Ltd v Westminister Bank Ltd (1962)
Mr Epstein had an account at the Westminister Bank. Some years after opening it he became a director of the plaintiff company, Orbit. Cheques on Orbit's account required the signatures of two directors. Before leaving for a business trip abroad, one director, Mr Woolf, signed a number of crossed blank cheque forms and left them with Epstein who took one, made it out to "Cash or order", added his own signature and the words "For and on behalf of Orbit Mining and Trading Co Ltd", and paid it into his private account. He did this on two other occasions. Epstein was authorised to sign cheques only for company business and so these three documents were fraudulent. The company claimed the money back and the bank claimed its statutory protection as collecting for a customer under S.4(2). The Court of Appeal found for the bank. "It cannot be the duty of the bank to keep itself up to date as to the identity of a customer's employer" (Harman, LJ). Epstein's signature as drawer of the cheques was illegible and the bank could not be expected to recognise the name signed as being the same as that of the holder of the account into which the mandate for payment (it was technically not a cheque as it was payable "To cash") was being paid.

Liability of Paying Bank to Drawer and to Rightful Owner of the Cheque

The main duty of a bank, as was stated above, is to pay its customers cheques quickly. In doing so it runs the risk of paying one to the wrong person. How may this occur? Say, A draws a cheque payable to B. X, a thief, steals the cheque and now wants to get the money. If it is an uncrossed cheque then X can go to A's bank and if the cheque is for a reasonable amount, he will probably be paid over the counter.

If it is a crossed cheque then the proceeds of the cheque can only be paid into a bank account. So X, the thief, must either forge B's indorsement and then pay the cheque into his own or another person's account; or X may open an account in the name of B and pay the cheque into that. The second method is obviously more difficult because it requires X to obtain references who will state that he (X) is in fact B.

These then are the two methods by which a thief may obtain the proceeds of a stolen cheque. Note that in either of these two situations A's bank (the paying banker) will pay the proceeds of the cheque to the wrong person. On the face of it that bank will then be liable to A (for paying A's money to someone other than A had designated) also to B the rightful owner of the money (for wrongfully interfering with B's goods).

The bank on which the customer has drawn his cheque is called the paying bank because that bank will be paying the money to the bank into which the cheque has been paid for collection called the collecting bank.

The paying bank then will be liable to its customer and to the rightful owner of the money and the collecting bank will be liable only to the rightful owner of the money.

If this state of affairs had been allowed to continue then banks would have found it very difficult to operate. Consequently Parliament stepped in and provided the following protection for banks.

Banker's Protection

Paying Banker

A banker is under a duty to pay his customers cheques quickly and in doing so it may be that he pays the wrong person.

1.   *Section 59* of the *Bills of Exchange Act 1882* provides protection for

a bank which pays the holder of a bearer bill and that holder was not entitled to the money.

The section reads

A bill is discharged by payment in due course by or on behalf of the drawee or acceptor. "Payment in due course" means payment made at or after maturity of the bill to the holder thereof in good faith and without notice that his title to the bill is defective.

It will be noticed that reference is made to a bill and not merely a cheque, so this section covers all bills of exchange; also payment must be to the "holder". Now the only person who can be a holder of a cheque to which he is not entitled is the bearer of a bearer cheque. If it is an order cheque then the indorsement must have been forged by the thief and so consequently the person to whom he negotiates the cheque cannot be "a holder" because of the forged indorsement.

Therefore Section 59 in not of great importance to bankers because it only applies to bearer cheques which are not particularly common.

2. *Section 60* of the *Bills of Exchange Act 1882* provides protection if the bank pays out on a cheque bearing a forged indorsement. The section reads

---

"Where a bill payable to order on demand is drawn on a banker, and the banker on whom it is drawn pays the bill in good faith and in the ordinary course of business, it is not incumbent on the banker to show that the indorsement of the payee or any subsequent indorsement was made by, or under the authority of the person whose indorsement it purports to be, and the banker is deemed to have paid the bill in due course, although such indorsement has been forged or made without authority".

It will be seen that Section 60 covers the situation where there is a forged indorsement, also the protection only applies to cheques. In addition, in order to get the protection, the banker must have acted in good faith and in the ordinary course of business.

Probably the good faith of a banker would not be doubted but the requirement that payment must be made "in the ordinary course of business" was examined in *Baines v National Provincial Bank (1927)*.

In that case the bank cashed a cheque payable to Mr Wood at five minutes past three o'clock, which was five minutes outside normal banking hours. In the ordinary course of business the bank ceased trading for that day at 3 p.m. The next day Mr Baines cancelled payment on the cheque but the cheque had already been paid the day previously. Mr Baines then claimed the bank had not acted in the ordinary course of business.

The court held that normally paying a cheque outside banking hours would not be in the ordinary course of business but five minutes leeway was permitted so far as people already on the bank's premises were concerned. The meaning of payment in due course was further considered in

Auchteroni and Co v Midland Bank Ltd (1928)

In this case a fraudulent person presented a bill to the paying bank and was paid cash over the counter. The court held this was unusual but did not deprive the bank of its protection under S.59.

Examples of payments *not* in the ordinary course of business would be

a.   Payment to a tramp, postman or office boy.
b.   Payment after hours – but a few minutes could make no difference particularly if the payees were in the building.

3.   *Section 80* of the *Bills of Exchange Act 1882* provides

---

Protection to banker and drawer where cheque is crossed. Where the banker, on whom a crossed cheque is drawn, in good faith and without negligence pays it, if crossed generally, to a banker, and if crossed specially, to the banker to whom it is crossed, or his agent for collection being a banker, the banker paying the cheque, and, if the cheque has come into the hands of the payee, the drawer, shall respectively be entitled to the same rights and be placed in the same position as if payment of the cheque had been made to the true owner thereof.

In other words if a banker pays out on a cheque according to the crossing and if he does so in good faith and without negligence then he is protected if he pays to the wrong person.

The above are the main sections which protect the paying banker. Section 59 applies to bills of exchange, generally where payment is to a holder of the bill. Section 60 covers the case of a forged indorsement on a cheque and section 80 deals with crossed cheques.

Analogous instruments

The above protection is extended to instruments other than bills of exchange and cheques by the following provisions:

Section 1 of the Cheques Act 1957

Protection of bankers paying unindorsed or irregularly indorsed cheques

1. Where a banker in good faith and in the ordinary course of business pays a cheque drawn on him which is not indorsed or is irregularly indorsed, he does not, in doing so, incur any liability by reason only of the absence of, or irregularity in, indorsement, and he is deemed to have paid it in due course.

2. Where a banker in good faith and in the ordinary course of business pays any such instrument as the following, namely:

    a. a document issued by a customer of which, though not a bill of exchange, is intended to enable a person to obtain payment from him of the sum mentioned in the document;

    b. a draft payable on demand drawn by him upon himself, whether payable at the head office or some other office of the bank; he does not, in doing so, incur any liability by reason only of the absence of, or irregularity in, indorsement, and the payment discharges the instrument.

Section 1 of the *Cheques Act 1957* gives to a paying banker the same protection that he will get in the case of unindorsed or irregularly indorsed cheques to banker's drafts and conditional orders – crossed or uncrossed. Section 1 extends the protection given to a paying banker if he pays to the wrong person

1.   a banker's draft
2.   a mandate for payment. This is not a cheque but is intended to enable a person to obtain payment from the banker.

The bank must of course be acting in good faith and in the ordinary course of business.

A banker's draft is drawn by a banker upon himself and it is not "addressed by one person to another". A conditional order lacks an essential requirement of a cheque which is that it must be an unconditional order.

Section 1 of the Cheques Act 1957 does away with need for an indorsement on cheques except for the purpose of negotiation.

However on 23 September 1957 the *Committee of London Clearing Banks* issued a memorandum to their members.

This requires a paying bank to obtain indorsement of a cheque if it is either (a) a cheque marked "R" (by this the drawer signifies that he requires a receipt for payment of the cheque) or (b) an open cheque presented at the counter for payment in cash.

In addition promissory notes, travellers cheques and ordinary bills of exchange will also require indorsements.

Section 5

Application of certain provisions of Bills of Exchange Act 1882, to instruments not being bills of exchange

The provisions of the Bills of Exchange Act 1882, relating to crossed cheques shall, so far as applicable, have effect in relation to instruments (other than cheques) to which the last foregoing section applies as they have effect in relation to cheques.

Section 5 of the *Cheques Act 1957* gives to a paying banker the same protection he will get under *Section 80* of the *Bills of Exchange Act.*

Section 5 applies to instruments other than cheques (i.e. instruments that do the work of cheques but do not comply with the definition of a cheque) e.g.

Banker's drafts
Conditional Orders
Drafts drawn upon the Paymaster-General or the Queen's and
Lord Treasurer's Remembrancer.

Therefore Section 80 gives similar protection to a paying banker in
respect of these instruments if they are crossed, as he gets for crossed
cheques.

Section 19 of the *Stamp Act* covers crossed or uncrossed bankers
drafts.

Collecting Banker

If a banker collects the proceeds of a cheque for his customer he will
incur liability in conversion if the cheque did not belong to his
customer. The rogue may have opened an account in the name of the
payee named on the cheque or he may have forged the payee's
indorsement and paid the cheque into his own account. In either
case the banker who collected the proceeds of the cheque will have
done so (albeit innocently) for the wrong person. He will therefore,
prima facie, be liable to the rightful owner of the money. The
collecting banker may be protected as follows:

By *Section 4(1) of the Cheques Act 1957,*

Where a banker, in good faith and without negligence;

1. receives payment for a customer of a cheque or other
    instrument specified in Section 4(2). The instruments
    referred to in Section 4(2) are:

    a. cheques
    b. any document issued by a customer of a banker
        which, though not a bill of exchange, is intended to
        enable a person to obtain payment from that banker
        of the sum mentioned in the document
    c. any document issued by a public officer which is
        intended to enable a person to obtain payment from
        the Paymaster General or the Queen's and Lord
        Treasurer's Remembrancer of the sum mentioned in
        the document but is not a bill of exchange.
    d. any draft payable on demand drawn by a banker

upon himself, whether payable at the head office or some other office of the bank; or

2.   having credited a customer's account with the amount of the cheque, etc, receives payment thereof for himself, and the customer had no title (e.g., because the indorsement was forged), or a defective title (e.g., he obtained the cheque by fraud).

3.   The banker does not incur liability to the true owner of the instrument by reason only of having received payment thereof.

Before the banker can claim the benefit of the protection, however, he must satisfy the following conditions;

1.   *Good faith*: He must have acted in good faith. This means that what he does when collecting the cheque must be done honestly.

2.   *Customer*: Section 4(1) confers protection only where the person for whom payment is collected is a customer.

A customer is a person who has a banking account with a banker even if the cheque with which he opened the account is the subject-matter of the action in respect of which the banker claims the protection of section 4(1): *Ladbroke & Co v Todd (1914)*. On one occasion thieves intercepted letters which Ladbrokes the bookmakers, had sent to clients containing their winnings cheques. The thieves took out the cheques and substituted forgeries. One such cheque was for £75 11s 3d payable to a Mr Jobson and crossed "A/c payee only".

One of the thieves took this cheque to the John Bull Bank, which was owned by Mr Todd, and opened an account in Jobson's name using the stolen cheque as an initial deposit and asked for that cheque to be specially presented. This was done and the cheque was paid. The next day "Mr Jobson" withdrew the money from his account and disappeared. Mr Todd said that he had not made any enquiries at all about "Mr Jobson" because he was obviously a University man and told a plausible story about not wishing his usual banker to see a cheque drawn by a bookmaker. The court held that "Mr Jobson" was a customer of the bank from the moment his account was opened but that the banker had been negligent in not making enquiries, for example, at the college he claimed to attend, which would have revealed him as an imposter.

The account may be a deposit or a current account: *Great Western Railway Co v London and County Banking Co Ltd (1901)*.

Section 4(1) applies to all cheques, whether crossed or uncrossed. It also applies to bankers' drafts, conditional orders and Paymaster-General's warrants (see Section 4(2) of the Cheques Act 1957).

3. *Without Negligence*: The banker must have collected without negligence. The meaning of negligence must be ascertained from the cases, but Section 4(3) of the Act provides that he is not to be treated as having been negligent by reason only of his failure to concern himself with the absence of, or irregularity in, indorsement of an instrument.

   Whether the banker has been negligent or not will be decided by reference to the practice of reasonable men carrying on the business of banking and endeavouring to do so in a manner calculated to protect themselves and others against fraud.

Through the cases it has been established that a bank may be negligent in the following areas:

1. *Opening an account*
   Failure of the bank to obtain or follow up references when an account is being opened for a prospective customer may be negligence. If the banker acts on the reply from only one referee, he is not necessarily negligent, though where the prospective customer is a foreigner, it may be desirable for the bank to confirm the reply by an examination of the customer's passport: *Marfani & Co v Midland Bank Ltd (1967)* Marfani & Co's office manager, calling himself Mr Eliaszade (with whom the company did business) cultivated the acquaintance of a restaurant proprietor called Akkadas Ali. Shortly before Mr Marfani left to visit Pakistan, the office manager opened an account in the name of Eliaszade at the Midland Bank giving Ali's name as a reference. Ali was well known as a substantial customer of the bank and he had previously introduced good new customers. The office manager then got Mr Marfani to sign a cheque for £3,000 payable to Eliaszade, pretending that money was owed to him in the normal course of business. He

paid this cheque into his account, withdrew the money and disappeared. The bank claimed statutory protection as collecting for a customer but Marfani & Co claimed the bank had been negligent. The court found for the bank but said, "If the defendant bank here exercised sufficient care, it was in my view only just sufficient." The bank had not enquired about the employment of "Eliszade" and had presented the cheque before receiving Ali's reference.

Lumsden & Co v London Trustee Savings Bank (1971)
In this case a collecting banker was found guilty of conversion without the protection of Section 4, Cheques Act 1957 in that he failed to obtain a satisfactory introductory reference relating to a new customer. The latter was a stranger who offered the name of "Dr Blake" as a referee who replied favourably to the bank but did not supply the name of his own bankers. The bank was informed that Dr Blake had recently arrived in the UK from Australia. Cheques drawn by Lumsden & Co were misappropriated and passed through the defendant bank, the proceeds being quickly withdrawn. The whole story of the thief turned out to be a lie which would have been revealed, said the court, if the defendant bank had been more diligent, demanding at least the sight of the "Dr Blake" with his passport.

The case is notable, however, for the fact that the damages awarded to the plaintiffs, were reduced by 10% because they had been contributorily negligent in not drawing the cheques correctly.

2. *In collecting for a customer who is an employee a cheque drawn by or in favour of the employer*
When opening an account, the banker is under a duty to inquire as to the name of his new customer's employer if the banker knows that the customer occupies a position which involves the handling and opportunity of stealing his employer's cheques.

If the customer is a married woman, the banker must inquire as to the name of her husband's employer. *Savory & Co v Lloyds Bank (1932)*. E B Savory & Co were London stockbrokers and two of their clerks, Perkins and Smith, from time to time misappropriated bearer cheques drawn by their employers payable to stock jobbers and paid them into London branches of Lloyds Bank for the credit of, in the case of Perkins, his account at the Wallington branch of that bank and in Smith's case for his wife's account at the Redhill, and later, the Weybridge branches of that bank. The branches of Lloyds Bank that conducted these accounts had not, on opening the accounts

a.   in the case of Perkins, ascertained the name of his employers and
b.   in the case of Mrs Smith, ascertained the name of her husband's employers.

The bank failed to obtain statutory protection from its common law liability for conversion since it was considered to be guilty of negligence in two respects, viz.,

a.   the branches which maintained the accounts were not possessed of information to enable the bank to keep watch on what was paid into the account so to detect any misappropriation of the employers' cheques.
b.   the London branches failed to pass on to the "home" branch details of the cheques paid in by Perkins and Smith and cleared by the London branches on behalf of the "home" branches.

However in 1968 – the Marfani case – Diplock LJ said of Savory's case that it depended on its own facts and there were matters to arouse suspicions in the social conditions of the 1920's. The case is merely an illustration of the principle that a banker must exercise reasonable care in all the circumstances of the case. Savory was decided in the light of banking practice as it was at that time.

3.   *In not enquiring further into circumstances which should have set the alarm bells ringing*
Where there is evidence on the face of the cheque of possible misappropriation the banker who fails to inquire further may be negligent. In the following cases further inquiry will be needed before a banker:

a.   Collects payment for a private account a cheque payable to a public official. *Ross v London County, Westminster and Parr's Bank Ltd (1919)*

b.   Collects for an employee's private account or his wife's account cheques drawn by or in favour of his employer. *Savory (E B) & Co v Lloyd's Bank Ltd (1932)*

c.   Collects for a customer's private account cheques payable to the customer as "agent for the Marquis of Bute". *Bute v Barclays Bank Ltd (1954)*

McGaw had been the Manager of three sheep farms owned by the Marquis of Bute. After the termination of his employment he received three warrants totally £546, being subsidies, payable to McGaw "for the Marquis of Bute". They were collected and credited to McGaw's private account without enquiry by Barclays Bank, Barnsley.

In defence, Barclays Bank stated that:

(i)   As the warrants were payable to McGaw he was the true owner notwithstanding that he was accountable for the proceeds to the Marquis.

(ii)   The Marquis was estopped against the bank since he knew that the warrants would be issued payable to McGaw.

(iii)   The bank was entitled to statutory protection if its defence in a had failed.

The court held that although the warrants were payable to McGaw, the intention of the drawer was that the Marquis should receive the money and not McGaw – the latter was merely accountable to the Marquis. Consequently conversion of the warrants had taken place and the bank was guilty of conversion. The statutory protection it claimed was lost because the court declared that it was clear that McGaw was to receive the money only as an agent and so such documents should not have been credited to the agent's private acount without enquiry.

d.   Collects for a director's private account a cheque payable to his company. The bank was unaware the company had an account at another bank. *A L Underwood Ltd v Bank of Liverpool and Martins Ltd (1924)*.

e.   Collects a cheque marked "acount payee" or "account payee only" for some other account. *Ladbroke v Todd (1914)*

f.   Collects an amount inconsistent with the status of the customer: *Nu-Stilo Footwear Ltd v Lloyds Bank Ltd (1956)*

Nu-Stilo Footwear Ltd v Lloyds Bank Ltd (1956)

Nu-Stilo Footwear employed M as its Secretary. M opened an account at Lloyds Bank in the false name of B saying he, B, was a freelance agent just commencing business. For references he gave his real name and address and later, when Lloyds Bank followed up the reference he, not surprisingly, said that "B" was a suitable person to be given banking facilities. Subsequently 9 cheques drawn by Nu-Stilo, most of them payable to B were collected by Lloyds Bank for "B's" account. Since the total of these cheques was £4,855 the court ruled that the amount was inconsistent with B's commencing business as a freelance agent. Consequently negligence was attributed to the bank which therefore failed to get the statutory protection it claimed.

Banker acting both as collecting and paying banker

Where a banker acts in the dual capacities of collecting and paying banker, he must, to escape liability to the true owner of the cheques he has dealt with (in an action for conversion), bring himself within the scope of the statutory protection afforded to both the paying and collecting banker. In other words, he cannot, for example, say "I concede I was negligent when I was acting as collecting banker but in my separate capacity as the paying banker, I am entitled to the protection of Section 1 of the Chques Act 1957."

In *Carpenters' Co v British Mutual Banking Co (1937)* a clerk of the Carpenters' company procured cheques from the company dishonestly and paid them into his private account at the defendant bank, which also acted as the company's bankers. The bankers claimed to be protected either by Section 60 or Section 82 (now Section 4 of the Cheques Act 1957). It was held that, although the bankers were protected by Section 60, they had been negligent in the collection of the cheque and were therefore liable to the company.

Collecting banker as holder for value

It should be remembered that a banker may collect the proceeds of a cheque in one of two capacities.

1. He may collect as agent of his customer and then *Section 4 of the Cheques Act 1957* may protect him.

2. He may collect the proceeds of the cheque for himself. In order

for that situation to arise he must have given value for the cheque. In that case he will come within the definition of a holder for value or in due course and so will be able to sue the drawer of the cheque. The fact that the cheque, paid in by the customer, will probably not be indorsed will not affect the situation. *Section 2 of the Cheques Act 1957* provides that a banker who gives value for, or has a lien on, a cheque payable to order which the holder delivers to him for collection without indorsing it has such (if any) rights as he would have had if upon delivery, the holder had indorsed it in blank. In other words the unindorsed cheque will be treated as a bearer cheque.

A banker will be deemed to have given value for a cheque if

a.   He lends further sums to the holder on the strength of the cheque.

b.   If he pays over the amount of the cheque or part of it in cash or on account before it is cleared.

c.   If he agrees either then or earlier, or as a course of business, that the customer may draw against the cheque immediately, before it is cleared.

d.   If the cheque is paid in specifically to reduce an existing overdraft.

e.   If he gives cash over the counter for the cheque at the time it is paid in for collection.

f.   If he has a lien on the cheque.

Section 2 of the Cheques Act 1957 covers only cheques and it will not apply if the cheque bears a forged indorsement.

Westminster Bank v Zang (1965)

The application of Section 2 of the Cheques Act is illustrated by the above case, the facts of which are:

Zang lost money gambling. He asked Tilley who was then watching if he could let him have £1,000 in return for a cheque. Tilley gave Zang the money in return for the cheque. Tilley had taken the £1,000 from a company, Tilley Autos Ltd. He was the company's managing director and controlling shareholder. Consequently he paid it in for the company's account but as the cheque had been made payable to himself he should have indorsed it before paying it in. This he did not do and this omission was not noticed by the

collecting branch cashier. On presentation the cheque was dishonoured and Tilley borrowed it to sue Zang on it but abandoned his
action. The bank later sued Zang themselves because Tilley Autos'
account was overdrawn. To do so successfully they had to establish
that they were holders for value.

The bank lost the action because even though *Section 2* of the
Cheques Act could be satisfied, the bank was held not to have given
value for the cheque. The bank's argument, that by crediting the
cheque to the account of Tilley Autos Ltd, and reducing the
company's overdraft by £1,000 they had given value, was dismissed
on the ground that the bank's paying-in slip had a note to the effect
that the bank reserved the right to refuse to pay against uncleared
effects. This prevented an implied agreement from arising in the
circumstances. The bank lost its lien when it lent the cheque to
Tilley.

It was further held that the words "for collection", which appear
in *Section 2 of the Cheques Act 1957*, are not to be confined to cases
where the bank is to collect for a customer's account. It applies if the
cheque is being collected for any account.

Electronic Transfer of Funds

The physical movement of paper used in the transfer of funds is a
very expensive process. Consequently in recent years a number of
electronic systems have been developed using computers and
designed to reduce the amount of paper used.

B.A.C.S. (Bankers' Automated Clearing Service)

B.A.C.S. Ltd is the company which operates the service. It deals
with standing orders, direct debits, salary credits and other credits,
such as traders settling amounts due. The B.A.C.S. system is used by
the banks and by customers. The user prepares details of the
transactions i.e. sort code number, account number, account name,
amount and reference number. The details are sent to the B.A.C.S.
computer centre at Edgware, Middlesex. They are contained on a
tape or disc and are then read by computer at the centre. The entries
are then sorted electronically, placed on magnetic tapes which are
then passed to the appropriate bank. The advantages are – reduced
clerical costs, lower bank charges cash flow benefits, interest saved
and increased security.

C.H.A.P.S. (Clearing House Automated payments system)
This is a high value clearing system which is operated electronically. At present the system is available for payments of £5,000 or more. The settlement bank transmits the payment to the computer systems of the other settlement banks. When a payment has been fed into the system it cannot be stopped and so the funds are guaranteed as having been cleared. The C.H.A.P.S. system has taken over from the Town clearing which only applies to the City of London. This new system operates throughout the U.K. and is used when a guaranteed and speedy method of payment is required. Apart from that, the payee's bank account is credited immediately the payer orders his settlement bank to make the transfer.

E.F.T.P.O.S. (Electronic funds transfer at point of sale)
This is the technical name for the system which makes use of plastic cards – either debit cards issued by banks or building societies, or by credit cards. This method of transfer of funds sometimes goes under the names of – "Connect" "Switch", "P.D.Q." or "Accept".

When the customer presents his card the retailer "swipes" it through the electronic reader. Details of the transaction are transmitted to a central computer, the cost of the goods is checked against the cardholder's balance in his bank or building society. The customer's account is then debited and the retailer's account is credited.

It it is an "off-line" E.F.T.P.O.S. system then all the transactions for a day are collected together and then sent to the central computer by disc or tape or the bank's own computer system is used.

The advantages to the customer are: convenience, no need to write a cheque. To the retailer: it means greater efficiency, less cash to handle and a guaranteed payment once acceptance has been made.

A.T.M.S. (Automated Teller machines)
Most banks now have an A.T.M. outside their premises. The user operates the A.T.M. by inserting his card into the machine and keying in his P.I.N. (Personal identity number). The machine looks up the account in the bank's computer and then carries out the orders of the user. These may be:

Cash withdrawal
statement request

cheque book request
some machines will also accept deposits and carry out payment of bills.

The advantages to a customer are that these machines allow him to pay bills and withdraw cash without drawing a cheque. Over the years the banks have co-operated and created shared A.T.M. networks e.g.

Midland, National Westminster, TSB and Clydesdale Barclays, Lloyds, Royal Bank of Scotland and the Bank of Scotland.
Link Co-op bank, Girobank and some building societies.
Matrix a building society network.

1992

The transfer of funds is being currently studied in view of the advent of the single market which will be brought about by 31 December 1992.

The European Commission is critical of many of the existing transfer procedures as they are often slow, expensive and labour intensive. The European consumer organisation has calculated that simply exchanging £100 through each of the E.C. countries will lose £50 in charges. This risk has been reduced by the success of E.R.M. in bringing about greater exchange rate stability. Also in the final stages of EMU the risk would disappear but pending a single currency, one option would be for national bank notes to carry an indication of their ECU value printed on them. Banks would then exchange them at par value for notes of other Member States. These disadvantages are not faced by business in the USA. A New York based business man investing in Texas has no such problems because the value of the dollar is always the same anywhere in the USA. A similar arrangement was followed in the U.K. after the merger of Scotland and England. For 100 years after the union in 1707 bank notes in Scotland showed values both in pounds sterling and Scottish pounds. The Commission considers the ACHs (Automated Clearing houses) should be expanded and standard practices be adopted in order to provide efficient cross border services. This will require wider banking co-operation including central bank involvements. Priority is likely to focus on improvements in electronic payments via Eurocheques. However if machine readable code lines for electronic processing can be standardised in the E.C. ordinary cheque usage could increase.

Since 1987 progress has been made with the acceptance of payment cards at ATMs in all Member States. The U.K. leads with nearly 16,000 but surprisingly Germany had fewer than 6,000 in June 1989.

Chapter Eleven

Corporate Insolvency

Often the words insolvency, bankruptcy and winding-up or liquidation become intermixed in a person's mind. However one should be clear to what one is referring when using these words. Insolvency simply means inability to pay ones debts. Assuming B owes A £1,000 then A may have to establish his right to that sum of money by going to a court of law. If A wins then he can say he has obtained judgment against B and so B becomes a judgment debtor and A is the judgment creditor. But A still has not received his money.

If that is the case A must consider enforcing his judgment against B and will have to seek the help of the court. This may consist of the court ordering the bailiffs to distrain on B's goods, to sell them and from the proceeds to pay A. Other methods would be – if B is employed to get an attachment of earnings order by which B's employer is ordered to deduct a certain sum each week or month from B's wages and to pay the money deducted to A. However all these methods are only used in order to assist A to recover his money. If B owes money not only to A but also to C, D, E and F etc it might mean by concentrating on one creditor the other creditors could be unfairly treated and may not be able to recover any part of their debt. In that case it may be advisable from the point of view of all the creditors that a united front is maintained against B and that he is made bankrupt. The main purpose of bankruptcy proceedings is to ensure that each creditor is dealt with fairly. Also when one considers the assets of B a personal action against him would only succeed in gaining control of assets he owns at that time. Whereas a feature of bankruptcy is that it may be possible in certain cases to follow assets which formerly belonged to the debtor and to recover them so that they can be distributed amongst the creditors. In the case of companies the procedure for collecting in their assets and distributing them amongst the creditors is called winding-up or a liquidation. One point to be observed is that a human person is made bankrupt because he cannot pay his debts; a company may be wound up for reasons other than that it cannot pay its debts although the insolvency of a company is probably the main reason why it is wound up.

Thus insolvency means inability to pay debts and from that there may follow the formal procedures of winding-up or liquidation in the case of a company or bankruptcy in the case of an individual. However if these formal procedures are adopted it may result in there being less for distribution amongst the creditors because the expenses of these formal procedures will have to be paid before there is any distribution. Consequently it may be preferable for the creditors to come to some arrangement with the debtor company or the individual debtor. These voluntary arrangements are a feature of the new legislation contained in the *Insolvency Act 1986* and the Act facilitates the making of such arrangements.

Corporate Insolvency

The various methods of dealing with an insolvent company other than having it wound up are:

1. *Bank rescues.* Sometimes, instead of winding up a company it is advisable to lend it more money, in the hope that it will become profitable and eventually the creditors will recover the full amount of their debts. In such a case if a bank lends money then it will take a fixed debenture as security.
2. *Receivership.* An ordinary receiver is one appointed by the creditors under power contained in the debenture certificate. An administrative receiver is a receiver or manager of the whole of the company's property. He is appointed by the holders of any debentures secured by a floating charge.
3. *Administration Order.* The Insolvency Acts, have introduced a new procedure whereby the court may make an "administration order" in regard to a company. The effect of this is to place the management of the company in the hands of an administrator and while the administration order is in force no resolution may be passed nor any order made for the winding up of the company, nor may an administrative receiver be appointed.

    The appointment of an Administrator may be blocked by the holder of a floating charge but not by the holder of a fixed charge.

The administrator is given specific powers in particular to carry on the business of the company, to take possession of the company's property and to raise or borrow money and in that connection to grant security over the property.

Voluntary arrangements

These may be arrangements, assignments or compositions.

An *arrangement* may include a reorganisation of the company's share capital so the creditors can convert some debts into ordinary shares.

A *composition* is an agreement of creditors not to take action against the company in return for payment by the company of part of their debts.

An *assignment* involves a transfer of the company's property to the creditors or to a nominee of them all *S.425 Companies Act 1985*

In addition the *Insolvency Act 1986* has created a new scheme of voluntary arrangements. This requires supervision by a nominee, who must be an insolvency practitioner.

If these voluntary arrangements are unsuccessful it may be necessary to have the company wound up.

Winding up

The procedures for the winding up of a company are contained in the *Insolvency Act 1986* which consolidates parts of the *Companies Act 1985* and the *Insolvency Act 1985*. A company is usually wound up because it is unable to pay its debts but it may be wound up also on technical grounds such as the company did not commence business within a year after it was incorporated, or the number of its members has been reduced below two. Also a company may be wound up merely because the shareholders wish it to be wound up.

A company may be wound up compulsorily by the court or voluntarily by its members or creditors.

Winding up by the Court

The court may order the winding up of a company only if one or several of the following grounds for winding up are present. Applications to the court is made by petition, called a *winding-up petition* which if successful will result in the court making a winding-up order.

Grounds for petition: under section 122 of the *Insolvency Act 1986*, a company may be wound up by the court if:

1. the company has by special resolution resolved that the company be wound up by the court; or
2. the company does not commence its business within a year from its incorporation or suspends its business for a whole year.
3. the number of members is reduced below two.
4. the company is unable to pay its debts.
5. the court is of opinion that it is just and equitable that the company should be wound up.

Company unable to pay its debts

Section 123 of the *Insolvency Act 1986* provides that a company may be deemed unable to pay its debts in the following cases;

1. If a creditor to whom the company is indebted in a sum exceeding £750 has served on the company (at its registered office) a written demand for the payment of the debt and the company has for three weeks thereafter neglected to pay the sum or to make some other arrangement satisfactory to the creditor about its payment; or
2. If in England and Wales, execution or other process issued on a judgment of any court in favour of a creditor of the company is returned unsatisfied in whole or in part. Execution is where a judgment creditor is seeking to enforce his judgment against the debtor company.
3. If it is proved in any other way to the satisfaction of the court that the company is unable to pay its debts. In this case, the court has a discretion and the amount owed need not exceed £750. Usually, the fact that the petitioner has made repeated demands for payment, and that the company has neglected to pay affords *cogent evidence* that the company is unable to pay its debts. Unless the company bona fide disputes the claim, a winding-up order will be made.
4. Asset Test: if it is proved to the satisfaction of the court that the liabilities of the company exceed its assets. S.123.

Just and Equitable

The power of the court to wind up a company on "just and equitable grounds" is discretionary. What is "just and equitable" will depend upon the allegations made by the petitioner. In the following situations the courts have made winding-up orders.

1. Where the main object of the company can no longer be realised.
2. If the company is a "bubble", i.e. if it never had any business or assets.
3. If the company was formed for purposes of fraud or to conduct illegal business.
4. That the articles of association provided for a winding-up in the event which has happened.
5. That in a small private company, the company was in substance a partnership and the facts would justify the dissolution of a partnership. This happens usually where the relationship between the persons owning its share capital is analogous to a partnership relationship: *Re Yenidje Tobacco Company Ltd (1916)*.

Who can petition for winding-up?

A petition may be presented by the following:

1. The company or its directors
2. A creditor
3. A contributory
4. The Official Receiver
5. Department of Trade and Industry or Bank of England may petition in special cases.

A petition by the company would be very unusual because it only needs to pass an appropriate special resolution to be wound up.

Contributories also are not very common because they only exist in the case of shares which are not fully paid. The liquidator must prepare a list of persons who are liable to contribute to the assets of the company in the event of its being wound up. "A" list contains the names of present members of the company and "B" list the names of past members who ceased to be members within a year preceding the winding-up. In the event of a person on "A" list being unable to contribute the unpaid amount of his share, a person on "B" list may be asked to contribute – but only in respect of debts incurred before he ceased to be a member. The more likely petitioner will of course be a creditor.

The Official Receiver may petition if the company is in voluntary liquidation and he feels that the interests of creditors or contributories are in danger.

The Secretary of State for the Department of Trade and Industry may petition under *Section 440 of the Companies Act 1985* if it appears that it is expedient in the public interest that the company should be wound up on the basis of information he has been given from his inspectors.

Consequences of a winding-up order

If a winding up petition is successful, the court will make an order for winding up.

The order relates back to the date of the commencement of the winding-up. Under *Section 129 Insolvency Act 1986* the winding-up commences either:

1.   at the time of the presentation of the winding-up petition, or
2.   where, before a petition was presented, the company was in voluntary liquidation, on the passing of the resolution for voluntary winding up.

The effect of a winding-up order is:

1.   To make void all dispositions of the company's property and any transfer of shares made after the commencement of the winding-up is void. S.127 unless sanctioned by the court.
2.   Any attachment, sequestration, distress or execution against the estate of the company after the commencement of the winding-up is void. S.128.
3.   After a winding-up order has been made or a provisional liquidator has been appointed, no action can be proceeded with or commenced against the company except by leave of the court. S.130(2).
4.   The Official Receiver becomes provisional liquidator until he or another person is made a liquidator. S.136(2)(3).
5.   The employment of employees and other agents of the

company is terminated. Further the directors are dismissed
and their powers to act on behalf of the company cease.

6.   All invoices, orders for goods or business letters of the company
      must state that the company is in liquidation. S.188.

Proceedings after a winding-up order has been made
The court may require a statement of affairs to be produced by the
official receiver. He must also carry out two investigations:

1.   if the company has failed – into the reason for the failure.
2.   in any case, into the promotion, formation, business dealings,
      and affairs of the company.

In order to assist him in his investigation, he may apply to the
court for the public examination of:

1.   any one who has been an officer of the company
2.   has acted as liquidator, administrator, receiver or manager of
      its property or
3.   anyone else who has been concerned in the promotion,
      formation or management of the company.

The official receiver must apply for a public examination if so
requested by one half of the creditors or three quarters of the
contributories. S.133(2).

Appointment of liquidator
The official receiver becomes the first liquidator until another person
is appointed. Within 12 weeks of the winding up order the official
receiver must decide whether or not to summon separate meetings of
the company's creditors and contributories in order to choose a
liquidator. If he decides not to call a meeting he must notify the
creditors and then he may be obliged to call a meeting if requested by
one quarter in value of the creditors.

The official receiver may apply to the Secretary of State for the
appointment of a liquidator.

Duties and powers of the liquidator
He is not a trustee for the individual creditors but is the agent of the
company. However he will be liable in damages to any creditor for
breach of any of his statutory duties.

He must

1.   assist the official receiver
2.   take into his custody the property of the company
3.   settle the list of contributories
4.   summon meetings of creditors
5.   summon a final meeting in accordance with S.146.

He may

1.   bring and defend actions in the name of the company
2.   carry on the business of the company so far as is necessary for the winding-up
3.   pay any classes of creditors
4.   compromise or make arrangements with creditors
5.   he may disclaim any onerous property such as unprofitable contracts or any property which is unsaleable.

Voluntary winding up

The main attraction of voluntary winding up from the members' point of view is that there are not a great many formalities to be complied with.

A voluntary winding up may be either

1.   a members' voluntary winding-up or
2.   a creditors' voluntary winding-up. S.90.

Whether the winding-up is a members' or creditors' voluntary winding-up, it is initiated by the members of the company passing an appropriate resolution to that effect and not, as in the case of a compulsory winding-up, by a petition to the court.

Voluntary Winding-up Resolutions

Under section 84 of the *Insolvency Act 1984*, a company may be wound up voluntarily:

1.   When the period, if any, fixed for its duration by the articles expires, or the event, if any, occurs, on the occurrence of which the articles provide that the company is to be dissolved, and the company in general meeting passes a resolution requiring the company to be wound up (in this case an *ordinary resolution* will suffice) or
2.   If the company resolves by special resolution that the company be wound up voluntarily; or

3.   If the company resolves by *extraordinary resolution* to the effect that it cannot by reason of its liabilities continue its business, and that it is advisable to wind up.

The reason for allowing an extraordinary, instead of a special resolution in the last case is to dispense with the requirement of twenty-one days' notice when the company is insolvent and that winding-up is urgent.

What determines the type of voluntary winding-up is whether or not a *declaration of solvency* can be made by the directors. This is a statement by the majority of them that they have inquired into the company's affairs and have formed the opinion that the company will be able to pay its debts in full together with interest within a specified period not exceeding 12 months from the commencement of the winding-up.

The declaration must be made within the five weeks immediately preceding the date of the passing of the winding-up resolution. The declaration must be filed with the registrar within fifteen days of the passing of the resolution. It must embody an up to date statement of assets and liabilities of the company.

If the declaration is made, the winding up proceeds as a member's voluntary winding up. If the declaration is made by the directors without reasonable grounds, the makers are liable to a fine or imprisonment or both. The fact that after the declaration the company's debts are not paid in full within the stipulated time raises a presumption that it was made by the directors without reasonable grounds. S.89(5).

Members' voluntary winding-up

This is entirely managed by the members and the liquidator is appointed by them. No meeting of creditors is held. Until the liquidator has been appointed the directors cannot exercise their powers without the sanction of the court; except those which relate to the disposal of perishable goods.

If the liquidator is of the opinion that the company will in fact be unable to pay its debts in full in accordance with the declaration of solvency then he must call a creditors meeting within 28 days, giving them 7 days notice by post and advertising it in the Gazette.

The liquidator must lay before the meeting a statement of the affairs of the company. The effect of holding this meeting is that the winding-up proceeds as if a declaration of solvency had not been made i.e. as a creditors' voluntary winding-up. S.96.

Creditors' voluntary winding-up

The company must call a meeting of the creditors for a date not later than 14 days after the passing of the resolution for voluntary winding up. This meeting must also be advertised in the Gazette.

The notice must name the insolvency practitioner who will act.

The business of the meeting is for the creditors:

1. to receive the directors' statement of the company's affairs together with a list of the creditors and the estimated amount of the claims; S.99
2. to appoint a liquidator. S.100
3. to appoint a liquidation committee. S.101.

The effect of a voluntary winding-up

1. As from the date of the passing of the resolution to wind-up, the company must cease to carry on business except so far as is required for beneficial winding-up.
2. No transfer of shares can be made without the sanction of the liquidator.
3. On the appointment of the liquidator the powers of the directors cease except so far as the company in general meeting, the liquidator (in a members' voluntary winding-up) or the creditors or committee of inspection (in a creditors' voluntary winding-up) may sanction their continuance. S.103.

Powers and duties of the liquidator in a voluntary winding-up

1. He can without sanction, commence or defend legal proceedings on behalf of the company.
2. He can carry on the business of the company, so far as it is beneficial for the winding-up.
3. He can exercise all the powers of a liquidator in a compulsory winding-up.
4. He may apply to the court to determine any question arising in the winding-up or to exercise any of the powers which the court

could exercise if the company were being wound up by the court.

In the case of a compulsory winding up, when the affairs of the company have been completely wound up the liquidator may give notice to the Registrar that the final meeting has been held and that the winding-up is complete. Three months after the registration of the notice the company will be automatically dissolved.

In a voluntary winding-up the three months period begins with the registration of the liquidator's final account and returns.

When a company has been dissolved the court may within 12 years make an order declaring the dissolution void.

Summary – Corporate insolvency
1. A company may be wound up or liquidated.
2. A company may be wound up by the Court in which case this is called a Compulsory winding up.
3. Alternatively a company may be wound up voluntarily.
4. In that case the company must pass the appropriate resolution for a voluntary winding up.
5. Such a voluntary winding up may be a members' voluntary winding up or a creditors' voluntary winding up.
6. Whether or not the directors can make the declaration of solvency to the effect that all debts will be paid in full within twelve months, will determine whether the creditors can take a hand in the winding up proceedings.

Chapter Twelve

Individual Insolvency

Voluntary arrangements

Deeds of arrangement

A debtor is sometimes able to make a private arrangement with his creditors known as a deed of arrangement (or assignment) as prescribed by the *Deeds of Arrangement Act 1914*. By such a deed a debtor assigns his property to a trustee as a representative of the creditors, and this deed must be distinguished from a scheme or arrangement.

A deed of an arrangement is any instrument, whether under seal or not, made for the benefit of creditors generally or made by an insolvent debtor for the benefit of three or more creditors. It may be

1. An assignment of property.
2. A deed or agreement for a composition; and in cases where the creditors obtain control over the debtor's property.
3. A letter of licence.
4. An agreement for the carrying on or winding up of the debtor's business.

A deed of arrangement will be void unless it is registered at the Department of Trade within seven days after first execution and is properly stamped. A deed for the benefit of creditors generally is also void unless assented to by a majority in number and value of the creditors before or within twenty-one days of registration, and within twenty-eight days of registration a statutory declaration must be filed confirming that the assents have been obtained. Within a further seven days the trustee under the deed must give security unless the creditors dispense with it, and in default the court may declare the deed void or appoint a new trustee.

The problem with a deed of arrangement is that it does not prevent a dissenting creditor from petitioning for a bankruptcy order. A deed of arrangement is outside the bankruptcy provisions.

In addition, voluntary arrangements may be made under the *Insolvency Act 1986*.

Composition and Scheme of Arrangement

The debtor may submit a *composition* or a *scheme of arrangement* to a meeting of his creditors. The distinction between *a scheme* and *a composition* is that where a debtor makes over his assets to be administered by a trustee, that is a scheme; but a debtor keeps his assets and undertakes to pay over to the creditors a certain sum, that is a composition: *Re Griffith (1986)*. Any composition or scheme of arrangement must normally offer at least 25p in the £, and must be approved by a majority in number and three – fourths in value of the creditors. Where this is done, the composition or scheme will be considered by the court and if it provides for the payment of the preferential creditors and is one which the court considers reasonable, and calculated to benefit the general body of creditors, the court will sanction it. However, if the debtor fails to pay any instalment due under the scheme, or the scheme cannot, in consequence of legal difficulties or for any sufficient cause, proceed, or where approval of it was obtained by fraud, the scheme may be annulled and the court retains the right to adjudicate without starting bankruptcy proceedings again.

Interim Order

When an individual intends to make a proposal to his creditors on the above lines then an application may be made to the court for an "interim order". The application may be made by the debtor, or, if he is an undischarged bankrupt, by him, the trustee of his estate or the official receiver.

An "interim order" lasts for 14 days in the first instance and its effect is to stay any actions against the debtor and no bankruptcy petition may be presented against him.

An "interim order" will only be made if the court is convinced that the debtor is serious in attempting to reach agreement with his creditors. A nominee, who must be an insolvency practitioner, is appointed and the debtor must give him details of the arrangements he is trying to make.

The petition for a bankruptcy order to be made against the debtor
The petition may be filed by:

1. the debtor himself
2. the supervisor of a voluntary arrangement
3. the Official Petitioner where a criminal bankruptcy order has been made
4. more usually by a creditor who must show:

    a. that he is owed at least £750,
    b. it is a liquidated sum,
    c. it is unsecured,
    d. the debtor is unable to pay the debt.

Inability to pay his debts is proved by the creditor showing

1. that he has served a *statutory demand* on the debtor and it has been ignored for three weeks, or
2. enforcement proceedings in relation to a judgment against the debtor have not been satisfied.

The three weeks may be dispensed with and the petition may filed earlier if it can be shown that the assets of the debt may be reduced during that petition.

After the presentation of the petition
Any disposition of property or payment of money made after petition has been presented is void if the debtor is eventually adjudged bankrupt, unless the court approves the transaction. If a person has dealings with the debtor after the presentation of the petition and before the granting of the bankruptcy order then that person may be protected if he acted in good faith for value and without notice of the presentation of the petition.

The court can stay any action, execution or legal process against the property or person of the debtor. Also the court may consider it necessary, for the protection of the debtor's estate, to appoint an interim receiver. This will usually be the Official Receiver. He will have all the powers of a receiver and manager appointed by the High Court. He will have power to sell perishable goods and any goods which are likely to diminish in value if not sold.

Bankruptcy Order

It is within the discretion of the court whether or not to make a bankruptcy order. If it does so then it will terminate any interim receivership and the debtor becomes an undischarged bankrupt and loses ownership of his assets.

The Official Receiver becomes the manager of the bankrupt's estate pending the appointment of a trustee in bankruptcy. He can sell perishable goods and goods which will diminish in value if not sold.

The bankrupt must prepare a statement of affairs within 21 days and if he refuses or neglects to do so can be punished for contempt of court.

The Official Receiver can at any time apply to the court for a public examination of the bankrupt.

The Trustee in Bankruptcy
Appointment. The trustee may be appointed by creditors, the court or the Secretary of State. Usually the creditors will appoint. They will do so when the Official Receiver, who commences to act when the bankruptcy order is made, calls a meeting to consider the appointment. The meeting must be called within 12 weeks of his taking office. If the Official Receiver decides not to call a meeting then he will become the trustee in bankruptcy.

The court may appoint as trustee the insolvency practitioner who reported on the debtor's affairs or if the bankruptcy order follows upon a scheme or composition it can appoint the supervisor of the scheme.

If the creditors fail to appoint a trustee then the Secretary of State may do so.

Functions. The trustee must collect, realise and then distribute the assets of the bankrupt. He has all the powers of a receiver appointed by the High Court. He has power to carry on the business of the bankrupt and to mortgage assets to raise money. He also has power to disclaim onerous contracts which are unprofitable and property which is unsaleable.

Control of the trustee. The trustee is subject to the general control of the court. The creditors may also appoint a committee to exercise certain function. The trustee is of course liable for misapplication of the estate, misfeasance or breach of duty and the court has full discretionary powers to order a remedy.

Assets in the bankruptcy

The bankrupt's estate "comprises all property belonging to or vested in the bankrupt at the commencement of the bankruptcy". The bankruptcy commences on the date when the bankruptcy order is made. The bankrupt's tools, books, vehicles and other items used by him in his employment and provisions necessary for the domestic needs of the bankrupt and his family are exempt.

If an income payments order is made then a proportion of the income of the bankrupt will automatically pass to the trustee as in the case of profits of the business.

The trustee succeeds to the bankrupt's property on the "commencement of the bankruptcy". Bankruptcy commences on the day of the bankruptcy order.

Any disposition of property by the bankrupt between the date of presentation of the petition and the date when the bankrupt's estate vests in the trustee in bankruptcy is void.

However persons who took property or money from the bankrupt before the date of the bankruptcy order in good faith, for value and without notice of the presentation of the petition may be allowed to keep these transfers.

Persons who took property from the bankrupt after the bankruptcy order are given no protection and will have to appeal to the court.

Family homes

The *Matrimonial Homes Act 1983* gives a right to a spouse who is not the legal owner of the matrimonial home to register a charge on the home which cannot be upset except by an order of the court. This situation is accepted by the *Insolvency Act* and application must be made to the court if it is desired to realise the bankrupt's interest in the home.

Duration of Bankruptcy

In the majority of cases bankruptcy will end automatically after 3 years have elapsed since the bankruptcy order was made. The Official Receiver can inform the court that the bankrupt has failed to comply with his obligations and the court may order that the time under the 3 year period shall stop running.

Where the bankrupt has been an undischarged bankrupt within

15 years before his current bankruptcy he will not be discharged automatically but must apply to the court for discharge after 5 years have elapsed.

Banks and bankruptcy

The problem with bankruptcy is that it is a long drawn out process. Firstly there is the bankruptcy petition but of course that does not necessarily mean that the customer will be made bankrupt. If a banker learns, as he may well do, that a customer is in financial difficulties he should discuss the matter with the customer. He should also watch the situation closely so that he will know when a bankruptcy petition has been presented. At that stage he should stop the account. The wisest course for the banker is to open a suspense account when he learns of the presentation of the petition and to place any credits into that account.

Suspense acct

When the banker learns of the presentation of the petition he should close the customer's account and suggest to the customer that he obtains the consent of the court if he wishes to operate an account. Otherwise the bank may be held liable for operating the account. *Re. Gray's Inn Construction Co Ltd (1980)*.

Principles common to corporate and individual insolvency

1.   It is a well founded principle of insolvency law that all creditors must be treated equally or pari passu.

Exceptions to this rule are

1.   preferential creditors are paid out in preference to ordinary creditors
2.   secured creditors also get priority.

Any contractual arrangement for a creditor e.g. a bank to receive priority would be unacceptable but non-contractual rights such as a right of combination or lien will be unaffected.

non contractual rights eg setoff or lien unaffected

British Eagle International Airlines Ltd v Compagnie Nationale Air France (1975)
2.   It is important to consider the effect upon a bank account of the presentation of a petition to make an individual bankrupt or for a company to be wound up. In this connection Sections 127 and 284 are of importance.

Section 127 provides that "In a winding-up by the court any disposition of the company's property and any transfer of shares, or alteration in the status of the company's members made after the commencement of the winding-up is, unless the Court otherwise orders, void".

The effect of this section is that cheques paid out of an account in credit may have to be refunded to the liquidator and cheques paid into an overdrawn account may have to be returned to the liquidator. Also debts in an overdrawn account arising after the date of the petition would cause an increase in the debt owed to the bank which the bank could not prove.

Thus, once a winding up petition has been presented against a company the bank must stop the account. *Re Grays Inn Construction Co Ltd (1980)*

More recent cases include *Re Tramway Building and Construction Co Ltd (1988)* and *Re Pressdee Ltd (1985)*.

In the cases of an individual insolvency *Section 284* will apply. The effect of this section is similar to that of section 127. It provides that any payment to a bank, after the presentation of the petition, shall be held by the bank for the trustee unless it can show that it acted in good faith, a transaction took place for value, and had no notice that the petition had been presented.

Once the bank becomes aware of a bankruptcy petition, it should stop the account and allow no further payments to be made from it: Sometimes it may be possible for the liquidator or trustee in bankruptcy to recover money or property transferred to third parties. This situation may arise because the bankrupt or company has been involved in a transaction at an undervalue, a fraudulent transaction or a preference. See items 3, 4 and 5.

3. **Transaction at an undervalue**

This will arise where the debtor has transferred property and has either received no consideration for it or the consideration was less than the market value of the property. It also arises where the debtor has entered into a transaction in consideration of marriage. Liability will arise from the fact of the transaction and the state of the debtor's mind will be irrelevant.

The period during which transactions at an undervalue may be avoided by the trustee in bankruptcy is 5 years before the presentation of the petition for a bankruptcy order.

If the trustee can "avoid" a transaction it means that the trustee can recover the property from the person who acquired it. The bankrupt must have been insolvent at the time of the transaction. Transactions within 2 years of the petition are affected irrespective of the bankrupt's insolvency. Also, if an "associate" is involved, insolvency is presumed. If any property is transferred at an undervalue during the relevant periods, it may be recovered by the trustee.

An associate includes spouses and other relatives, partners etc. The same principles apply in the case of companies and transactions at an undervalue may be avoided by the liquidator. However, where a company is concerned the basic period is 2 years and not 5 years before the relevant time and in the case of a company this is the date of the presentation of the petition (compulsory winding up) or the date of the resolution (voluntary winding up).

4. **Preferences**

These arise if the debtor does anything which results in the creditor being in a better position, in the event of a bankruptcy of the debtor, than he would have been in if that things had not been done. The periods during which the preference transactions must have occurred are:

1.   if the transaction is not at an undervalue and is entered into with an associate of the debtor – *2 years* before the presentation of the petition. (An associate is the bankrupt's spouse or former or reputed spouse and any brother, sister, uncle, aunt, nephew or niece of them) or
2.   if the person preferred is not an associate and the transaction is not at an undervalue – 6 months before the presentation of the petition.

The same periods apply in the case of a company.

For a transaction to amount to a preference there must have been the intention on the part of the debtor to improve the position of the recipient of the preference.

Also the debtor must have been insolvent at the time of the transaction. Insolvency is defined as "where the debtor was unable to pay his debts as they fell due; or where the value of the debtor's assets was less than his liabilities, including contingent and prospective liabilities.''

The recipient of the preference may not always be a creditor who receives payment but may sometimes be a bank to which the debtor makes payment, not to favour the bank, but to favour the guarantor of his debt. However the bank may be protected so long as it received the benefit in good faith, for value and without notice of the relevant circumstances.

Where a bank is involved in a possible preference transaction it will be protected

1.   If it received payment in good faith and for value and without notice of bankruptcy proceedings.
2.   If the bank has to repay a credit received, the court may permit it to retain the security.
3.   In practice a bank will include a clause in its security forms allowing it to retain the security until the danger of preference has disappeared.

Re. KM Kushler (1943)

In practice banks will usually include a clause in their security documents by which they will be allowed to keep the security until the danger of preference has disappeared.

The periods which apply are 6 months in the case of an ordinary guarantee but 24 months if the guarantee was given by a spouse, partner or company with which the customer was connected.

In the case of preferences as in undervalues the court may make an order, the effect of which will be to put the parties back to their original positions which they occupied before the transaction.

Preferences are not prohibited unless the individual is insolvent at the time of the transaction or becomes insolvent because of it.

5. Fraudulent transactions

Sometimes a transaction may be at an undervalue and is made with the intention of putting the assets beyond the reach of actual or potential claimants. Undervalue has the normal meaning of the word mentioned above. However a fraudulent undervalue has no restriction as to when it is made and so the periods which are relevant to an ordinary undervalue transaction do not apply to a fraudulent undervalue. *Insolvency Act 1986* Ss.423–425.

Summary – Individual insolvency
1. If the creditor can only get his money by making the debtor bankrupt then the creditor must petition the Court for a Bankruptcy Order.
2. If the order is made then the Official Receiver is appointed as temporary trustee in bankruptcy until a trustee in bankruptcy is appointed.
3. A trustee succeeds to the bankrupts property on the day of the Bankruptcy Order.
4. Because of the period between the presentation of the petition to make an individual bankrupt or for a company to be wound up and the date of the making of Bankruptcy/Winding up Order, then any person who has dealt with the bankrupts/ companies property during this period must be protected.
5. Section 127 of the Insolvency Act 1976 as regards companies, Section 284 as regards individuals make void any transfer of property of a company or individual after the presentation of the petition unless it can be shown that the person concerned had no notice of the petition.
6. Undervalue arises where the debtor has transferred property and has received no value or less than the market value for it.
7. A preference arises where the debtor has transferred property with the intention of putting the creditor in a better position than he would have been in had not the transaction taken place.

Chapter Thirteen

Realisation and Distribution of Assets

When it is desired to realise any security of an individual or of a company it may become necessary for a person to be appointed to deal with the business of realising the assets and distributing the proceeds amongst the debenture holders or creditors. Under the Act, there are a number of "office holders" who may act in connection with an insolvent company. These include an *administrator* appointed under an administration order, a *liquidator* whether under a compulsory or voluntary winding-up and an *administrative receiver* under a floating charge. The *Insolvency Act 1986* allows the court to order anyone who holds information or has records concerning the company to produce these to the "office holder". Clearly, this could affect the bank. Similar powers may also be obtained by the trustee in a personal bankruptcy.

Where individuals are concerned a receiver will only be appointed if it is desired to realise land. The power to appoint a receiver will arise and become exercisable in the same way as the power of sale. In practice an individual will probably only consider appointing a receiver if the land has been leased and it is considered that the proper course is to defer selling the land, and to continue to receive the rents.

Such rents collected by the receiver must be applied by him in:

1. discharge of expenses in connection with the property such as taxes and rates.
2. payment of interest on prior incumbrances.
3. payment of insurance premiums.
4. payment of repairs and his own commission.
5. payment of interest under the mortgage.
6. discharge of the principal debt.

More commonly a receiver will be appointed by a bank when it is owed money by a company or by an individual. The bank will have such power conferred in its debenture form. The receiver may realise the security whether or not a liquidation or bankruptcy has occurred.

Administrative Receiver

The receiver appointed under a floating charge is called an administrative receiver if the charge covers the whole of the company's property. He must be an insolvency practitioner.

If an application is made for the appointment by the court of an administrator under the *Insolvency Act 1986 S.9* then the court will give notice of this application to any holder of a floating charge. If the court is satisfied that an administrative receiver is in office it shall dismiss the application to appoint an administrator. If the bank hs not appointed an administrative receiver than it will have 5 days in which to do so. If it does not do so within that period the court will make an administration order.

The effect of the administration order is that the bank may be prevented from realising its security. The bank will not be deprived of its security rights but may only receive the proceeds when the security has been realised. Once an administrator is appointed no debenture holder can realise his security except with the court's consent. An administrator must consider the interests of the company and of the general creditors.

For this reason a bank will in future usually take a floating charge so that it will be in a position to appoint an administrative receiver. The bank will then be able to realise its security if it wishes.

Within 3 months of appointment the administrator must produce proposals for the creditors and if he fails to do so the administration order will lapse.

A receiver may be appointed by the bank under the power conferred on it by the debenture form. He must be appointed in writing not necessarily under seal. The appointment takes effect when it is received by the receiver who must accept by the end of the following business day and the acceptance must be confirmed within 7 days.

After appointment the receiver must notify the company and the creditors within 28 days. The debenture holder must notify the Registrar of companies within 7 days and a note is made in the register of charges.

As stated earlier, a receiver appointed under a floating charge is an administrative receiver and is merely a receiver under a fixed charge.

A receiver is the agent of the company and so can bind the company by his transactions. However he is also personally liable on contracts he makes. He must have regard for the interests of the company and when selling the assets he must take reasonable care to get the best price available *Cuckmere Brick Co Ltd v Mutual Finance Ltd (1971)*.

[margin note: Personal liability of receiver]

The powers of an administrative receiver are contained in the *Insolvency Act 1986* (Part III) and include the making of reports and the calling of creditors' meetings.

The order in which the disposition of assets is to take place follows that used by a liquidator i.e.

1. The rightful owners of the property.
2. Costs and expenses.
3. Holders of fixed charges.
4. Preferential creditors.
5. Holders of floating charges.
6. Unsecured creditors.
7. Any surplus for the members of the company.

It very often happens that soon after a receiver has been appointed a liquidator is appointed to wind up the company. When that occurs the receiver's powers cease. He ceases to be the agent of the company but he does not automatically become agent of the debenture holder.

It is in the bank's interests for it to appoint an administrative receiver, as if the court appoints an administrator the bank may be prevented from realising the asset. Therefore a bank will invariably take a floating charge which will enable it to block the appointment of an administrator.

Distribution of the Assets

To prove a debt means to claim for it in a bankruptcy or winding up proceeding. Debts which may be claimed are said to be provable and they are

1. Debts which existed before the date of the bankruptcy order/ winding up order.
2. Debts for which the debtor my become liable because of an

obligation incurred before the commencement of the bankruptcy/winding up.

3. The interest on a debt but that does not apply to interest payable after commencement of the bankruptcy/winding up.

4. Amounts specified in a criminal bankruptcy order.

The first three of these apply to companies and individuals alike. The last one only to individuals.

Order of application of assets in payment of debts

Once the liquidator/trustee has "collected" in all the property of the bankrupt or company he must proceed to pay those creditors who are entitled to be paid.

Secured creditors

The respective rights of secured and unsecured creditors must be maintained.

A secured creditor is one who has some mortgage, charge or lien on the debtor's property. In order that the respective rights of secured and unsecured creditors may be maintained secured creditors are allowed to rely primarily on their security for payment. In this respect they have four clear choices:

1. they may rest entirely on their security and not prove in the bankruptcy or winding up at all; or

2. they may realise their security and prove only for the deficiency; or

3. they may value it and prove for the deficiency, after deduction of the assessed value, in which case the liquidator/trustee may redeem the security at such assessed value; or

4. they may surrender the security to the liquidator/trustee and prove for the whole debt in the winding up or bankruptcy.

Once a secured creditor has exhausted his rights against his security, any balance of the debt owed to him is owed to him as an ordinary unsecured creditor.

As soon as the above considerations are disposed of, the liquidator/trustee can proceed to make actual payments to unsecured creditors in the following order.

1.   Costs, charges and expenses properly incurred in the winding up/bankruptcy, including the remuneration of the liquidator/trustee.

2.   Preferential debts

   a.   Deductions from wages which should have been made under the PAYE scheme in the 12 months before the relevant date or the date of the making of the winding up/bankruptcy order.

   b.   Value added tax payable in the 6 months before the relevant date.

   c.   Social security contributions for 12 months before the relevant date.

   d.   State and occupational pension scheme contributions which the debtor should have made.

   e.   Employees' arrears of wages for 4 months before the relevant date up to a maximum of £800 per employee.

   Loans made for the payment of wages would be included here, consequently a bank which lends money for this purpose would be treated as a preferential creditor.

The "relevant date" in a compulsory winding up means, when a provisional liquidator was apppointed, the date of his appointment; otherwise it means the date of the winding up order. In the case of a voluntary winding up the date of the passing of the resolution for winding up. Schedule 19 *Companies Act 1985.*

3.   Holders of floating charges. These rank behind the preferential creditors even though the floating charge crystallises before liquidation. This provision only applies to companies.

4.   Ordinary unsecured creditors: If after payment of the preferential creditors in full, there are still funds left, the next class of creditors to be paid is the ordinary unsecured creditors. They also rank equally amongst themselves and abate *pari passu* if the company's/individual's assets are insufficient.

5.   Interest on debts since the bankruptcy/winding up commenced.

6.   Non-provable debts: In the unlikely event that the

liquidator is able to pay all the above creditors in full, and if there are still assets available, he must then pay the debts which are normally not provable in winding up, such as unliquidated damages in tort. This is because, in such a case, the company is solvent and by section 611, *Companies Act 1985*, all debts may be proved.

7. If after paying the above, there is still some money left, it goes to the members of the company according to their rights in a winding up. Sometimes preference share-holders take the capital in preference to ordinary share-holders.

The order of priority in the case of an individual is the same, except that "floating charges" do not apply and any assets remaining after "interest on debts" has been paid goes to pay any debts owed to the bankrupt's spouse. Finally any surplus is returned to the bankrupt.

Wages Accounts

In 2(e) above we have seen that arrears of wages rank as a preferential debt. By subrogation this privilege applies also to persons who have made advances for the purpose of paying the wages. The person who lent the money shall rank as a preferential creditor to the extent that the employee would rank as a preferental creditor i.e. £800 per employee.

A person (company, partnership or sole trader) which is borrowing from a bank for the payment of wages is often requested to open a special wages account to which all cheques for salaries and wages may be debited. It becomes essential therefore for bankers and the borrowers to know precisely what payments may be debited to the wages account with a view to obtaining preferential treatment.

It is not legally necessary to open a separate wages account to establish a preferential claim – *Re Rampgill Mill Ltd (1967)* however the advantages of doing so are:

1. it avoids disputes as to the reason for borrowing money.
2. it avoids the operation of the "Rule in Clayton's case".

If a bank has a preferential and a non-preferential debt then any money it receives it would obviously wish to appropriate to the non-preferential debt so as to keep the preferential debt as large as possible to be proved in the winding up.

In *Re Unit 2 Windows Ltd (1985)* the court held that the correct solution was to apply the money received proportionately between the preferential debt and the non-preferential debt.

All preferential payments rank equally among themselves and must be paid in full *in priority* to all other debts. If there are insufficient funds to pay them in full they abate proportionately.

Summary – Realisation and distribution of assets
1.   When it is desired to realise any security of an individual or of a company. It will be necessary for a person to be appointed to realise the assets and to distribute them.
2.   Such persons may be a liquidator, an administrator or an administrative receiver.
3.   An administrator may be appointed by the Court but this will not be convenient for a bank as it may be prevented from realising its security.
4.   If the bank holds a floating charge it will be able to block the appointment of an administrator by appointing its own administrative receiver and so will be able to realise its security.
5.   A receiver is appointed by debenture holders.
6.   A liquidator is appointed to wind up a company.
7.   Debts must be paid off in a certain order.
8.   Preferential debts are paid off immediately after payment of the costs of the liquidation and so it will be to the advantage of a bank to ensure that its debts are ranked as preferential debts e.g. a debt used by a company to pay its wages.

Chapter Fourteen

Securities – Land

It is a fact of life that when a lender lends money to a borrower, the lender will inevitably require security to be given for the loan. Admittedly there are a few occasions when no security is required but this is not normal practice particularly if the sum of money lent is large and the loan is for a substantial period of time.

The simplest form of giving security was the pledge. In this case a pawnbroker was usually involved. The borrower went to him and physically handed over something of value such as a watch or necklace. In return the pawnbroker lent a sum of money and when the loan was repaid or redeemed then the security wsa returned to its owner.

[handwritten margin note: pledge: handover something]

The limitations affecting these procedures are obvious. The amount of the loan would be restricted to a proportion of the value of the asset that could be physically deposited with the lender. During the period of the pledge the lender did not own the asset but if the loan was unredeemed than the lender could sell the asset six months after the failure to repay the loan and could recoup himself from the proceeds.

A development of the pledge is the mortgage or charge. In this case the borrower keeps possession of the asset which is to constitute the security and merely gives rights to the lender. The most important of these rights is of course the right to sell the asset. Thus the assets are said to be mortgaged or charged in favour of the lender. The difference between a mortgage and a charge is a technical one and depends on the type of document used. The effect is the same.

It is important to bear in mind that the actual security transaction is a separate one from that which concerns the lending of the money.

$$A \xrightarrow{\text{loan}} B$$

A lends B money that – is the loan transaction. Collaterally or alongside this transaction runs the security transaction.

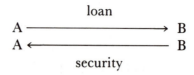

This is why an American thinking of lending money to you will be interested to know what "collateral" you have. It is a short form of referring to the security.

Note that as regards the loan transaction A can sue B at any time for the return of the money. A loan is a contract and as any simple contract must be sued upon within 6 years of its coming into force otherwise no action may be taken, the same limitation period applies to a loan. So if A has lent B the money more than 6 years ago he will no longer be able to sue to recover it, unless a deed was used.

Separate from the loan transaction is the security transaction. Now it may not be necessary for any action to be taken on this. Most borrowers probably repay their loans. However in the event of this not happening then A can enforce the rights he has been given by B as security.

The important point to remember is that, leaving a pledge aside where the lender takes physical possession of the security, when a person gives security for the loan he has received, he transfers rights to the lender. The most important right being the right to sell the security if the borrower defaults.

So once again, we are in the area of rights, because this is what the law is always concerned with. Thus it is necessary to consider the rights that exist over the various things that may be used as security for a loan, and also to consider how such rights may be transferred.

Property

At this point we must consider the division of property which is anything that a person may own. So all property is classified as illustrated in the diagram opposite.

The securities we shall consider will be land and personal property in the form of life assurance policies and shares. In addition we must examine guarantees which can be used as security for a loan if the borrower himself does not have any security.

Negotiable instruments will be treated separately as they are a very special form of chose in action.

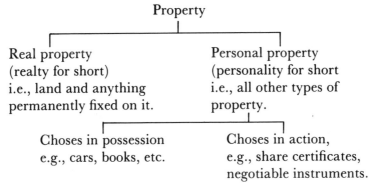

So all property is classified in this way.

Land

This is usually considered by students to be the most difficult of the things that can be offered as security. Land law has its origins in the past centuries when land and animals on the land were the only things of any value and capable of ownership. So it came to be all property (i.e. everything that a person may own) was divided into land and personal chattels (which word was derived from cattle or the animals on the land). This division of property remains with us today.

Rights of ownership
The interesting point about a piece of land is that more than one right may exist over it. Firstly there are rights of ownership. Unlike personal property where a person either owns the article, or not, in the case of lend where there are several different kinds of rights of ownership known as estates. These estates are either freehold or leasehold or to put it in another way, a person may have a freehold right or a leasehold right over a piece of land. The most important freehold right that can exist over a piece of land is that known as the "fee simple estate". This is a right of ownership that may be inherited and the owner of it may dispose of it during his lifetime or by his will. It is a right of ownership that is virtually absolute ownership. There are other lesser freehold rights such as a life estate. As its name indicates this right of ownership lasts for the life-time of the owner and this may not be inherited nor may it be disposed of by the owner. Upon his death it will be transferred automatically to another person who has been designated to receive the ownership of the land when the life estate is terminated.

Apart from a freehold estate there may be a leasehold estate. A lease is a contract and basically the difference between a freehold estate and a lease is that the lease will terminate at some time and the ownership of the land will revert to the person who granted the lease; also a lease may contain a number of conditions which will be binding on the lessee. However, when one considers the difference between a freehold estate and a lease of 999 years it should become clear that there is little difference during the initial period of the lease. It may be transferred, in the same way as a freehold interest in land and it may be disposed of by will. Of course as the period of the lease nears its end then the owner of it will be aware that he will lose his right of ownership and so the value of the lease will diminish. Both freehold and leasehold rights are rights of ownership and they merely differ in certain respects.

So you see a person can say that he owns a piece of and, but a number of different types of ownership exist. He may "own" the land as a freeholder and have a fee simple over the land; or he may be a leaseholder and have a lease. He may have a life interest in the land.

Rights other than rights of ownership
Also someone other than the person who has the right of ownership over a piece of land may have rights or interests as they are called. For example a person may have fishing rights, a right of way or a right to dig sand or gravel. Also a mortgagee will have a right (basically a right of sale) over the land.

Law and Equity
Apart from the different kinds of estates that may exist over a piece of land such as fee simple, leasehold or life interest, there are in fact two types of right i.e. a legal right or equitable right.

The creation of equitable rights goes back centuries to the time when there were two different courts, one to administer legal rights and the other equitable rights.

The person who owned the legal rights had the paper ownership of the land and the equitable owner had the beneficial ownership. Often of course the two types of ownership were joined and one person held both of them. At other times the ownership might be split as in the case of a trust where the trustee has the legal ownership. If there is a conflict between the person holding the legal right and the one holding the equitable right then equity always wins. So if one person had rights which are upheld by a court of law then he may be restrained from exercising those rights by an injunction being issued against him. This would be a remedy recognised by the Court of Equity.

Since the *Judicature Acts 1873–1875* both equity and law may be administered in the courts of law.

Equitable rights may be created intentionally as when a person leaves land to a person A to hold in trust for his children X, Y, Z. In this case A will have a legal title and the children will get an equitable title.

An equitable title may arise also when a person intends to transfer his legal title but neglects to make the transfer in the manner laid down by law. Thus a person may mortgage his land but not use a deed, (which is required by law). In that case the mortgagee will get an equitable mortgage.

If a person who only has a legal right to the land attempts to sell both the legal and equitable rights in the land then he may be prevented if the beneficiaries (owners of the equitable title) have registered their interests in the land. If the beneficiaries have not registered their interests and the purchaser takes for value and without knowledge of the interests of the beneficiaries then he may get both the legal and equitable rights on the land.

As far as mortgages are concerned these may be legal or equitable and may exist over unregistered or registered land.

Unregistered and registered land

In this country at present there are two types of land and whether it is registered or unregistered refers to whether or not the owner's title to the land is entered on the Land Register.

The difference becomes apparent when the land (or the ownership in the land) is conveyed from one person to another.

Unregistered Land

Transfer of Unregistered Land

Even though we may speak of "transfer of land", what we really mean is the transfer of the owner's title to it. A landowner's title may be either freehold or leasehold.

In the transfer of unregistered land the vendor must produce a bundle of documents which shows all the major transactions affecting the land. This bundle is the evidence by which the seller is able to demonstrate to the purchaser his title to the land. Only documents affecting legal title are kept.

The vendor must demonstrate his title by establishing a *good root of title*, at least fifteen years old, then through a *good chain of title* to the *holding deed*.

Good Root of Title

This document will form a starting point for checking the title of the vendor.

A good root is a deed of conveyance or a deed of mortgage. It must be at least fifteen years old (Law of Property Act 1969, S.23, reducing the period from thirty years).

It must cover all the essential facts concerning the lands, e.g., it must describe the land, and identify the owner of the legal interest.

Good Chain of Title

Every time a legal interest in land is transferred, it must be done by deed. Except in the case of registered land, every deed forms a link in the chain of title. It shows how the land has been dealt with in the past and also how the present owner derives his title.

A good chain of title will show in chronological order the major transactions affecting the land. These will include marriages, deaths and even, where appropriate, bankruptcies – so that a coherent story comprising the sequence of titles and ownerships over the fifteen period may be told.

The Holding Deed

This is the last of the series of deeds in the chain of title and is the one that transfers the land to the vendor.

Abstract of Title

This does not form part of the title to land. It is merely a summary of the deeds and other supporting documents constituting the chain of title. It is usually prepared by the solicitor of the vendor. An abstract of title should begin with a good root of title such as a conveyance of the fee simple on sale. After a summary of the good root of title, there will follow short summary (called the "recital") of the material parts of all the deeds, wills, births and marriage certificates, and other records affecting the title. An abstract must also show that receipts are given for any consideration money. A purchaser of freehold or leasehold land has a legal right to demand an abstract of title going back for fifteen years.

Charges on the Land

In addition to rights of ownership over a piece of land there may be other rights that may exist over the same piece of land. From a banker's point of view the most important is the land charge such as a mortgage or charge. This is discussed in more detail in Chapter 15. if this has been given by the vendor of the land to another person, the bank will wish to know about it before it decides whether or not it wishes to make the loan. Also if the bank has agreed to take a charge over the land it will wish its own charge to be registered so as it will be protected and it will serve as notice to any future prospective purchasers of the land of the bank's interest.

Registration of Incumbrances or Charges

The 1925 property legislation provided for the registration of a number of charges and interests affecting land. Under the *Land Charges Act 1925*, any person having certain rights over land of another must register those rights, otherwise the rights will be void against a purchaser for value who acquires a legal interest in the land.

Only charges capable of registration can be registered; but registration constitutes actual notice of the existence of the charge and the fact of its registration to all persons and for all purposes connected with the land affected, as from the date of the registration.

The object of the system is to enable a purchaser to discover easily what charges exist on the land he is purchasing. Indeed, any third party interested in the land can search in the Register of Charges. If there are no charges registered he can assume that none affects the land.

Land charges are registered against the name of the owner (i.e. proprietor) of the land at the time the charge is registered. Five registers are kept at the Land Registry in London where an alphabetical list of the estate owners is kept.

The Registers

1.   *The Register of Pending Actions*
     A pending action is any action, information or proceeding pending in any court relating to any interest in land. It includes a petition for a bankruptcy order. A purchase of the land is not bound by an unregistered pending action unless he has actual or express notice of it.

2.   *Register of Annuities*
     No annuities are registered in this register after 1925.

3.   *Register of Writs and Orders Affecting Land*
     The matters entered in this register are writs and orders affecting land made for the purpose of enforcing a judgment or an obligation to the Crown, and orders appointing a receiver or sequestrator.

4.   *Register of Deeds of Arrangement Affecting Land*
     A deed of arrangement is any document whereby control is given over a debtor's property for the benefit of creditors generally or, if he is insolvent, for the benefit of three or more of his creditors.

5.   *Register of Land Charges*
     There are six classes of land charges, from A to F.
     Classes A and B are charges imposed on land by statute.
     Class C. This class comprises the most important charges. There are four categories:

     (i)   Puisne mortgages, e.g., a legal mortgage if not protected by deposit of title deeds.
     (ii)   A limited owner's charge, i.e., an equitable charge in favour of a tenant for life or statutory owner under any statute – e.g., one who has paid death duties in respect of the estate in which his interest lies.
     (iii) A general equitable charge, e.g., an equitable mortgage which is not protected by deposit of title deeds. Annuities created after 1925 are registered here.
     (iv)   An estate contract, i.e., a contract to create or convey a legal estate.

     Class D. There are three categories:

     (i)   Charges in favour of the Inland Revenue
     (ii)   Restrictive covenants

(iii) Equitable easements.

Class E. This consists of annuities created before 1926 which should have been registered in the register of annuities but were not.

Class F. A charge affecting any land by virtue of the *Matrimonial Homes Act 1983.*

Land charges (other than floating charges) created by a company must be registered at the Companies Register as well as in the Land Charges Register.

Operation of the Register

An intending purchaser of unregistered land will need to know two things in particular:

1. Does the vendor have title to convey the land?
2. If he does, are there any incumbrances or charges on land which he must know?

Question 1 may be answered from the examination of the title deeds explained earlier on.

An intending purchaser of land can discover what registrable charges and incumbrances exist on the land by making a search of the relevant register. Two methods of search are possible.

1. *A personal search*, i.e., he may go to the Land Registry and search the register himself; or
2. *An official search.* He may request an official to search for which an official certificate may be given.

An official search is preferable for two main reasons:

1. The certificate of search is conclusive in favour of a purchaser and so exonerates him from any liability in respect of rights which it fails to disclose.
2. The certificate provides protection against incumbrances registered in the interval between search and completion of the contract of sale.

Registered Land

In 1925 the *Land Registration Act* introduced a system of registration of title (ownership) over land. This system has the following advantages.

1.   Simplicity
2.   Cheapness
3.   State-guaranteed title.

Simplicity
The pile of title deeds grows in bulk as time goes on. When land is registered the title is checked for the last time by the state lawyers and a certificate of title issued. Thereafter any transfer is achieved by completion of a simple form of transfer which is then lodged at the Land Registry together with the registered Land Certificate. The old certificate is then cancelled and a new one issued in the name of the new owner. The procedure is similar to the transfer of shares in a company.

The forms dealing with registered land transfer are free from legal technicalities. The law governing unregistered land is difficult to understand and the constant re-checking of title over and over again upon every transfer of the land constitutes an expensive duplication of work.

Information about registered land is generally available from the register. This means that a person interested in the land should in theory be able to know:

1.   What land it covers and what rights are attached to it?
2.   Who owns the land?
3.   What charges are registered against the land, what restrictions are imposed on the owner as to its use and what rights are exercisable over it?

The insistence that every title on the register should have a plan attached to it facilitates easier identification and description of the land in words is greatly curtailed.

Cheapness
The contract of sale is simpler, as the stipulations affecting the land need not be set out in full. As the transfer is by reference to the

register there is little checking of title and the legal costs involved are therefore reduced.

State-Guaranteed Title

The State guarantees the title to registered land. This means that unless the proprietor has acted fraudulently, he is secure in the knowledge that he cannot be left without the land or its value if the vendor did not after all have title.

A title far from perfect can be made perfect by the fact of its being registered.

Note: Registration of title is subject to one limitation. Only legal estates in the land can be registered. This means only the fee simple absolute in possession and the term of years absolute can be registered.

In order to implement the system the *Land Registration Act 1925* created a register in which everything known about a piece of land is to be recorded. Thereafter, all dealings with that land are to proceed with reference only to the register.

Title can be registered only after the title deeds have been checked in the usual way.

It was pointed out earlier how the transfer of unregistered land must be preceded by the vendor producing a bundle of documents which show all the major transactions affecting the land.

Where title to land has been registered, the land is then known as registered land. The transfer of registered land proceeds on a different principle; once the title is registered, its past history is irrelevant. Thereafter any transfer of the land is achieved by substituting the purchaser's name for that of the vendor.

Registration of title at present may be either permissive or else it is obligatory if the land is in a "compulsory area". Further, not all titles in the compulsory areas must be registered.

Compulsory Registration

After registration of title has become compulsory within a particular area the following transactions give rise to compulsory registration:

1. the sale of the freehold;
2. the grant of a lease for a term of more than 21 years;
3. the assignment of a lease having more than 21 years to run.

As to leases;

1.   Where the lessor has registered his freehold title, a lessee must register any lease of more than 21 years irrespective of whether the land is in an area of compulsory registration or not.
2.   If the area is one of compulsory registration the lessee must register any lease of more than 21 years even if the freehold title is not registered.
3.   If the area is not one of compulsory registration and the lessor's title is not registered then a lease of any number of years is not normally registrable.

When the title to the land has been investigated a Land Certificate is issued to the owner and he will then be recorded as registered owner in the Register.

THE REGISTER

The register of any individual title consists of three parts:

The Property Register;
The Proprietorship Register;
The Charges Register.

1.   *First Part: The Property Register*
This describes the property concerned in words and also by a plan. It may also describe any other things included and owned by the proprietor – e.g. easements or restrictive covenants of which the registered land is the dominant tenement.

With leasehold property, the following additional information will be given;

1.   the date of the lease;
2.   a description of the parties to it;
3.   the title number of the lessor's title if his title was registered;
4.   the duration (i.e. term) of the lease; and
5.   the rent payable and any premium paid.

2.   *Second Part: The Proprietorship Register*

1.   This sets out the full names of the proprietor of the land, his address and the nature of his title.
2.   A proprietor may have;

    a.   absolute title.
    b.   qualified title.
    c.   possessory title.

Further in the case of leaseholds, he may be registered with good leasehold title. If the Registrar is satisfied as to the freehold title and any superior leasehold title, he may, and if the proprietor applies, he must, convert good leasehold into absolute title.

Absolute title

1. In the case of freeholds, this gives the first registered proprietor the equivalent of the fee simple in possession in unregistered land subject only to:

    a. overriding interests.
    b. minor interests of which he has notice; and
    c. entries on the register – e.g. any restraint on the proprietor's right of disposition.

2. In the case of leaseholds, absolute title gives the first registered proprietor the leasehold interest subject to a–c above and also any liability expressly imposed by the lease.

Qualified title: This is granted where absolute title is asked for, but the Chief Land Registrar concludes that the title is valid for a limited period only or that it is subject to some reservation.

In the case of freeholds, this has the same effect as an absolute title except that the property is held subject to some defect or right specified in the register.

Qualified title to leaseholds has the same effect as an absolute or good leasehold title, as the case may be, except for the specified defect. If Registrar is satisfied he must convert a qualified title to absolute freehold or good leasehold. Qualified titles are rare in practice.

Possessory title: This is granted where the applicant cannot establish his title in the normal way by title deeds and other documentary evidence but his title is based on possession of the land or his receipt of the rents and profits.

An applicant for possessory title must produce declarations establishing possession and the declaration should also set out any known incumbrances on the land, such as rights of way.

In both freeholds and leaseholds, first registration with possessory title has the same effect as registration with absolute title except that the title is subject to all defects existing at the time of the first registration. Possessory freehold may be upgraded to absolute freehold and possessory leasehold to good leasehold.

Good leasehold title: This is equivalent to an absolute title to leaseholds, except that the lessor's right to grant the lease is not guaranteed.

3.   *Third Part:* The Charges Register.

This records mortgages, charges, leases which affect the land.

Overriding interests and minor interests are not included here.

Minor Interests

These are defined by the *Land Registration Act S.3* and are interests which require protection by entry on the register otherwise they will not bind a purchaser for value of the legal estate if he has no knowledge of the minor interest. Minor interests do not include overriding interests, registered estates and charges.

A minor interest may be protected by:

1.   *Notice*: This ensures that any disposition of the freehold land by the proprietor will only operate subject to those interests protected. Important interests which may be so protected are:

   a.   Leases which are not overriding interests.
   b.   Land charges – e.g. estate contracts, restrictive covenants and equitable esements; (in the case of unregistered land, such charges must be registered as Class C charges).

2.   *Restriction*: A restriction is an entry which prevents dealings in registered land until certain conditions or requirements set out in the restriction have been complied with. Its object is to record on the register any impediments that affect the proprietor's freedom of disposal.

   Such an entry may be made in the case of strict settlements and trusts for sale affecting registered land.

3.   *Caution*: Generally notices and restrictions are possible only with the proprietors consent and the land certificate must be available. When that consent cannot be obtained a caution may be registered in the proprietorship register. The effect of this is to require the Registrar to give the cautioner warning that if he does not object to some proposed dealing with the land within 14 days the registration will be made.

4.   *Inhibition*: The court or the Registrar, upon the application of any persons interested, may order an inhibition to be entered upon the proprietorship register.

Such an entry prevents any dealings with the registered land or registered charge, either generally, or for a given time, or until the occurrence of an event named in the order.

Such an entry will be most appropriate in those cases where for reasons of urgency, the other kinds of entry cannot be used.

Overriding Interests

These comprise all interests, rights and powers not entered on the register but subject to which dispositions are to take effect.

A comprehensive list of these interests is provided in Section 70 of the *Land Registration Act 1925*. Examples are:

1. Rights of common, public rights and *profits a prendre*.
2. Leases for not more than twenty-one years.
3. Rights of persons in occupation.

Overriding interests bind the proprietor of the registered land even though he has no knowledge of them and no reference to them is made in the register. The most important and difficult of overriding interests from the point of view of a bank are the rights of every person in actual occupation of the land, unless such a person has been questioned and the existence of his rights has not been disclosed. *Land Registration Act 1925 S.70(1)*

So if a bank is considering granting a loan to the legal owner of a house and intends to take a charge over the land, it must also make inquiries of any equitable owner of the property who is in actual occupation of it.

In this connection the relevant date of "actual occupation" has been held by the House of Lords in *Abbey National Building Society v Cann and others (1990)*, to be the date of completion.

In *Williams and Glyn's Bank Ltd v Boland (1979)* the House of Lords held that the wife had contributed financially to the purchase though her husband had the legal ownership. The wife therefore had an equitable interest in the land and this was an overriding interest. The bank should have made inquiry of the wife and if her interest had been disclosed she should have been asked to join in the mortgage or to waive her rights. The husband had the legal interest. He in effect was a trustee for sale: In *City of London Building Society v Flegg (1987)* the House of Lords held that if there are two trustees for sale, the over-reaching provisions apply and the two trustees can defeat an overriding interest.

Thus a bank may protect itself by getting a single trustee to appoint a co-trustee. Then if both sign the mortgage the bank is protected from any third party rights not entered in the register.

Unregistered Land

Overriding interests only apply to registered land. However a spouse in occupation of unregistered land may have an equitable interest in it.

Thus in the case of unregistered land and registered land a bank should

1.   ask the spouse to execute a postponement of her equitable interest or

2.   get both spouses, the one with the equitable interest and the one with the legal interest to join in the mortgage with the bank.

This should be the action to be taken by the bank unless it decides to make use of the judgment in Flegg's case.

The Matrimonial Homes Act 1983: Broadly, this Act deals with the right of one spouse to occupy the matrimonial home against the wish of the other spouse. As far as bankers are concerned the question will often arise in the form of defining the right of a deserted wife to remain in the matrimonial home, where that home is mortgaged to the bank; in other words, has the bank an undisputed right of possession;

The main provisions of the *Matrimonial Homes Act 1983* are:

1.   One spouse is given statutory "rights of occupation" in the dwelling-house of the other spouse, whether the latter spouse is the owner of the dwelling-house or not.

2.   "Rights of occupation" implies two things;

   a.   if the spouse entitled to these rights is already in occupation, a right not to be evicted or excluded from the house by the other spouse except with leave of court;

   b.   if the spouse is not in occupation, a right with the leave of the court to enter into occupation of the house.

3.   The Act does not apply to a house which has at no time been a matrimonial home.

4. A spouse's rights of occupation of the matrimonial home during the marriage are a charge on the other spouse's interest or estate in the house.

5. These rights of occupation do not constitute "overriding interests". In the case of unregistered land, they must be registered as a Class F land charge – a charge affecting any land by virtue of the *Matrimonial Homes Act 1983*, otherwise the charge is void. In the case of registered land, it must be protected by registering a Notice.

6. A spouse entitled to rights of occupation may waive them, by a release in writing. Furthermore, where such a spouse has registered the rights of occupation so that they constitute a charge on the home, he or she may agree in writing that any other charge on that estate or interest shall rank in priority to the charge to which the spouse is entitled.

Note: The practical significance of the above provisions for bankers is that where a banker agrees to take a matrimonial home as security for a loan, he must check the Land Charges Register to see whether any rights of occupation have been registered against it. If any have been registered, the property will not be a good security unless the spouse who registered the charge agrees in writing to allow the banker's mortgage to rank in priority to his or her own charge.

Also, whether or not a spouse's interest has been registered, he or she may still have an overriding interest. This may be discovered by examination of the property.

Summary – Securities, Land

1. It is the type of right of ownership over land which is of importance.

2. Also there may be rights other than rights of ownership over land; such as the right of a mortgagee.

3. Land may be unregistered or registered.

4. Ownership of unregistered land is proved by the title deeds. Other rights over such land are registered in the Land Charges Register.

5. Ownership of registered land is proved by registration of title

and the Land Certificate. Other rights over registered land must be protected.

6. Such rights over registered land are protected primarily by a caution or a notice.

7. Other rights over land such as the equitable right of a person in actual occupation of land is called an overriding interest and cannot be registered.

Chapter Fifteen

Mortgages and Charges over Land

A mortgage is a form of security created by the borrower of the money or the debtor when he transfers or creates a legal or equitable interest in property as security for the debt which he owes to the mortgagee or creditor. This method may be used when taking land, life policies or shares as security. However some variations do occur according to the particular security. For example in the case of life policies or shares these may be assigned into the name of the mortgagee (the bank). In the case of land the mortgagee does not become the owner of the land but acquires rights over the land.

Let us examine firstly a mortgage of land. Instead of a mortgage a bank will usually take a charge over the land. From the borrower's point of view there is really little difference between a mortgage and a charge but legally a mortgage transfers an interest in the property to the mortgagee whereas a charge merely gives the "chargee" or lender of the money certain rights over the property. As far as the lender is concerned he has as good protection with a charge as with a mortgage but it may be that the borrower prefers a charge because it will not appear on the title deeds, and some borrowers do not like it widely known that they have borrowed money. Also

1. it is simpler and so cheaper
2. it can be used for either freehold or leasehold interests and occasionally the chargeor's lease may contain a prohibition on sub-leasing.
3. it can be arranged more quickly.

Deed

At one time a deed was a document to which was affixed a blob of molten wax and on this was impressed the mark of the maker of the deed. This was a seal. At the time he was making his mark the words "I deliver this as my act and deed" were spoken.

In later years the molten wax was dispensed with together with the formality of speaking the words. In fact a red adhesive wafer was affixed to the document.

The present position is now stated in the *Law of Property (Miscellaneous Provisions) Act 1989*.

This now provides that it is unnecessary to seal a deed although the maker's signature must be attested. It must now be made clear that the document is intended to be a deed. As regards deeds executed by companies the new provisions as to sealing and witnessing do not apply.

A point to remember is that when a legal mortgage is made it must always be by deed. Thus if a mortgage is made *not* by deed it cannot be a legal mortgage. An equitable mortgage may be made by deed or not.

Mortgage of Unregistered Land

A mortgage may be either legal or equitable and it may be created with freehold land, leasehold land or an equitable interest in land.

Legal Mortgage

1. A legal mortgage of a freehold estate may be created by a demise for a term of years absolute subject to a provision for cesser on redemption.

    In the case of a leasehold estate it is created by a sub-demise for a term of years absolute subject to a provision for cesser on redemption – the term being one day shorter than the term vested in the grantor or

2. By a charge by deed expressed to be by way of legal mortgage.

    A demise means a long lease e.g. 4,999 years.

Equitable Mortgage

1. An imperfect legal mortgage will take effect as an equitable mortgage.

2. So will a mere deposit of title deed made for the purpose of creating a security. *Note*: that an equitable mortgage with deposit of title deeds cannot be registered.

3. A conveyance of the mortgagor's equitable interest to the mortgagee with a provision for the mortgagee to reconvey it to

him after repayment of the loan will also take effect as an equitable mortgage.

Where the mortgagor has only an equitable interest to offer, he cannot create a legal mortgage. In such a case, he can only give an equitable mortgage.

In practice an equitable mortgage will usually be made by the mortgagor leaving his title deeds or land certificate with the bank together with a Memorandum of Deposit. This document makes clear why the deeds have been left with the bank and the mortgagor will promise to execute a legal mortgage if required to do so.

Mortgage of Registered Land

There are two ways of creating a mortgage of registered land.

1. *By registered charge*
    This is a legal mortgage of registered land and so it must be created by deed but the wording may be in any form.

    Once the chargee is registered as the proprietor of the charge, a charge certificate will be issued to him and the land certificate must be deposited at the Land Registry until the charge is cancelled – usually on the payment of the mortgage debt.

    A registered charge takes effect as a mortgage created by a charge expressed to be by way of legal mortgage.

2. *By deposit of Land Certificate*
    This is the usual method for creating an equitable mortgage of registered land.

    The proprietor of registered land or registered charge may create a lien by deposit of the land certificate or charge certificate with the bank.

    The lien is similar to a mortgage of unregistered land by deposit of title deeds, and takes effect subject to overriding interests and entries on the register.

    The mortgagee, by deposit of the land certificate, or charge certificate should give notice to the Registrar of his interest who will enter on the charges register a notice or a caution.

Priorities

The priority of a mortgage is of importance to banks because of course the lower down the list of interested parties the bank's mortgage is, the less likely is the bank to obtain payment in full.

UNREGISTERED LAND
Deeds deposited.

1. If title deeds are deposited – then no registration is possible.
2. It is immaterial whether the mortgage is legal or equitable.

Deeds not deposited.
Priority is determined by date of registration of mortgage in the Land Charges Register.

REGISTERED LAND
A legal mortgage is registered at the Land Registry and a charge certificate is issued. Date of registration determines priority and not the order in which the mortgages were created.

It makes no difference whether a mortgage is legal or equitable.

An equitable mortgage may be protected by:

Notice in the Charges Register
Provided the mortgagee can produce the Land Certificate.

Caution
This does not require production of the Land Certificate. The effect is that if anyone seeks to deal with the land the Land Registry will notify the mortgagee who lodged the caution. He has 14 days in which to act.

Notice of Deposit
If the mortgagee holds the certificate he may register notice of deposit in the Charges Register. The mortgagee will receive 14 days notice of any attempt to deal with the land.

Second Mortgage

This arises when some land already mortgaged to secure a debt is mortgaged for a second time with a provision that it should cease on redemption. It is possible to have any number of mortgages legal or equitable on the same land so long as the land is of sufficient value to cover all the loans. Normally a second or later mortgage will be legal and a second equitable mortgage is rarely taken by a bank.

A second legal mortgage of freehold land is created in the same way as a first mortgage – by a charge by deed expressed to be by way of legal mortgage or by the demise of a term of years absolute with the second mortgagee's term at least one day longer than that of the first mortgagee.

If the land is leasehold and a charge is not used then there must be a sub-demise (or sub-lease) for a term of years absolute.

As the second legal mortgagee will not be given the title deeds then the second mortgage must be registered as a puisne mortgage Class C (I) or if equitable as a general equitable charge Class C (III).

A second equitable mortgage is hardly ever taken by a bank.

When taking a second mortgage of registered land the mortgagee should protect it by registration; or by lodging a caution.

When a second mortgage is contemplated then the second mortgagee should immediately give formal notice to the first mortgagee asking him to state the amount of his loan and to confirm that he is under no obligation to make further advances. The reason for this is to avoid the possibility of tacking.

Tacking

This enables a mortgagee to modify the rules relating to priority of mortgages in his favour.

Tacking is only possible where:

1. The first mortgagee who wishes to tack does not have any knowledge of an intermediate mortgagee or
2. The first mortgagee was bound in contract to make further advances to the mortgagor or
3. The intermediate mortgagee agrees to the tacking.

Assume the owner of freehold or leasehold property created three mortgages in form of M1, M2 and M3. As the mortgage M1 is the first it will usually be accompanied by the title deeds and need not be registered.

The mortgages M2 and M3 will not therefore be accompanied by the deeds and so must be registered. If they are legal mortgages they must be registered as a Class C (I) (puisne mortgage). If they are equitable they must be registered as Class C (III) (general equitable charge).

The order of priority will be M1, M2 and M3.

Assume that a person borrows these amounts of money from two people, A and B. So A lends money and this is covered by Mortgage 1. B lends money covered by Mortgage 2 and then A is asked for another loan covered by Mortgage 3.

A will naturally prefer to be able to tack his second loan M3 on to M1, and so gain priority for M3 over M2. This will only be possible if A know nothing about this intermediate loan from B and provided A had an agreement to advance further sums. To prevent this tacking, B must notify A of the loan he intends to make. Thus if a bank takes a second mortgage it must inform the first mortgagee. *Dearle and Hall (1828)*.

Consolidation

A right to consolidate is a right of a mortgagee who has lent two sums of money, each secured by separate charges on different pieces of land, not to allow one mortgage to be paid off (redeemed) unless the other is also redeemed.

For example, A has borrowed money from X and has mortgaged Greenacre to cover a loan of £10,000 and later mortgages Blackacre to cover a loan of £12,000. He then finds that the value of Greenacre has increased considerably whereas the value of Blackacre has dropped. He now wishes to redeem the mortgage over Greenacre leaving X with the mortgage over. Blackacre which may not be sufficient to cover the loan. In *Jennings v Jordan (1881)* Lord Selborne stated that the mortgagee "could treat them as one, and decline to be redeemed as to any, unless he is redeemed as to all."

However the rule was considered to be unfair to borrowers (mortgagors) and so it was abolished by the *Conveyancing Act 1881* and confirmed by the *Law of Property Act 1925*. Both Acts permit the statutory rule to be excluded and of course banks usually do this by adding a clause in their mortgage deeds excluding the operation of Section 93 of the *Law of Property Act 1925*. It would not be to a banker's advantage to permit a mortgagor to pick and choose which security he wished to redeem.

Sub-mortgage

This is a mortgage of a mortgage. It can only be understood by remembering that we are dealing as always with rights and a right is a thing of value. So the right of the original mortgagee can be used as security if he now wishes to borrow money himself.

A sub-mortgage is created by the grant of a sub-term out of the mortgagee's own term or by a legal charge.

A sub-mortgage of registered land is made by lodging the sub-charge in duplicate with the charge certificate at the Land Registry. A certificate of sub-charge will then be issued. Another method is to protect the sub-charge by filing a caution.

An equitable sub-mortgage can be taken either by a deposit of the original mortgage, accompanied by a memorandum of deposit or by a general equitable charge.

In the case of registered land, if the charge certificate is deposited the sub-mortgagee can lodge a notice of deposit of the charge certificate or can file a caution.

Mortgage forms

Referring back to the methods of creating a legal or an equitable mortgage we must remember that in the case of a legal mortgage it must be by deed, and in the case of an equitable mortgage it may be made quite informally. An equitable mortgage will exist if the intention of the parties is clear and this will usually be evidenced by a memorandum of deposit; so if the mortgagor deposits his title deeds or land certificate with the bank this will create an equitable mortgage.

If no documents are lodged but an intention is expressed that will be sufficient and of course if the mortgagor only has an equitable interest his mortgage must be equitable.

An equitable mortgage will be used in the case of a short-term loan or where speed is important in arranging it. Sometimes the owner of the land may not want a legal mortgage to appear as a registered charge on the records. An equitable mortgage will be cheaper to take than a legal one and is often taken prior to taking a legal mortgage. In fact, one of the most important clauses in the memorandum of deposit is an undertaking by the mortgagor to execute a legal mortgage if required to do so.

The main disadvantage of an equitable mortgage is that the mortgagee does not have a statutory legal right to sell the land. However this is taken care of in the memorandum of deposit when the mortgagor promises to execute a legal mortgage if required to do so. Furthermore if the equitable mortgage is by deed then the mortgagee will obtain a power of sale. This is done by inserting a clause by which the mortgagor gives power of attorney to a bank official or there may be a clause by which the mortgagor acknowledges that he holds the property upon trust for the bank. Also he gives power to the bank to remove him from the trust and to appoint some other person as trustee. Either clause allows the bank to sell the legal estate or to appoint a receiver, similar to the powers of a mortgagee in a legal mortgage.

Legal mortgage
These are a few of the more important clauses to be found in a bank's mortgage form.

1.   Continuing Security

The Mortgagor as beneficial owner charges by way of legal mortgage all and every interest in or over the property referred to in the Schedule hereto which the Mortgagor has power at law or in equity so to charge (the Mortgaged Property) and/or the proceeds of sale thereof as a continuing security to the Bank for the discharge on demand of:

1.   all present and/or future indebtedness of the Mortgagor to the Bank on any current and/or other account with interest and bank charges and
2.   all other liabilities whatsoever of the Mortgagor to the Bank present future actual and/or contingent and
3.   all costs charges and expenses howsoever incurred by the Bank in relation to this Mortgage and such indebtedness and/or liabilities on a full indemnity basis

and for payment of interest on the foregoing day by day from demand until full discharge such interest to be chargeable at the rate of interest payable or deemed to be payable by the Mortgagor (whether before or after judgement) as calculated and compounded in accordance with the practice of the Bank from time to time.

The document will usually be phrased in such a way as to ensure that the security will cover any debt outstanding, as banks frequently lend money by way of a fluctuating overdraft.

2. Insurance

The Mortgagor will keep the Mortgaged Property in a good state of repair and condition and will keep it insured against such risks and in such office and for such amounts as the Bank may from time to time approve. If the Mortgagor fails to maintain or insure the Mortgaged Property the Bank may do so at the expense of the Mortgagor without thereby becoming a mortgagee in possession.

The bank wishes to be certain that the property is to be insured and the liability to do that belongs to the mortgagor.

3. Power of sale

Section 103 of the Law of Property Act 1925 shall not apply to this Mortgage and the statutory power of sale and other powers shall be exercisable at any time after demand.

The two points to note here are

1. when the power to sell the property arises and
2. when the power to sell becomes exercisable.

As regards 1. the power to sell will arise as soon as the legal date for payment has passed S.101 *Law of Property Act 1925* and the mortgage debt has not been paid. However, it may not be exercised S.103 *Law of Property Act 1925* until:

1. notice requiring payment of the mortgage money has been served on the mortgagor and he has failed to pay it after the expiration of three months from the service of the notice; or
2. some interest (i.e. not necessarily all) is in arrears and unpaid for two months after becoming due; or
3. the mortgagor has broken some provision in the mortgage deed other than the covenant for repayment of the mortgage money or interest on it.

This is the general law on the topic but bankers seem to take the view that 3 months is too long a period to wait before exercising the power to sell and so S.103 is excluded and the sale will take effect whenever the banker wishes.

When selling, the mortgagee must have due regard for the mortgagor's interests, but he is not liable, merely because the price he has realised is less than the market value of the property. He must act honestly and fairly *Tse Kwong Lam v Wong Chit Sen (1983)* and *Cuckmere Brick Co Ltd v Mutual Finance Ltd (1971)*.

If the mortgagee realises more than his debt, he must hand over the balance to any subsequent mortgagee who has given him notice; otherwise to the mortgagor.

4. Power to appoint a Receiver

At any time after the power of sale has become exercisable the Bank or any Receiver appointed hereunder may enter and manage the Mortgaged Property or any part thereof and provide such services and carry out such repairs and works of improvement reconstruction addition or completion (including the provision of plant equipment and furnishings) as deemed expedient. All expenditure so incurred shall be immediately repayable by the Mortgagor with interest at the rate aforesaid and shall be a liability charged on the Mortgaged Property. Neither the Bank nor any Receiver shall be liable to the Mortgagor as mortgagee in possession or otherwise for any loss howsoever occurring in the exercise of such powers.

Banks often take power to appoint a receiver and rules similar to those relating to the sale of the property will apply.

If there is no such power, then the power to appoint a receiver will be implied in all mortgages created by deed unless the mortgage deed shows a contrary intention.

The power arises and becomes exercisable if the same events occur as with the power of sale.

The receiver has power to recover the rents and profits by action and to give effectual receipts.

Apart from the payment of taxes, rates and other outgoings on the property and his commission, the receiver must apply the balance in discharge of the mortgage interest and also in the reduction of the mortgage debt.

5. Consolidation

> Section 93 of the Law of Property Act 1925 shall not apply to this deed.

The right of the mortgagee to consolidate as explained earlier will usually be retained by the bank's inserting a clause to this effect, therefore Section 93 of the *Law of Property Act 1925* shall be excluded.

6. Restrictions on leasing

> The Statutory powers of leasing or of accepting surrenders of leases conferred on mortgagors shall not be exercised by the Mortgagor nor shall the Mortgagor part with possession of the Mortgaged Property or any part thereof nor confer upon any person firm company or body whatsoever any licence right or interest to occupy the Mortgaged Property or any part thereof without the consent in writing of the Bank but the bank may grant or accept surrenders of leases without restriction.

The Law of Property Act 1925 S.99 provides that a mortgagor in possession may grant agricultural or occupation leases for any term not exceeding fifty years and building leases for any term not exceeding nine hundred and ninety-nine years.

Once again the bank will deprive the mortgagor of this power.

Remedies of Legal Mortgagee
It will be seen from the foregoing that a mortgagee has a number of remedies against the mortgagor. These are

1. Right to sell the property
2. Right to appoint a receiver
3. Right to apply for an order of foreclosure
4. Right to take possession
5. Right to sue the mortgagor on his personal covenant to repay.

Equitable mortgage
This form is rather simpler than the legal mortgage form and is called a memorandum of deposit. Clauses similar to those in a legal mortgage appear in the equitable mortgage form such as

1.   continuing security
2.   exclusion of S.103 *Law of Property Act 1925* (exercise of power of sale)
3.   exclusion of power of leasing.

The most important clauses in the equitable mortgage form are:

1.   Undertaking by mortgagor to execute a legal mortgage if required to do so.
2.   The appointment of a bank official as an attorney of the mortgagor. The purpose of this being to enable the bank to sell the security.

The importance of these two clauses is that an equitable mortgagee has no power of sale and so he must get the permission of the court, unless he has managed to get the mortgagor to execute a legal mortgage or failing that he has arranged for the mortgagor to appoint a bank official as his attorney or trustee.

For this to happen the memorandum of deposit must be under seal.

If the equitable mortgage form is by deed then the powers of the equitable mortgagee are the same as the powers of a legal mortgagee.

In addition the mortgagee has the right to request the equitable mortgagor to execute a legal mortgage.

Discharge of Mortgage

Legal mortgage
In the case of unregistered land a vacating receipt may be signed. This is usually indorsed on the mortgage deed and is signed by the mortgagee and names the person who pays the money. This operates as a surrender of the mortgage term to or a reconveyance to the mortgagor and discharges the mortgage.

Section 115 of the *Law of Property Act 1925* further provides that a mortgagor may require a reconveyance, surrender, release or transfer to be executed in place of the receipt.

In the case of registered land, Form 53 must be completed by the mortgagee and this must be sent to the Land Registry.

In all cases where the mortgage or charge has been protected by registration then this registration must be cancelled.

Equitable mortgage

This is discharged by way of receipt or cancellation of the memorandum of deposit and the return of the title deeds. If the charge has been registered then the Land Registry must be notified and in the case of registered land a notice or caution should be cancelled.

Summary – Mortgages and charges

1. A mortgage is the procedure by which the owner (mortgagor) of land or other property gives rights to the lender of money (mortgagee).
2. The most important of these rights is the right to sell the property.
3. A legal mortgage can only be created by deed.
4. If the intention is clear e.g. by depositing the title deeds or land certificate, then it may be an equitable mortgage.
5. Tacking arises when the original lender is allowed to tack on the security covering a later loan even though there has been an intermediate lender. Banks taking a second mortgage must avoid this situation by giving notice to the first mortgagee.
6. Nowadays banks take a charge instead of a mortgage. There is basically no difference except in the form that the document creating the charge takes.

Chapter Sixteen

Securities – Life Policies

It really does not matter whether the word "insurance" or "assurance" is used; although "assurance" is usually linked with life because the death of a person is the only certain thing in an uncertain world. So although it is of little importance whether the word "insurance" or "assurance" is used it is of importance to understand something about the contract of insurance.

Like any contract it is an agreement whereby the parties make promises to each other. In this particular contract, one party approaches the insurance company and pays, or promises to pay a sum of money called a premium and in return the insurer promises to pay out a sum of money if a certain thing occurs in the future. In the case of life assurance the thing referred to is the death of the life insured.

On the face of it, it appears that a contract of insurance is like a wager – which is also a contract in which one party agrees to pay a sum of money to the other party dependent upon the happening of some uncertain future event. A contract of insurance is enforceable whereas a wager is not. *Gaming Acts 1835–1968.*

Insurable Interest

The difference between a wager and a contract of insurance lies in the fact that in the latter there must be "an insurable interest". *Life Assurance Act 1774.*

An insurable interest has not been defined by Parliament but in *Halford v Kymer (1830)* it was stated that a person who will suffer pecuniary loss as a consequence of the happening of the risk insured against, as opposed to a chance of winning money as in the case of a wager, can be said to have an insurable interest.

It is up to the courts to decide whether an insurable interest exists as they have so decided in the following cases:

1. a creditor may insure the life of his debtor. *Anderson v Edie (1795)*. Thus according to Paget a bank may insure the life of its debtor but in practice never does so, preferring to take as security, a policy on the life of another person.

2. A guarantor may insure the life of the principal debtor.

3. An employer may insure the life of his employee. *Hebdon v West (1863)*. In this connection an employer will frequently insure his employees' lives and agree that any benefits be paid to their next of kin.

4. A litigant may insure the life of his judge. This has been done in a long and complicated will case and it was apparent that if the judge were to die a retrial would necessitate heavy additional expense.

5. A husband or wife can insure the life of the other spouse.

6. A father does not have an insurable interest in the life of his child unless he can show some pecuniary interest e.g. the daughter is looking after him. He can of course take out a policy on his child for his child's benefit.

7. An assignee such as a bank does not need to have an insurable interest – *Ashley v Ashley (1829)*.

Special features of life assurance

1. *Surrender value*

Usually a policy of life assurance will be used as security because in a policy of this sort a residual fund of money, will have been built up over the years the policy has been in force and so long as the premiums continue to be paid the residual value will increase. The particular value referred to is known as the surrender value of the policy. It is that amount which must be ascertained when a bank is considering taking a policy as security. A policy has a capital value which is the amount which the policy will be worth at maturity. However before that date every policy will have a value (a surrender value) which will be paid by the insurance company if the assured gave up the policy and stopped further payments of the premium.

The surrender value depends on the age of the assured and the duration of the policy. It is greater on policies of long duration and on lives where the age is considerably advanced, than on those of short duration and on young lives. It has no direction connection with the number of premiums paid although it will increase with the payment of each premium.

Usually policies less than three years old do not have a surrender value.

2.   *Uberrimae Fidei* (of the utmost good faith)

A contract of life assurance comes within the group of contracts that require that absolute disclosure must be made of all relevant facts that might influence the other party in his decision whether or not to enter the contract.

In *London Assurance v Mansel 1879* the defendant wished to insure his life with the plaintiffs. The proposal form asked Mansel to state whether he had been insured at any other offices and whether he had been declined. He replied that he was "Insured now at two offices for £16,000 at ordinary rates. Policies effected last year".

The proposal was accepted but when London Assurance discovered that his life had been declined by a number of offices, the court held that they were entitled to have the contract set aside.

3.   *Suicide*

Life policies usually nowadays provide for the payment of the sums assured not only on natural or accidental death but also on death by suicide while sane or insane, if the suicide does not take place before a given period from the date of taking out the policy, has expired.

As a matter of strict law, the House of Lords held in *Beresford v Royal Insurance Co Ltd (1938)* that where the assured had committed suicide while sane, with a view to benefitting his estate, it was contrary to public policy to compel the insurance company to pay the sum assured to the deceased assured's estate.

Since the passing of the *Suicide Act 1961*, suicide is no longer a crime. Therefore, where the assured commits suicide in order to enrich his estate by the policy money there does not appear to be any reason why the policy moneys should be withheld. However, payment in such circumstances would probably still be considered "contrary to public policy". Therefore insurance companies usually include a suicide clause in their policies providing for payment provided the death does not take place within a certain period of the date of taking out the policy.

4. *Age*

A peculiarity of life assurance used to be that the company would issue the policy without proof of age. It will not of course pay out benefits without the age being "admitted" or proved in some way. It is a point that should be borne in mind when taking a policy as security. If the age has been mistated through an innocent mistake then the premium can be adjusted. However if the age was purposely mistated in order to gain some benefit, e.g. to avoid a medical examination then the insurance company may decide not to pay out benefits.

5. *Assignment of Policies*

By Section 1 of the *Policies of Assurance Act 1867* a policy may be assigned, usually a deed is used.

The assignee will take subject to the interests of any other party and notice must be given to the insurance company of the assignment. *Section 136 of the Law of Property Act 1925* also provides that debts and the legal choses in action may be assigned, again provided

1. the assignment is in writing
2. the assignment is absolute and not by way of charge only and
3. notice must be given to the debtor, trustee or other person who holds the funds assigned.

The policy must usually be assigned by the beneficiary and not by the life assured where they are different persons. This then may cause problems if the policy is a "settlement policy" or a "trust policy" under *Section 11 of the Married Womens Property Act, 1882*. Such a policy is taken out by the husband on his own life for the benefit of his wife and/or children. Thus a trust is created in favour of the beneficiaries. Because a man may marry more than one wife, although not at the same time, and may have children from a number of wives then the beneficiaries must be explicitly stated. "For the benefit of my wife and children" would not be very clear. This would only be so if the wife and children were named e.g.; "For my wife A and my children X, Y and Z".

From the point of view of taking an assignment it is necessary for all the beneficiaries to be designated and in the case of children that they are of full age, otherwise an assignment would not be possible.

Also the question of undue influence should be considered and independant legal advice should be available in order to avoid such a suggestion.

Types of Policies

Endowment Policies
The most common policy nowadays is the endowment policy which is taken out for a certain period of time and provides for the payment of a capital sum at maturity or on the death of the assured whichever occurs first.

These policies form the basis of private occcupational pension schemes. The capital sum payable at maturity, which is the retirement age of the assured, can be commuted to a pension in whole or in part.

In addition to endowment policies there is a *whole life policy* that provides for the payment of a capital sum upon the death of the assured. Premiums are cheaper than on endowment policies but the benefits are of course much more restricted.

Family protection policies These provide for the payment of a capital sum on a sliding scale e.g. £10,000 if the assured dies during the first five years of the policy, dropping to £2,000 at maturity date. As its name implies these policies are suitable for parents with young children as some protection is given to them during their earlier years.

Industrial policies are usually for very small amounts and are not usually acceptable as a security for that reason.

Settlement policies These were mentioned when discussing assignment by beneficiaries and it is necessary to get all the beneficiaries to join in the assignment. This cannot happen if the beneficiaries are not named or if children, they are minors.

Taking the Security

As always there may be a legal or an equitable mortgage. In the case of the legal mortgage, as with shares, the life policy is assigned to the bank.

Legal Mortgage

To create a legal mortgage, the policy must be assigned in writing normally by deed thereby transferring the assured's right to recover the policy moneys to the mortgagee; subject to cesser on redemption.

To complete the mortgagee's title the *Policies of Assurance Act 1867* requires that notice must be given to the insurance company of the assignment.

The notice must state the date and purpose of the assignment and it must be addressed to the company's principal place of business. The Act makes it obligatory for insurance companies to acknowledge receipt of the notice when requested to do so by the mortgagee.

Under the Act, the legal mortgagee may sue for the policy moneys in his own name provided the following conditions are satisfied;

1.   that at the time of the action, he has the equitable right to receive the sum assured; and
2.   that he has an assignment either by indorsement on the policy or by a separate instrument.

All parties having an interest in the policy must sign the deed of assignment.

Equitable Mortgage

A mere deposit of the insurance policy with a bank with intention to give a security will constitute an equitable mortgage and will give the bank the rights of an equitable mortgagee. Usually, the deposit will be accompanied by a written memorandum explaining the purpose of the deposit.

In the case of equitable mortgages, when the policy moneys moneys become payable, the insurance company will require a discharge from the assured as well as the mortgagee.

Notice, though not required by law, must for obvious reasons be given to the insurance company. If an equitable mortgagee fails to give notice, he may lose his priority to a subsequent mortgagee who does give notice.

The important clause of the Memorandum of Deposit is that by which:

"The Mortgagor hereby irrevocably appoints the Bank to be the Attorney of the Mortgagor (with full power of substitution and delegation) in the Mortgagor's name and on the

Mortgagor's behalf and as the Mortgagor's act and deed to sign or execute all deeds instruments and documents which may be required by the Bank pursuant to this deed or the exercise of any of its powers.

The effect of this clause is to allow the Bank to convey the legal estate in the security to a purchaser.

Enforcing the Security

Legal Mortgage
If the policy moneys have become payable because the life assured has died or the policy has matured then the bank merely has to claim the money and furnish proof of death.

Surrender of the policy: if the policy moneys have not become payable then if the bank encashes the policy, only the surrender value will be payable. This will be very much less than the capital value and so to the disadvantage of the assured. However it may be the only choice available to the bank.

Sale of the policy: an alternative to surrender of the policy is to sell it to a company which specialises in that type of investment, or to a relative of the mortgagor.

Loan: Finally it may be possible for the bank to obtain a loan from the insurance company using the policy as security. If the amount of the loan is sufficient to repay the bank overdraft then this method would be preferable to surrendering the policy.

Equitable Mortgage
In the case of an equitable mortgage the personal representatives of the deceased must join with the bank in claiming the money from the insurance company.

If the mortgagor has not died then his co-operation would be required, obtained if necessary, by a court order.

However if the equitable assignment has been executed under seal then a power of attorney clause will have been incorporated in the deed and this will give the bank a power of sale.

Release of the Policy
Once the loan has been repaid the mortgagor is entitled to the return of his policy. In the case of a legal mortgage the bank will usually

indorse a release under seal. Sometimes it may be a reassignment, although this is no longer necessary. The insurance company should be notified of the release.

In the case of an equitable mortgage there is no need for any reassignment or for an indorsed receipt. It is quite sufficient to write "cancelled" across the memorandum of deposit and to return it with the policy to the mortgagor. Again the insurance company should be notified of the release.

Summary – Securities – Life policies
1. An insurable interest determines whether or not the contract is a wager or a contract of insurance. A person who will suffer percuniary loss if the things insured against occurs can be said to have an insurable interest. A wager is of course not legally enforceable.
2. In taking a life policy as security the important thing is to consider its surrender value. This is the value of the policy at the time the loan is made.
3. The Policies of Assurance Act 1867 permits the assignment of policies provided it is in writing and the insurance company has been notified.
4. If the assignment is made formally by deed it will be a legal mortgage, otherwise it will be an equitable mortgage.

Chapter Seventeen

Securities – Stocks and Shares

The word "security" may be used to refer to stocks and shares, unit trusts, local authority loan stock, investments in building societies and Government stocks.

So we must now consider how these securities may be used as security for a loan.

The securities referred to above consist of rights to sums of money which are evidenced by documents called share certificates, debentures, bonds etc.

These documents are choses in action as are bills of exchange and cheques but the latter are of course negotiable. When a banker is presented with one or other of the above mentioned securities which the borrower proposes to use as security for his loan, the banker must consider how to take the security.

In the case of land being used as a security the borrower either leases his land or gives the banker a charge over it if it is unregistered; or creates a registered charge or an equitable charge over it if it is registered land.

In the case of securities the borrower must either transfer the security into the name of the banker (or his nominee) or grant him a charge over the security.

Transfer of securities
We must now consider the method of transferring ownership of the security, which is to be used as security.

Bearer securities present no problem because ownership in these may be transferred by mere delivery of the document of title.

Foreign government stocks are often in bearer form also the stocks of USA companies are usually in that form. The certificate has a combined transfer form and power of attorney on its reverse side and this must be signed by the registered holder when he wishes to transfer it.

In this country bearer securities are comparatively rare.

Unit Trusts. These provide the investor with the means of investing his money in a wide portfolio and this is done on his behalf by the managers of the trust.

To transfer unit trusts a deed or any form of transfer approved by the trustees must be used. If a holder wishes to realise them then he will normally sell them back to the managers by completing a form of renunciation on the back of his certificate.

Building Society Shares

These are not freely transferable and must be realised by withdrawing the money.

Inscribed stocks

These are not very common and only certain Commonwealth Governments issue them. The buyer of such stock has his name entered in the inscription books of the registering authority and he is issued with a stock receipt or certificate of inscription. The stock may only be transferred if the holder or his authorised agent attends at the office of the registration authority.

Registered stocks and shares

Most stocks are in this form and the names of the holders together with a note of the amount they hold are entered in the register of the issuing authority.

The registers of British Government stocks are kept by the Bank of England but there are National Savings Stock registers for some of these stocks.

Details of shareholders' holdings of shares issued by companies are entered in each company's register of shareholders. Transfer of these shares is by a transfer form which was introduced by the *Stock Transfer Act 1963*.

The transferor must fill in a share transfer form stating both his own name and that of his transferee and other relevant details, such as the number of shares to be transferred.

When all the necessary details have been entered the share transfer form together with the share certificate in the name of the transferor are sent to the company. The company will then delete the transferor's name from the register of members and substitute for it the name of the transferee.

Finally, the company will cancel the transferor's share certificate and issue a new certificate in the transferee's name.

In recent years changes have occurred in Stock Exchange dealings. In 1986 the Stock Exchange was subjected to a radical re-organisation. Alongside these fundamental changes a change in the method of transferring ownership of shares also has been gradually taking place. These new computerised methods go under names such as TAURUS, TALISMAN or SEPON. Nevertheless irrespective of the method of transfer the important point is who has the legal ownership of the shares?

The advantages of taking stocks and shares as security

1.   The value of the security can easily be ascertained by consulting the financial columns of certain newspapers and in particular the *Financial Times* and the *Stock Exchange Daily Official List*.
2.   Certain stocks such as gilt-edged securities have a greater stability of value than others.
3.   Minimum formalities to be observed when taking the security – in the case of bearer securities these are virtually non-existent.
4.   There is a ready market on the Stock Exchange to enable these securities to be marketed.

Disadvantages

1.   The value of stocks and shares can fluctuate rapidly and as in October 1987 their value can dramatically be decreased.
2.   There is the possibility of theft of the share certificates.
3.   In the case of partly-paid shares there is a danger that a customer may not be able to pay a call that is made.

     Furthermore if the banker took a legal mortgage of the partly-paid shares then he would be liable to pay the call. However partly-paid shares are not very common nowadays.
4.   The price of quoted shares can be easily ascertained but shares which are not quoted have to be valued by an accountant by reference to the value of the assets of the company.

Mortgage of stocks and shares

Like mortgages of land, mortgages of shares may be either legal or equitable.

LEGAL MORTGAGE OF SHARES: The borrower must transfer his shares into the name of the lender bank or its nominee. The procedure is identical with that for the transfer of the shares.

However, in order to establish that the transfer is only to constitute a mortgage, it will be accompanied by a memorandum of deposit which will explain the purpose of the transfer. *[memorandum of deposit]*

The advantage of taking a legal mortgage of shares is that the bank acquires a legal title in the shares and because the shares are in its name the bank is able to sell them whenever the occasion arises without having to seek the co-operation of third parties. *[obtain title]*

Disadvantages are:

1. As mentioned if the shares are partly paid, the bank may find itself having to pay a call made by the company. Also if the company is wound up within 12 months of the bank having transferred the partly paid shares then the bank may still be liable to contribute unless the person to whom the shares were transferred is in a position to do so. *[contribution by bank]*

2. The customer may wish to mortgage the shares in a company of which he is a director and which he holds because the Articles require directors to hold a certain number of shares called qualification shares. If therefore he were to use these shares as security and to give a legal mortgage to the bank then he would cease to be legal owner of them and would have to forfeit his position as director. In that case it would only be possible to take an equitable mortgage.

3. Occasionally the articles of the company whose shares they are may prohibit a transfer into the name of another company e.g. the bank's nominee.

4. If a signature on a transfer form is forged and the bank as transferee sends this to the company so that it may be registered as the new legal owner of the shares then the bank will be liable to the company for impliedly stating that the transfer was genuine. *Sheffield Corporation v Barclay (1905)*.

EQUITABLE MORTGAGE OF STOCKS AND SHARES

Such a mortgage may be created quite informally for anything showing an intention to charge the shares to secure a debt will be sufficient.

In practice, an equitable mortgage of shares is created by the deposit of the share certificate with the mortgagee accompanied by a memorandum of deposit signed by the mortgagor. This will protect the bank should the borrower attempt to get his share certificate back at a time when he has not repaid the loan by alleging that he gave the share certificate to the bank for safe custody and not by way of security.

The advantage of taking an equitable mortgage of shares is basically its simplicity. Little formality is involved and so the costs are less then in the case of a legal mortgage. Particularly where the customer may wish to keep changing his portfolio it is convenient for the bank that the shares remain in the name of the mortgagor.

However precisely because the shares do remain in the name of the equitable mortgagor then a number of difficulties and dis-advantages stem.

Disadvantages of an equitable mortgage

1.   The main danger for a bank is that the mortgagor might have created an earlier equitable interest in the shares and so the bank's interest would be subordinated to that. "Where equities are equal, the first in time shall prevail".

     In *Coleman v London County and Westminster Bank Ltd (1916)* Annie Coleman held some debentures as a trustee and then gave an equitable mortgage to the bank as security for a loan.

     When the bank learned of the equitable interest of the beneficiary of the trust it requested Annie Coleman to execute a legal mortgage. However the court held that the bank could not improve its position by taking a legal mortgage as it already knew of the equitable interest that existed.

2.   An important drawback to taking an equitable mortgage of any security is the fact that the mortgagee cannot sell it without the assistance of a third party. Usually of course the memorandum of deposit will state that the mortgagor promises to execute a legal mortgage if called upon to do so. A way round this difficulty, in the case of shares, is for the mortgagee to get the mortgagor to sign a transfer form but leaving it undated. This is called a "blank" transfer.

3.   Stemming from the fact that in an equitable mortgage the

shares remain in the name of the mortgagor another difficulty arises, namely that, dividends, bonus and rights issues and general correspondence will be sent directly to the mortgagor.

In the case of a bonus or a rights issue this means that additional shares are issued by the company to existing, registered shareholders either with (rights) or without (bonus) payment. In both cases the additional shares issued will mean that the value of the security taken by the bank will be reduced. If there is a one for three issue and the bank holds 3,000 shares worth £3,000 then after the issue 1,000 shares will go to the mortgagor and because of the additional shares in issue the value of the bank's holding will be reduced to £2,250.

This situation can be avoided by the bank's getting the mortgagor to agree that any bonus or rights issue will form part of the security charged in favour of the bank.

4. The company may have a lien over the shares owned by a shareholder who owes a debt to the company. This is a danger as far as a bank is concerned which takes an equitable mortgage. It may be avoided by the bank informing the company that it has taken a charge over the shares. Such action by the bank may be ignored by the company within the provisions of S.360 of the *Companies Act 1985* stating that a company cannot enter on its register notice of any trust. However, the receipt of such information by the company will prevent it from exercising its lien in priority to the banks. *Bradford Banking Company Ltd v Henry Brigg, Son and Company Ltd (1886)*.

In the case of companies whose shares are quoted on the Stock Exchange their articles may not contain any provisions as to a lien being exercisable so this point will in practice, only arise in the case of shares in unquoted companies.

5. A point to be borne in mind when taking an equitable mortgage of shares is that a dishonest mortgagor may represent to a company that he has lost his share certificate and would like a replacement. If an indemnity were given the company would issue a duplicate certificate and the mortgagor would thus be able to sell his shares to the obvious detriment of the bank. To protect itself from this eventually the bank may serve a "stop notice" on the company. The effect of this is that if the shareholder wishes to register a transfer of his shares the

company will notify the bank which will be given 14 days in which to take some action such as obtaining an injunction.

Enforcing the Security

If the bank needs to sell the shares there is of course no difficulty in the case of a legal mortgage nor in the case of an equitable mortgage when a blank transfer has been taken. If that is not the case then the assistance of a third party is required such as the customer or possibly the court.

Discharge of the Security

When the loan is repaid then the mortgage must be vacated.

In the case of a legal mortgage the shares are re-transferred to the mortgagor and the memorandum of deposit is destroyed or returned to him.

Where there is an equitable mortgage the share certificate is returned together with the memorandum of deposit.

If a stop notice has been served on the company this must be withdrawn and any blank transfer will be destroyed.

Summary – Securities – stocks and shares
1.   Security may take a number of forms – the most common being shares in a registered company.
2.   Such shares may be transferred either by a share transfer form or by one of the modern computerised methods.
3.   No matter what the method of transfer may be, if there is an agreement between the transferor and the transferee that the transfer is to support a loan then it will be legal mortgage.
4.   If there is no actual transfer into the name of the mortgagee then the mortgage will be equitable.
5.   An equitable mortgage will usually be accompanied by a blank transfer so as to facilitate the legal transfer of the shares should that later become necessary.

Chapter Eighteen

Securities – Guarantees

Guarantees must be distinguished from indemnities and from letters of comfort.

A guarantee is a promise to be answerable for the debt, default or miscarriage of another person.

An indemnity is a promise to be primarily liable.

This subtle distinction can be better illustrated by referring to *Birkmyr v Darnell (1704)*.

If two come into a shop and one buys, and the other says to the seller "Let him have the goods, if he does not pay you, I will", this is a guarantee. But if he says "Let him have the goods, I will be your paymaster" or "I will see you paid" this is an indemnity.

In a guarantee the guarantor is in fact saying "Try and get your money from him – if you don't succeed I will pay you." The guarantor has secondary liability.

In an indemnity the person say the indemnity is saying "Don't worry, whatever happens I will see you get paid." He is assuming primary liability.

Now this may seem to be an unimportant distinction but its importance is that in a contract of guarantees the guarantor will not be liable if for some reason the primary debtor is not liable. Therefore a bank will always insert into the contract of guarantee an indemnity clause. The effect of this is to make the guarantor liable in any event.

A letter of comfort appears to be in the nature of a guarantee or an indemnity but is merely a statement of intent or an agreement of honour. Consequently it is not legally enforceable.

The wording of the letter of comfort is very important. In *Kleinwort Benson Ltd v Malaysian Mining Corporation Berhad (1989)* the Court of Appeal held that a letter of comfort given by the defendant to the plaintiffs was a statement about the defendants' policy regarding their intention at the time they wrote the letter and was not intended to be a promise as to their future conduct. Accordingly it was not contractually binding and the only obligation on the defendants was a moral one.

Instead of relying on some security provided by the debtor, in the case of a guarantee the creditor (the bank) will be relying on the contract with the guarantor. It is therefore of the utmost importance that the bank should be able to enforce that contract if the need should arise.

The main factors that may render the contract invalid are misrepresentation, undue influence and mistake. If the guarantor can prove that any of these factors was present when he entered the guarantee agreement then he may be able to have the contract set aside and so the bank will lose its security.

Misrepresentation

May be the cause of mistake in the other party's mind. The misrepresentation need not have been intentional or with intent to deceive and it is unthinkable that a bank would ever deceive with intent. In *Mackenzie v Royal Bank of Canada (1934)* the bank inadvertently advised Mrs M that unless she executed a guarantee as security for an account in which her husband had an interest, certain securities would need to be realised. The court held that the guarantee was unenforceable because of the misrepresentation.

Mistake

The leading case on this topic is *Saunders v Anglia Building Society (1970)* where an old lady believed she was signing a deed assigning her interest in property to her nephew and in fact she assigned the property to another person. The House of Lords held that a person could escape liability on a contract he had signed if he believed it to be different in nature from the one he thought he was signing provided he had not been negligent. A person who has made a mistake as to the contents of the document which he has signed can never escape liability. *Howatson v Webb (1907)*. It will be normal practice therefore for a bank to require the proposed guarantor to sign the guarantee at the bank. The customer or debtor should never be asked to get the guarantor to sign because there might be a risk of his misrepresenting the nature of the document.

Undue Influence

May arise where the parties are unequal in bargaining power. *National Westminster Bank plc v Morgan (1985)* has decided that undue influence cannot be proved to exist unless the transaction in question is one which is "manifestly disadvantageous" to the weaker party. In that case National Westminster Bank had agreed to lend Mr and Mrs Morgan £14,500 to pay off their loan from the Abbey National Building Society who had threatened to take possession of their home. The bank manager called on Mrs Morgan's home to obtain her signature to the mortgage form, (her husband had already signed). Mrs Morgan was concerned at the possibility of her husband using the loan for business purposes. Nevertheless she signed the form and later, after her husband had died, and the bank sought to enforce its charge over their home she claimed that undue influence had been brought to bear upon her.

The House of Lords held that the transaction had not been unfair to Mrs Morgan and ordered that possession of the house should be given within 28 days.

Thus undue influence will only exist if the parties are unequal in bargaining power and it can be shown that the stronger party is getting some advantage over the weaker.

Where the bank is a party to the transaction there may be a suggestion that undue influence was exerted by the bank. In *Lloyds Bank Ltd v Bundy (1975)* an old farmer was called upon to give a guarantee and other security to cover a loan to his son. The Court of Appeal held that the old man had placed his confidence in the bank and this had been misplaced. However it is generally accepted that his case was decided on its own unusual circumstances and that undue influence will usually be quite difficult to prove.

In addition to being directly affected by a charge of undue influence the bank may be indirectly involved.

In *Bank of Montreal v Stuart (1911)* a representative of the bank obtained the signature of Mrs Stuart on a guarantee form. When the bank attempted to enforce the guarantee Mrs Stuart claimed she had been the victim of undue influence exerted by her husband and this was known to the bank's representative. The bank was therefore unable to enforce the guarantee.

The contract of guarantee

The extent to which a bank should explain the meaning of documents to a party was considered in *Cornish v Midland Bank plc (1985)*. In this case it was stated that *O'Hara v Allied Irish Banks (1985)* was correct in deciding that a bank has no duty to explain the terms of a document to a guarantor who is not a customer of the bank. However as regards customers of the bank, normal banking practice and professional standards would require that silence by the bank would be a breach of its duty. However it would not be feasible for a bank to explain all the legal intricacies of a form of guarantee. The bank should at least explain the main terms.

In arranging a contract of guarantee the guarantor may ask questions concerning the debtor's account. In *Hamilton v Watson (1845)* it was held that a bank had no duty to inform a substitute guarantor that it had asked the debtor for payment of the debt or for some fresh security and had received neither.

The bank may not disclose details of the debtor's account if asked for information by the guarantor. In practice this difficulty is circumvented by calling a tripartite meeting of bank, debtor and guarantor. It is usually stated that a contract of guarantee is not a contract uberrimae fidei i.e. of the utmost good faith.

This means that the principal creditor or the principal debtor need not disclose material information to the guarantor before he agrees to be guarantor. For example, in *Cooper v National Provincial Bank (1945)*, the principal creditor (the bank) failed to disclose the following to the guarantor before he signed the guarantee:

1. That the customer's husband was an undischarged bankrupt.
2. That the husband had authority to draw on the customer's account which the guarantor was guaranteeing.

In an action by the bank against the guarantor, he sought to escape liability by arguing that the bank should have informed him of the above facts. The courts held that the bank was under no duty to volunteer information about the customer's account to the guarantor and the non-disclosure by the bank did not avail him.

Further, in *National Provincial Bank v Glanusk (1913)* the customer was in the habit of overdrawing his account and the bank did not volunteer this information to the guarantor. The guarantor was held liable on his guarantee.

However, if the guarantor questions the banker with reference to such matters as might help him to decide whether to accept his liability as guarantor, he must give a lucid reply not capable of being misinterpreted.

Joint and Several Guarantees

There may be more than one guarantor and in this case they will be asked to agree to be jointly and severally liable. If they do so agree then each guarantor will be personally liable for the full amount of the sum covered by the guarantee e.g. if the guarantee is for £1,000 and X and Y have agreed to joint and several liability then the bank can sue each for £1,000 and recover from either or it can sue them separately and successively. The joint and several liability clause permits the bank to sue the guarantors jointly or separately and if one has died then his estate will continue to be liable.

A point to be borne in mind when taking a guarantee from multi-guarantors – all must sign before the guarantee is effective. In *National Provincial Bank of England v Brackenbury (1906)* four parties had agreed to joint and several liability for a loan, three signed and the bank advanced the money but the fourth party died before signing. The court held that the three who had signed were released from their liability. In *James Graham and Co (Timber) Ltd v Southgate – Sands and Others (1985)* the Court of Appeal held that when one guarantor's signature has been forged his fellow guarantor is released from liability.

Capacity of Guarantor

The famous case – *Coutts and Co v Browne-Lecky (1947)*, decided that because a loan to a minor was "absolutely void" (*Infants Relief Act 1874*), the guarantor of his loan could not be made liable in an action on the guarantee.

It was because of this case that banks decided to convert their forms of guarantee into indemnities.

An indemnifier will be liable notwithstanding any legal incapacity on the part of the debtor.

However Coutts would be decided differently today because the *Minors' Contracts Act 1987* states that the *Infant Relief Act 1874* (which invalidated certain contracts made by minors e.g. loans) shall not apply. Thus a minor can be made liable for a loan. However it is still true that guarantees given by minors are void.

Partnerships

No partner can make the partnership liable on a guarantee he has signed unless it can be shown that the guarantee was necessary for the carrying on of the partnership business. In *Brettel v Williams (1849)* the defendants were railway contractors who entered into a sub-contract with a firm of brick-makers. One of the partners of the defendant firm guaranteed the payment by the brick-makers of the bills for the coal used in connection with the contract. It was held the guarantee was not necessary for carrying on the business of the partnership and so did not bind the other partners. Therefore a bank will always ask all the partners to sign the guarantee form.

Companies

Since February 1991, presumably a company will have the necessary power to give a guarantee. In addition the person who signs the guarantee form on behalf of the company must be suitably authorised or it may be that the guarantee is sealed. In each case the bank must obtain an authenticated copy of the resolution conferring the necessary authority.

Rights of the guarantor – Against the Bank

As will be appreciated when we consider the typical clauses to be found in a bank's form of guarantee, the bank will attempt legally to limit the rights remaining to a guarantor. However the guarantor will still retain certain rights such as

1. He has a right to request to know from the bank the extent of his liability. The bank must be careful not to break its duty of confidentiality it owes to its customer and so when answering the guarantor it may notify him of the exact amount if the debit balance on the customer's account is less than the limit of the guarantee but may only say the guarantee is being relied upon if the debit balance is higher.

   However if the loan is £15,000 or less, it will be protected by the *Consumer Credit Act 1974*. In that case the guarantor is entitled to know the amount still owing by the principal debtor.

2.   As soon as the debt becomes due, the guarantor may apply to the creditor and pay him off, and then, after giving him an indemnity for costs, he can sue the principal debtor in the creditor's name or in his own name.

3.   If the guarantor pays off the debt he is entitled to be subrogated to all the rights possessed by the creditor in respect of the guaranteed debt. In particular, he is entitled to all securities held by the creditor or a proportion of them corresponding to the amount guaranteed by him, but he must pay off all his liability before he can get at the securities.

Against the debtor

1.   As soon as the bank becomes entitled to sue the guarantor, the latter is entitled to call upon the debtor to pay the bank so as to relieve him (the guarantor) from his liability under the guarantee).

2.   Once the guarantor pays either the whole or any part of the guaranteed debt to the bank he may bring an action against the debtor for reimbursement. In *Thomas v Nottingham Football Club (1972)* it was decided that the guarantor may call upon the debtor for reimbursement once the bank's right against the guarantor has become fixed. In this case that occurred because the guarantor had determined his guarantee with the bank.

3.   If the debtor is bankrupt the guarantor may prove in his bankruptcy for the sum he has actually paid to the bank, or for his contingent liability.

Against the co-guarantors

1.   The main right here is a right of contribution from co-guarantors. This right arises when two or more persons are guarantors for the same principal debtor and the same debt, although their obligations may be expressed in different documents.

2.   The guarantor seeking contribution must have paid more than his share under the guarantee.

3.   Before recovering contribution, the guarantor who has paid the debt must bring into account all securities he has obtained from the creditor in respect of the debt.

Determination of the guarantee

As we noticed above, if there is misrepresentation, mistake or undue influence present then the contract between the bank and the guarantor may be avoided. In addition if the guarantee is entered into it may be determined if any of the following events occur.

1. *Payment by the debtor*
    Payment by the debtor will usually discharge the liability of the guarantor, provided such payment was not a fraudulent transaction.

2. *Payment by the guarantor*
    Will obviously terminate his liability. He has fulfilled his duty on the contract he made with the bank.

3. *Death of the guarantor*
    Notice of the death of the guarantor will terminate, for the future, the liability of the guarantor's estate unless it has been agreed that the personal representatives of the guarantor shall continue to be liable until they have given notice of termination.

4. *Insanity of guarantor*
    The same principles apply as on the death of the guarantor also the

5. *Bankruptcy of the guarantor* will result in the same situation.
    If there is a joint and several guarantee and the bank receives notice of the death, insanity or bankruptcy of one of the guarantors it must stop the account so as to prevent the application of the rule in Clayton's case and to preserve the liability the guarantor's estate who has become insane or bankrupt.

6. *Death, insanity or bankruptcy of debtor*
    If any of these events occurs the bank should stop the debtor's account and notify the guarantor. It may be necessary for the bank to prove in the bankruptcy of the debtor as well as calling upon the guarantor to pay. In this way the bank has two sources of repayment.

A bank guarantee form

1. *The consideration clause*

In Consideration of the Bank at the request of the Guarantor entering into and/or giving time credit banking facilities or other accommodation under the Agreement the Guarantor hereby guarantees payment to the Bank on demand of all present future actual and/or contingent obligations of the Debtor to the Bank whether incurred solely severally and/or jointly in connection with the Agreement.

Although strictly it is unnecessary for the consideration to be stated in a contract of guarantee it is nevertheless normal practice to do so. The guarantor is promising to answer for the debt of the debtor and so the bank in return must provide consideration for that promise. Past consideration has no value and so the bank promises for the present to grant banking facilities and for the future to continue to grant banking facilities etc.

If it is a dormant account that is being guaranteed, care must be taken because of the past consideration rule. The bank may call in the existing loan and then promise not to sue the debtor for a period of time.

In *Provincial Bank of Ireland v Donnell (1934)* the bank had no intention of making further loans and so the guarantee agreement failed for want of consideration.

2. *The Operative Clause or the Whole Debt Clause*

The guarantor in consideration of the Bank giving time or credit or banking facilities to the debtor:

---

1. Guarantees to discharge on demand the Debtor's Obligations with Interest from the data of demand and

2. Agrees that if any of the Debtor's Obligations are at any time void or unenforceable against the Debtor for any reason the Guarantor would have been liable had the Debtor's Obligations not been void or unenforceable and further agrees to discharge that liability on demand with Interest from the date of demand.

   Provided That the account recoverable from the

Guarantor under this Guarantee shall not exceed the total of Pounds (£   ) together with Interest on that sum since the date on which Interest was last compounded in the books of the Bank and Interest on that total from the date of demand and Expenses.

This clause states the obligation of the guarantor.

Note The guarantor guarantees payment of *all* sums of money and then it is stated that the total amount recoverable from him shall not exceed £x.

Even where there is a limitation of the guarantor's liability, bank guarantee forms nevertheless insist that the guarantee must cover the entire amount advanced to the debtor and not merely to the limit of the guarantor's liability.

There are two main advantages to the bank in drafting the guarantee to cover the entire sum advanced rather than the limit of guarantee:

1. If the debtor becomes bankrupt and the guarantor pays the limit of his liability with some amount still owing to the bank from the principal debtor, the guarantor cannot prove in the debtor's bankruptcy in competition with the bank, because the guarantor can do so only if he has paid the whole of the guarantee debt.

2. A guarantor paying off a debt is entitled to claim from the bank securities which the debtor had deposited with the bank. To be able to do this he must pay off the entire debt covered by the guarantee and not the limit of his liability.

3. *Types of Guarantee*

This Guarantee shall be a continuing security and shall remain in force until determined by three months notice in writing from the Guarantor but such determination shall not affect the liability of the Guarantor for the amount recoverable at the date of the expiration of the notice.

A guarantee may be a specific guarantee or it may be a continuing guarantee.

Where the guarantor's promise to be liable secondarily refers to a specific transaction only, the guarantee is known as a specific guarantee. In this case, the guarantee is discharged as soon as the special advance or loan for which it was given is repaid.

If the guarantee is worded so as to cover advances made within an agreed limit so that the guarantor's liability attaches to the *fluctuating debit balance* for the duration of the guarantee it is known as a continuing guarantee. This may be revoked at any time by notice.

Whether a guarantee is a specific one or a continuing guarantee can only be determined from the wording of the contract itself.

Also the guarantor must give three months notice to determine the guarantee and so must his personal representatives.

4. *Sufficient demand*

I/we the undersigned hereby guarantee the payment or discharge to you and undertake that the undersigned will on demand in writing made on the undersigned pay or discharge to you all moneys and liabilities which shall for the time being be due owing or incurred by the Principal to you

---

The guarantor promises to pay on demand. The reason for that is that in *Parr's Banking Co Ltd v Yates (1898)* the defendant signed a guarantee that did not include the words "pay on demand". When sued by the bank he pleaded that the claim was statute barred because no fresh advances had been made to the debtor after the original one and that was over six years previously. The Court of Appeal accepted his argument.

A demand or notice hereunder shall be in writing signed by an officer or agent of the Bank and may be served on the Guarantor by hand or by post either by delivering the same to any officer of the Guarantor at any place or by addressing the same to the Guarantor at its registered office or a place of business last known to the Bank; if such demand or notice is sent by post it shall be deemed to have been received on the day following the day on which it was posted and shall be effective notwithstanding it be returned undelivered.

The right of action arises when the demand is made. To avoid the possibility that the guarantor might pretend he did not receive notice to pay, a demand is deemed to have been made when it has been posted to the guarantor.

5.   *Guarantor not to accept security from the debtor*

The Guarantor has not taken and will not take without the written consent of the Bank any security from the debtor in connection with this Guarantee and any security so taken shall be held in trust for the Bank and as security for the liability of the Guarantor to the Bank hereunder.

A clause binding the guarantor not to protect himself by taking security from the debtor. The object of such a clause is to ensure that in the event of the debtor becoming bankrupt and part of the overdraft not covered by the guarantee, the debtor's assets available for distribution will not be reduced by the guarantor holding on to it; i.e. relying on his security (being a secured creditor). Such clauses also state what will happen if the guarantor breaks his undertaking.

6.   *Indemnity Clause*

As a separate and independent stipulation (but without increasing the before-mentioned total amount recoverable hereon) the undersigned agree that all sums of money which may not be recoverable from the undersigned on the footing of a guarantee whether by reason of any legal limitation disability or incapacity on or of the Principal or any other fact or circumstance and whether known to you or not shall nevertheless be recoverable from the undersigned as sole or principal debtor(s) in respect thereof and shall be repaid by the undersigned on demand in writing made by you or on your behalf.

This clause will render the guarantor primarily liable notwithstanding that the original loan agreement between the bank and the debtor has become void for any reason.

See note on minors, page 213.

Sometimes called a conversion clause the effect of this is to make the guarantee into an indemnity.

7. *Conclusive evidence clause*

Certificate of Debtor's Obligations

A certificate signed by an official of the Bank as to the amount of the Debtor's Obligations or the amount due from the Guarantor under this Guarantee shall be conclusive evidence save in the case of manifest error or on any question of law.

This is an agreement by the guarantor that he will accept as conclusive evidence of the amount owed by the debtor to the bank a certificate signed by an officer of the bank. In *Bache and Co (London) Ltd v Banque Vernes et Commerciale de Paris S.A. (1973)* the Court of Appeal accepted a similar clause.

8. *Power to vary securities, to grant time to and to compound with the debtor*

The Bank may without any consent from the Guarantor and without affecting the Guarantor's liability hereunder renew vary or determine any accommodation given to the Debtor hold over renew modify or release any security or guarantee now or hereafter held from the Debtor or any other person including any signatory of this Guarantee in respect of the liabilities hereby secured and grant time or indulgence to or compound with the Debtor or any such person and this Guarantee shall not be discharged nor shall the Guarantor's liability under it be affected by anything which would not have discharged or affected the Guarantor's liability if the Guarantor had been a principal debtor to the Bank instead of a guarantor.

If it were not for this clause the guarantor would be released from his liability if the bank granted further time in which to pay to the debtor or if the bank came to some private agreement with the debtor. In order to maintain its complete freedom of action the bank relies on this clause.

9. *Guarantor's power to sue the debtor is restricted*

Preservation of Bank's claims against the Debtor

Until all claims of the Bank in respect of the Debtor's Obligations have been discharged in full:

1. The Guarantor shall not be entitled to participate in any security held by the Bank or money received by the Bank in respect of the Debtor's Obligations
2. The Guarantor shall not in competition with or in priority to the Bank make any claim against the Debtor or any co-guarantor or their respective estates nor make any claim in the bankruptcy or liquidation of the Debtor or any co-guarantor nor take or enforce any security from or against the Debtor or any co-guarantor
3. Any security taken by the Guarantor from the Debtor or any co-guarantor shall be held in trust for the Bank as security for the Guarantor's liability to the Bank under this Guarantee

---

When the guarantor pays any sum to the bank he may then sue the debtor. This may be disadvantageous to the bank hence the reason for this clause. Furthermore the guarantor promises not to prove in the bankruptcy or liquidation of the debtor.

10.   *The Consumer Credit Act 1974*

Important – You should read this carefully
Your Rights
The Consumer Credit Act 1974 covers this guarantee and indemnity and lays down certain requirements for your protection: If they are not carried out, the Bank cannot enforce the guarantee and indemnity against you without a court order.

Until the agreement between the Bank and the debtor has been made, you can change your mind about giving the guarantee and indemnity. If you wish to withdraw, you must give *WRITTEN* notice to the Bank which must reach it *BEFORE* the main agreement is made. Once it has been made you can no longer change your mind.

Under this guarantee and indemnity *YOU MAY HAVE TO PAY INSTEAD* of the debtor and fulfil any other obligations under the guarantee and indemnity. (But you cannot be made to pay more than he could have been made to pay unless he is under 18). However, if the debtor fails to keep to his side of the agreement, the Bank must send him a default notice (and a copy to you) giving him a chance to put things right before any claim is made on you.

If you would like to know more about your rights under the Act, you should contact either your local Trading Standards Department or your nearest Citizens' Advice Bureau.

Most bank lending will be for business purposes therefore the *Consumer Credit Act* will have no application because lending to Companies will not be caught by the Act; neither will loans to anyone if the amount exceeds £15,000. However a loan may be caught by this Act and so the above note will appear on the guarantee form to inform the guarantor/indemnifier of his rights.

Summary – Securities – guarantees
1. A guarantee is an agreement between the lender and the guarantor whereby the latter undertakes to pay the debt due to the lender if it is not repaid by the debtor.
2. A bank will therefore rely upon this agreement as security for its loan.
3. It must ensure that the contract will be enforceable in case that need arises.
4. Such matters such as mistake, misrepresentation or undue influence must be avoided as these may make the contract unenforceable.
5. As in any contract the guarantor will have rights against the bank and against the debtor.
6. The banks' form of guarantee are complicated documents and the example in the text should be studied.

Chapter Nineteen

Borrowing by a Company

As was mentioned earlier, a company may sometimes need to borrow money. A power to borrow money will presumably be implied into the objects clause of every company registered with the 'general trading' object. The directors are the persons who will actually arrange the loan on behalf of the company and so they too must have the necessary power to act. Sometimes the shareholders may wish to restrict their borrowing powers to a certain maximum amount.

Now that the doctrine of ultra vires has been abolished presumably a company will have implied power to borrow and to give security for the loan but the authority of the directors will still have to be considered. This, no doubt, may continue to be restricted if so desired, but such restrictions will not affect persons dealing with the company unless they are aware of them.

The same principles apply to securities given by companies as apply to securities given by individuals. Some must be by deed e.g. a legal mortgage and in that case the company's seal must be affixed. If the document may merely be signed, the person signing on behalf of the company must be authorised by resolution of the board of directors.

An important requirement as far as charges given by companies are concerned is that *Section 398 of the Companies Act 1985* provides that the prescribed particulars of the charge together with the instrument (if any) by which the charge is created or evidenced must be delivered or received by the Registrar of Companies in Cardiff for registration within 21 days after the date of the charge's creation.
Particulars may be delivered by any one interested in the charge. The company no longer receives a certificate. Instead the Registrar sends a copy of the particulars and a note of the date to the company, the chargee and any other interested person.
Examples of changes include:

1.　A charge securing any issue of debentures.

2. A charge on land.
3. A floating charge on the undertaking or property of the company.
4. A charge on goodwill, patent or trade mark.

A banker who proposes to lend to a limited company should therefore inspect the register before doing so to see whether any prior charges exist on the company's property.

Even though it is the duty of the company to register the charge, where the company defaults, the creditor himself may register it and recover from the company any fees paid by him.

Certain charges are not required to be registered:

1. where a company mortgages shares or assigns a life policy or pledges goods.
2. where a negotiable instrument is given to secure the payment of any book debts of a company.
3. where an unpaid vendor's lien exists.

S.399 of the *Companies Act 1985,* as amended by S.95 of the *Companies Act 1989* provides that if particulars are not delivered within 21 days the charge is void as against:

1. an administrator or liquidator; or
2. any person who for value acquires an interest in or right over any property subject to the charge. Where the relevant event (for 1, beginning of insolvency proceedings or for 2, the acquisition of the right or interest) occurs after the creation of the charge.

New S.400 of the *Companies Act 1985* provides that where particulars are delivered more than 21 days after creation the charge is not void where the relevant event occurs after the particulars are delivered. It is therefore no longer necessary to obtain court approval to register out of time.

However the charge will be void as against an administrator/ liquidator if at the date of delivery of the particulars the company is unable to pay its debts (as defined by S.123 of the *Insolvency Act 1986*); or becomes unable to do so as a result of the charge and insolvency proceedings begin within the relevant period (i.e. beginning with the date particulars are delivered – 6 months in the case of fixed charges, 1 year if a floating charge but extended to 2 years if in favour of a connected person).

S.401 of the *Company Act 1985* as amended by S.96 of the *Companies Act 1989* provides that where the registered particulars are incomplete or inaccurate, further particulars signed on behalf of the company and chargee may be delivered at any time.

Debentures

Section 744 of the Companies Act 1985 provides that a debenture includes debenture stock, bonds or any other securities of a company, whether constituting a charge on the assets of the company or not.

More usually a debenture is considered to be evidence of a loan and a certificate will be issued to the creditor.

A debenture created by a company in favour of a bank will usually give a fixed charge over certain assets of the company and a floating charge over the remainder of the assets.

Fixed and floating charge

A fixed charge may be a legal or an equitable mortgage of some fixed or specified assets of the company. The effect of this is that the assets may not be sold or destroyed by the company otherwise the security on which the mortgagee is relying would be affected. If certain assets such as raw materials or finished stock were to be the subject of a fixed charge then they could not be used in the manufacturing process or sold. Consequently a floating charge was devised which would float over certain assets, not fastening on to them until certain events occurred which would have the effect of crystallising the floating charge. The assets which are subject to the floating charge may be used in any way the company desires, even to the extent that they are used up entirely.

A floating charge will crystallise or become fixed if the company:

1.   defaults in payment of interest or capital or commits some

breach of another term of the debenture and the mortgagee takes some step such as the appointment of a receiver.

2.   goes into liquidation.
3.   ceases to carry on business.

Often a company will borrow money from more than one person and in that case the interests of the creditors are represented by a trustee whose powers are stated in the trust deed. If any breach of covenant occurs then a receiver can be appointed.

Debentures are similar to shares in that they can be transferred on the Stock Exchange. However in the case of a debenture the holder

1.   is a creditor and not a member of the company
2.   he receives interest and not dividends
3.   he has no voting rights
4.   in a winding-up a debenture holder is treated according to whether the debenture is secured or unsecured.
5.   a debenture may be repayable at a future date or may be irredeemable.
6.   debentures may be issued at a discount whereas shares may not as a rule be issued at a discount.
7.   a company may purchase its own debentures but it may only purchase its own shares in certain circumstances.

Debentures may be registered or issued to bearer. They may be secured or unsecured in which case they are called mortgage debentures or naked debentures.

If a bank lends money to a corporate customer it will use its own debenture form and the following are some typical clauses to be found therein.

Bank debenture form

The following clauses are usually contained in the bank's debenture form.

1.   _____

The Company hereby covenants to pay to the Bank on demand the sum of One pound (£1) and to pay and discharge on demand all monies obligations and liabilities which may now or at any time hereafter may be or become due owing or incurred by the Company to the Bank on any account (whether solely or jointly with any other person and whether as principal or surety) present or future actual or contingent of the Company to the Bank together with interest and other bank charges so that interest shall be calculated and compounded in accordance with the practice of the Bank from time to time as well after as before any demand made or judgment obtained hereunder.

The company agrees to repay all liabilities present, future actual or contingent together with expenses.

2.

The Company as beneficial owner and to the intent that the security created shall rank as a continuing security hereby charges with the payment or discharge of all monies obligations and liabilities hereby convenanted to be paid or discharged (together with all costs and expenses howsoever incurred by the Bank in connection with this Mortgage Debenture on a full indemnity basis):

a. by way of legal mortgage any property referred to in the Schedule hereto (the legally mortgaged property) and/or the proceeds of sale thereof

b. by way of specific equitable charge all estates or interests in any freehold and leasehold property (except the legally mortgaged property) now and at any time during the continuance of this security belonging to or charged to the Company (the equitably charged property) and/or the proceeds of sale thereof

c. by way of specific charge all stocks shares and/or other securities now and at any time during the continuance of this security belonging to the Company in any of its subsidiary companies or any other company and all dividends and other rights in relation thereto

d. by way of specific charge all book debts and other debts now and from time to time due or owing to the Company

e.   by way of specific charge its goodwill and the benefit of any licences

f.   by way of floating security its undertaking and all its property assets and rights whatsoever and wheresoever present and/or future including those for the time being charged by way of specific charge pursuant to the foregoing paragraphs if and to the extent that such charges as aforesaid shall fail as specific charges but without prejudice to any such specific charges as shall continue to be effective.

As continuing security the company creates a fixed charge over freehold and leasehold property, plant and machinery, stocks and shares etc. It also creates a floating charge over other property not subject to a fixed charge.

3.

With reference to the property assets and rights subject to the floating charge:

a.   the Company shall not be at liberty without the consent in writing of the bank to:

    i.   create any mortgage or charge ranking in priority to or pari passu with that charge and/or

    ii.   sell the whole or except in the ordinary course of business any part of the Company's undertaking

b.   the Company agrees to effect and maintain such insurances as are normally maintained by prudent companies carrying on similar businesses

c.   the Bank may by notice to the Company convert the floating charge into a specific charge as regards any assets specified in the notice which the Bank shall consider to be in danger of being seized or sold under any form of distress or execution levied or threatened and may appoint a receiver thereof.

The company agrees not to create any mortgage charge or lien on the property, to rank in priority to the floating charge.

4.   _____

With reference to the legally mortgaged property and the equitably charged property the Company agrees:

a.   to keep it in a good state of repair and condition and insured against such risks and in such office and for such amounts as the Bank may require or approve and that failure to do so will entitle the Bank to do so at the expense of the Company and as agent of the Company without thereby becoming a mortgagee in possession.

b.   that the statutory power of leasing and/or accepting surrenders of leases conferred on mortgagors shall not be exercised by the Company without the consent in writing of the Bank but the Bank may grant or accept surrenders of leases without restriction

c.   not to part with the possession of it or any part thereof nor confer upon any person firm company or body whatsoever any licence right or interest to occupy it or any part thereof without the consent in writing of the Bank

To keep insured the property charged.

5.   _____

Immediately upon or at any time after the presentation of a petition applying for an administration order to be made in relation to the Company or at any time after this security shall otherwise have become enforceable the Bank may by writing under the hand of any area director or manager of the Bank appoint any person (or persons) to be an administrative receiver (the Administrative Receiver) of the property hereby charged. Where two or more persons are appointed to be an Administrative Receiver the Bank will in the appointment declare whether any act required or authorised to be done by such Administrative Receivers is to be done by all or any one or more of such Administrative Receivers for the time being holding office. Any Administrative Receiver shall be the agent of the Company and the Company shall be solely responsible for his acts or defaults and for his remuneration and any Administrative Receiver shall have all the powers of an administrative receiver specified in Schedule 1 of the Insolvency Act 1986 or any statutory modification or re-enactment thereof.

The bank may appoint a receiver.

6. _____

Section 103 of the Law of Property Act 1925 (the 1925 Act) shall not apply to this security which shall immediately become enforceable and the power of sale and other powers conferred by section 101 of the 1925 Act as varied or extended by this security shall be immediately exercisable at any time after notice demanding payment of any moneys hereby secured shall have been served by the Bank on the Company.

Section 103 (power of sale) and Section 93 (consolidation) of the Law of Property Act 1925, shall not apply.

7. _____

The Company shall from time to time supply to the Bank such accounts or other information concerning the assets liabilities and affairs of the Company its subsidiary or asociated companies as the Bank may require.

The company will send to the bank copies of its trading account and Balance Sheet.

Floating Charge

The characteristics of a floating charge are set out in *Re. Yorkshire Woolcombers Association (1903)*.

1. It is a charge on a class of assets of a company present and future.
2. The class of assets is constantly changing from time to time.
3. The company may deal with the assets in any way that it wishes, until the holder of the charge takes some step to enforce it.

Useful though a floating charge is it should never be taken without the addition of a fixed charge. The floating charge is only appropriate for certain fluctuating assets. The disadvantages of a floating charge are:

1.   Because the company may continue to deal with the assets which are subject to a floating charge it may be that when the mortgagee seeks to enforce the charge there will be no assets left. To minimise this risk a bank may ask for statements of assets from the company from time to time.

2.   In the winding up of the company its preferential creditors e.g. the Inland Revenue will have priority over creditors holding a floating charge. Also creditors other than preferential may obtain priority over a creditor holding floating charge such as a landlord levying distress for rent or the sheriff seizing goods to satisfy a judgment.

3.   On the same point concerning priority of creditors it may be that a supplier has sold goods to the company and has included in the contract of sale a "Romalpa" clause. This is the name given to the clause that was examined by the court in *Aluminium Industrie Vaasen B. V. v Romalpa Aluminium Ltd (1976)*. The case concerned the sale of aluminium foil by a Dutch company to an English company. The seller had inserted a clause to the effect that the ownership of the foil should remain with the seller, that the product of the goods should be held by the buyer as "producing owner" and that it should be stored separately from other stock on the supplier's behalf as "surety" for the remainder of the price. Also that the products might be sold by the buyers as agents for the sellers.

When the buyer became insolvent it was held that the seller could assume ownership of the goods in the hands of the buyer thus defeating the receiver.

It seems therefore that if the goods sold remain identifiable then the seller may assert his ownership. However if the goods sold are mixed with other goods so that the original goods lose their identity then problems may arise. In *Borden (UK) Ltd v Scottish Timber Products Ltd (1981)* the original goods became mixed with others and there was no provision in the contract for ownership in the mixed product remaining with the original seller. Consequently the attempt by the seller to retain ownership of the goods he had sold, failed.

In *Clough Mill Ltd v Martin (1985)* the court considered the matter obiter and came to the conclusion that the retention of ownership clause (Romalpa clause) would be effective in relation to unmixed goods. If it had been intended that a charge be created over the goods sold that now form part of the mixed goods then this must have been registered.

It does seem therefore that the retention of ownership clause will be effective, if drawn correctly, in the case of unmixed goods provided such a clause provides for separate accountability for the proceeds in the event of a re-sale by the original buyer. There are considerable difficulties in the case of mixed goods.

Avoidance of a floating charge

4.   *Section 245 of Insolvency Act 1986* provides that – "where a company is being wound up a floating charge on its property created within 12 months of the commencement of the winding up is invalid (unless it is proved that the company, immediately after the creation of the charge, was solvent), except to the amount of any cash paid to the company at the time of or subsequently to the creation of, and in consideration for, the charge, together with interest on that account."

In this connection the rule in Clayton's case may operate in favour of the bank, because money paid into a company's account after the charge has been created will be linked with any debt outstanding when the charge was made. Therefore if the amount paid into the account after the charge was created, equals the debt the charge was intended to secure, the amount paid in will cancel the debt outstanding when the charge was made and the charge will be valid to secure loans made after the charge was created. *Re Yeovil Glove Co Ltd (1965)* which approved *Re Thomas Mortimer Ltd (1925)*.

If the charge was created in favour of a person connected with the company then a floating charge created within 2 years of the commencement of a winding up will be invalid whether or not the company was solvent.

Any charge made by a company within 6 months before commencement of a winding up (2 years, if a person connected with the company) is void if it is a preference of any of the company's creditors or within 2 years if it is a transaction at an undervalue.

5.   As a floating charge is an equitable charge, if the company which has given the charge later executes a fixed mortgage or charge

over assets comprised in the floating charge then the latter fixed charge may take priority over the floating charge.

This situation may be avoided by the bank's inserting a clause into its debenture form to the effect:

"The company covenants not to create any mortgage or charge to rank in priority to or pari passu with the floating charge."

In order to make this restriction binding on possible later chargees the restrictive clause must be stated in Form 395 when registering the debentures with the Registrar of Companies.

Summary – Borrowing by a company

1. When a company borrows money it will usually issue a debenture to the lender.
2. This debenture is evidence of the debt and states the rights of the parties.
3. A company may give a fixed charge or a floating charge over its assets.
4. A floating charge has a number of disadvantages but is useful to cover assets which are constantly changing.
5. The effect of Section 245 of the Insolvency Act 1986 should be noted.
6. The example of a bank's debenture form should be studied.

Appendix

Bank legal documents

1. Memorandum of Deposit of Securities

2. Legal Charge

3. Debenture (Royal Bank of Scotland)

4. Guarantee and Indemnity

5. Legal Mortgage of Life Policy

6. Debenture (Barclays Bank PLC)

7. Memorandum of Deposit

 **The Royal Bank of Scotland plc**

THIS IS AN IMPORTANT DOCUMENT. SIGN ONLY IF YOU WANT TO BE LEGALLY BOUND. YOU ARE RECOMMENDED TO TAKE INDEPENDENT LEGAL ADVICE BEFORE SIGNING.

Date: 19

Definitions

Mortgagor:

Bank: The Royal Bank of Scotland plc

Interest: Interest at the rate stipulated by the Bank from time to time or in the absence of a stipulation the rate of   % per
                   annum above the Bank's fluctuating Base Rate

Securities   All stocks shares bonds or other securities at any time deposited with or transferred to the Bank or its nominee by the
                   Mortgagor

Mortgagor's Obligations: All the Mortgagor's liabilities to the Bank of any kind (whether present or future actual or contingent and whether
                   incurred alone or jointly with another) including banking charges and commission

Expenses: All expenses (on a full indemnity basis) incurred by the Bank at any time in connection with the Securities or the
                   Mortgagor's Obligations or in taking perfecting enforcing or exercising any power under this deed with Interest from
                   the date they are incurred

Charge

1   The Mortgagor covenants to discharge on demand the Mortgagor's Obligations together with Interest to the date of discharge and
        Expenses and as a continuing security for such discharge and as beneficial owner charges to the Bank the Securities and all income
        derived from the Securities and all rights attaching to the Securities

Undertakings by Mortgagor

2.1   The Mortgagor undertakes to deposit with the Bank all documents relating to any bonus or rights or other issue of stock or shares in
        respect of the Securities

2.2   The Mortgagor undertakes to pay all calls or other payments due from time to time in respect of the Securities

Powers of the Bank

3.1   Section 103 of the Law of Property Act 1925 shall not apply and the Bank shall have the power to sell the Securities in whole or in part at
        any time after the date of this deed

3.2   The Bank may at its discretion pay any calls or other payments due from time to time in respect of the Securities or payable in respect of
        any rights attaching to the Securities

3.3   Section 93 of the Law of Property Act 1925 shall not apply to this deed

Restrictions on Charging

4   The Mortgagor will not without the Bank's prior written consent create or permit to arise any mortgage charge or lien on the Securities

Power of Attorney

5   The Mortgagor hereby irrevocably appoints the Bank to be the Attorney of the Mortgagor (with full power of substitution and delegation)
        in the Mortgagor's name and on the Mortgagor's behalf and as the Mortgagor's act and deed to sign or execute all deeds instruments and
        documents which may be required by the Bank pursuant to this deed or the exercise of any of its powers

Return of Similar Securities on Discharge

6   On discharge of this deed the Mortgagor will accept in place of all or any of the Securities delivery of other securities of the same class
        and denomination

Appropriation

7.1   Subject to Clause 7.2 the Bank may appropriate all payments received for the account of the Mortgagor in reduction of any part of the Mortgagor's Obligations as the Bank decides

7.2   The Bank may open a new account or accounts upon the Bank receiving actual or constructive notice of any charge or interest affecting the Securities and whether or not the Bank opens any such account no payment received by the Bank for the account of the Mortgagor after receiving such notice shall (if followed by any payment out of or debit to the Mortgagor's account) be appropriated towards or have the effect of discharging any part of the Mortgagor's Obligations outstanding at the time of receiving such notice

Preservation of other Security and Rights and Further Assurance

8.1   This security is in addition to all other security present or future held by the Bank for the Mortgagor's Obligations and shall not merge with or prejudice such other security or any contractual or legal rights of the Bank

8.2   The Mortgagor will at the Mortgagor's own cost at the Bank's request execute any deed or document and take any action required by the Bank to perfect this security or further to secure on the Securities the Mortgagor's Obligations

Notices

9.1   Any notice or demand by the Bank may be sent by post or telex or delivered to the Mortgagor at the above address or the Mortgagor's address last known to the Bank or if the Mortgagor is a company may be served personally on any director or the secretary of the Mortgagor

9.2   A notice or demand by the Bank by post shall be deemed served on the day after posting

9.3   A notice or demand by the Bank by telex shall be deemed served at the time of sending

Governing Law

10   This deed shall be governed by and construed in accordance with the laws of England

Interpretation

11.1   The expressions 'Mortgagor' and 'Bank' where the context admits include their respective successors in title and assigns

11.2   If two or more persons are included in the expression 'Mortgagor' then the use in this deed of the word 'Mortgagor' shall be deemed to refer to such persons both together and separately and the Mortgagor's Obligations shall be their joint and several obligations and each of them shall be primarily liable by way of indemnity for the liabilities to the Bank of the other or others of them

11.3   Interest will be calculated both before and after demand or judgment on a daily basis and compounded quarterly on such days as the Bank may select but after a demand Interest will also be calculated on the Mortgagor's Obligations together with accrued Interest as at the date of the demand

In Witness whereof this deed has been duly executed

Signed Sealed and **Delivered**   **Signed Sealed** and **Delivered**

by the first named Mortgagor   by the second named Mortgagor

in the presence of:—   in the presence of:—

Witness' name in full _____   Witness' Name _____

Signature _____   Signature _____

Address _____   Address _____

_____   _____

Occupation _____   Occupation _____

The Common Seal of the Mortgagor
was affixed in the presence of:—

Director _____   Secretary _____

**The Royal Bank
of Scotland plc**

The Royal Bank of Scotland plc releases to the within named
Mortgagor all the Securities comprised in the within written
Memorandum of Deposit

Signed Sealed and Delivered for and on behalf
of The Royal Bank of Scotland plc by
a duly authorised Attorney

**Memorandum of
Deposit of Securities
(without Transfers)**

Date:

Date _____ 19

Branch:

Granted by:

20329 (7/85)

The Royal Bank
of Scotland plc

THIS IS AN IMPORTANT DOCUMENT. SIGN ONLY IF YOU WANT TO BE LEGALLY BOUND. YOU ARE RECOMMENDED TO TAKE INDEPENDENT LEGAL ADVICE BEFORE SIGNING.

Date: 19

Definitions

Mortgagor:

Bank: The Royal Bank of Scotland plc

Interest: Interest at the rate stipulated by the Bank from time to time or in the absence of a stipulation the rate of   % per annum above the Bank's fluctuating Base Rate

Property:

(Land Registry Title No:)

Mortgagor's Obligations: All the Mortgagor's liabilities to the Bank of any kind (whether present or future actual or contingent and whether incurred alone or jointly with another) including banking charges and commission

Expenses: All expenses (on a full indemnity basis) incurred by the Bank or any Receiver at any time in connection with the Property or the Mortgagor's Obligations or in taking perfecting enforcing or exercising any power under this deed with Interest from the date they are incurred

Charge

1   The Mortgagor covenants to discharge on demand the Mortgagor's Obligations together with Interest to the date of discharge and Expenses and as a continuing security for such discharge and as beneficial owner charges the Property to the Bank (to the full extent of the Mortgagor's interest in the Property or its proceeds of sale) by way of legal mortgage of all legal interests and otherwise by way of specific equitable charge

Repair and Insurance

2 1   The Mortgagor will keep the Property in good condition and comprehensively insured to the Bank's reasonable satisfaction for its full reinstatement cost and in default the Bank (without becoming liable to account as mortgagee in possession) may enter and repair or insure the Property. The Mortgagor will deposit the insurance policy with the Bank

2.2 The Mortgagor will hold in trust for the Bank all money received under any insurance of the Property and at the Bank's option will apply the same in making good the relevant loss or damage or in or towards discharge of the Mortgagor's Obligations Interest and Expenses

Restrictions on Charging Leasing and Parting with possession

3 The Mortgagor will not without the Bank's prior written consent:–

3.1 Create or permit to arise any mortgage charge or lien on the Property and the Mortgagor requests the Chief Land Registrar to enter a restriction on the Register of any Registered Land that except under an order of the Registrar no disposition is to be registered without the consent of the registered proprietor of this deed

3.2 Grant or accept a surrender of any lease or licence of the Property

3.3 Part with or share possession or occupation of the Property

Powers of the Bank

4.1 The Bank may without restriction grant or accept surrenders of leases of the Property

4.2 Section 103 of the Law of Property Act 1925 shall not apply and the Bank may exercise its power of sale and other powers under that or any other Act or this deed at any time after the date of this deed

4.3 The Bank may under the hand of any official or manager or under seal appoint or remove a Receiver or Receivers of the Property and may fix and pay the fees of a Receiver but any Receiver shall be deemed to be the agent of the Mortgagor and the Mortgagor shall be solely responsible for the Receiver's acts defaults and remuneration

4.4 All or any of the powers conferred on a Receiver by Clause 5 may be exercised by the Bank without first appointing a Receiver or notwithstanding any appointment

4.5 The Bank will not be liable to account to the Mortgagor as mortgagee in possession for any money not actually received by the Bank

4.6 Section 93 of the Law of Property Act 1925 shall not apply to this deed

Receivers

5.1 A Receiver shall have full power to carry out work at or sell lease charge deal with dispose of and manage the Property and do anything which he considers conducive or incidental to managing and realising the Property or the income from the Property and he may borrow any money he requires for those purposes

5.2 A Receiver will have power to remove store and dispose of any furniture or goods found in the Property which the Mortgagor shall refuse or omit to remove and the Receiver will account to the Mortgagor for the proceeds of any sale after deducting all Expenses incurred under this sub-clause

5.3 In the case of Joint Receivers any power may be exercised jointly or severally

5.4 A Receiver shall apply all money he receives first in repayment of all money borrowed by him and his expenses and liabilities and in payment of his fees and secondly towards the remaining matters specified in Section 109(8) of the Law of Property Act 1925

Power of Attorney

6 The Mortgagor hereby irrevocably appoints the Bank and any Receiver severally to be the Attorney of the Mortgagor (with full power of substitution and delegation) in the Mortgagor's name and on the Mortgagor's behalf and as the Mortgagor's act and deed to sign or execute all deeds instruments and documents which may be required by the Bank or any Receiver pursuant to this deed or the exercise of any of their powers

Appropriation

7.1 Subject to Clause 7.2 the Bank may appropriate all payments received for the account of the Mortgagor in reduction of any part of the Mortgagor's Obligations as the Bank decides

7.2 The Bank may open a new account or accounts upon the Bank receiving actual or constructive notice of any charge or interest affecting the Property and whether or not the Bank opens any such account no payment received by the Bank for the account of the Mortgagor after receiving such notice shall (if followed by any payment out of or debit to the Mortgagor's account) be appropriated towards or have the effect of discharging any part of the Mortgagor's Obligations outstanding at the time of receiving such notice

Preservation of other Security and Rights and Further Assurance

8.1 This deed is in addition to all other security present or future held by the Bank for the Mortgagor's Obligations and shall not merge with or prejudice such other security or any contractual or legal rights of the Bank

8.2 The Mortgagor will at the Mortgagor's own cost at the Bank's request execute any deed or document and take any action required by the Bank to perfect this security or further to secure on the Property the Mortgagor's Obligations

Notices

9.1 Any notice or demand by the Bank may be sent by post or telex or delivered to the Mortgagor at the above address or the Mortgagor's address last known to the Bank

9.2 A notice or demand by the Bank by post shall be deemed served on the day after posting

9.3 A notice or demand by the Bank by telex shall be deemed served at the time of sending

Governing Law

10 This deed shall be governed by and construed in accordance with the laws of England

Interpretation

11.1 The expressions 'Mortgagor' and 'Bank' where the context admits include their respective successors in title and assigns

11.2 If two or more persons are included in the expression 'Mortgagor' then the use in this deed of the word 'Mortgagor' shall be deemed to refer to such persons both together and separately and the Mortgagor's Obligations shall be their joint and several obligations and each of them shall be primarily liable by way of indemnity for the liabilities to the Bank of the other or others of them

11.3 References to the 'Property' include any part of it

11.4 Interest will be calculated both before and after demand or judgment on a daily basis and compounded quarterly on such days as the Bank may select but after a demand Interest will also be calculated on the Mortgagor's Obligations together with accrued Interest as at the date of the demand

In Witness whereof this deed has been duly executed

Signed Sealed and **Delivered**
by the first named Mortgagor

Signed Sealed and **Delivered**
by the second named Mortgagor

in the presence of:–

Witness' name in full

Signature

Address

Occupation

in the presence of:–

Witness' name in full

Signature

Address

Occupation

05094 (6/85)

The Royal Bank of Scotland plc

The Royal Bank of Scotland plc releases and re-assigns to the within named Mortgagor all the Property comprised in the within written Legal Charge

Signed Sealed and Delivered for and on behalf of The Royal Bank of Scotland plc by a duly authorised Attorney

**Legal Charge
(Personal)**

Date:

Date   19

Branch:

Granted by:

Property:

05094 (6/85)

 **The Royal Bank**
of Scotland plc

Date: 19

Definitions

Company:

whose registered office is at

Bank: The Royal Bank of Scotland plc

Interest: Interest at the rate stipulated by the Bank from time to time or in the absence of a stipulation the rate
                               of   % per annum above the Bank's fluctuating Base Rate

Property: The whole and any part of the undertaking property and assets of the Company charged by
                               Clause 1

Registered Land: Description of Property   Land Registry Title Number

Company's Obligations: All the Company's liabilities to the Bank of any kind (whether present or future actual or contingent
                               and whether incurred alone or jointly with another) including banking charges and commission

Expenses: All expenses (on a full indemnity basis) incurred by the Bank or any Receiver at any time in
                               connection with the Property or the Company's Obligations or in taking perfecting enforcing or
                               exercising any power under this deed with Interest from the date they are incurred

Charge

1   The Company covenants to discharge on demand the Company's Obligations together with Interest to the date of
        discharge and Expenses and as a continuing security for such discharge and as beneficial owner charges to the
        Bank:—

1.1   By way of legal mortgage all the freehold and leasehold property now vested in or charged to the Company including
        any Registered Land

1.2   By way of fixed charge all estates or interests in any freehold and leasehold property now and in the future vested in or
        charged to the Company except the property charged by Clause 1.1

1.3   By way of fixed charge all the plant machinery and fixtures and fittings furniture equipment implements and utensils
        now and in the future belonging to the Company

1.4   By way of fixed charge all the goodwill and uncalled capital of the Company present and future

1.5   By way of fixed charge all stocks shares and other securities now and in the future belonging to the Company

1.6   By way of fixed charge all intellectual property rights choses in action and claims now and in the future belonging to the
        Company

1.7 By way of fixed charge all book debts and other debts (including any funds standing to the credit of the Company from time to time on any account with the Bank or any other bank or financial institution or organisation) now and in the future owing to the Company

1.8 By way of floating charge all the undertaking and all property assets and rights of the Company present and future not subject to a fixed charge under this deed

Restrictions

2 The Company will not without the previous written consent of the Bank:—

2.1 Create or permit to arise any mortgage charge or lien on the Property and the Company requests the Chief Land Registrar to enter a restriction on the Register of any Registered Land that except under an order of the Registrar no disposition by the proprietor of the land is to be registered without the consent of the registered proprietor of this deed

2.2 Dispose of the Property charged by Clauses 1.1 to 1.7 inclusive

2.3 Deal with the Company's book debts and other debts otherwise than by collecting them in the ordinary course of the Company's business and in particular the Company will not realise its book debts and other debts by means of block discounting factoring or the like

2.4 Dispose of the Property charged by Clause 1.8 other than in the ordinary course of business

2.5 Grant or accept a surrender of any lease or licence of or part with or share possession or occupation of its freehold and leasehold property or any part of it

Insurance

3.1 The Company will keep comprehensively insured to the Bank's reasonable satisfaction all of the Property which is of an insurable nature for its full reinstatement cost and in default the Bank may effect such insurance and for that purpose may enter the Property (without becoming liable to account as mortgagee in possession)

3.2 The Company will hold in trust for the Bank all money received under any insurance of the Property and at the Bank's option will apply the same in making good the relevant loss or damage or in or towards discharge of the Company's Obligations Interest and Expenses

Deeds Securities and Debts

4.1 The Company will from time to time deposit with the Bank all deeds documents of title and insurance policies relating to the Property

4.2 The Company will pay into the Company's account with the Bank (or such other account as the Bank may specify from time to time) all money which the Company may receive in respect of the Company's book debts and other debts

Repair

5 The Company will keep the Property charged by Clauses 1.1 to 1.3 inclusive in good condition and in default the Bank may enter and effect repairs (without becoming liable to account as mortgagee in possession)

Notice of Crystallisation

6 The Bank may by written notice to the Company convert the floating charge into a fixed charge as regards any of the Property specified in the notice

Powers of the Bank

7.1 The Bank may without restriction grant or accept surrenders of leases of the Company's freehold and leasehold property or any part of it

7.2 Section 103 of the Law of Property Act 1925 shall not apply and the Bank may exercise its power of sale and other powers under that or any other Act or this deed at any time after the date of this deed

7.3 The Bank may under the hand of any official or manager or under seal appoint or remove a Receiver or Receivers of the Property and may fix and pay the fees of a Receiver but any Receiver shall be deemed to be the agent of the Company and the Company shall be solely responsible for the Receiver's acts defaults and remuneration

7.4 All or any of the powers conferred on a Receiver by Clause 8 may be exercised by the Bank without first appointing a Receiver or notwithstanding any appointment

7.5 The Bank will not be liable to account to the Company as mortgagee in possession for any money not actually received by the Bank

7.6 Section 93(1) of the Law of Property Act 1925 shall not apply to this deed

7.7 The Bank may at any time (both before and after demand) set-off or appropriate any credit balance on any account of the Company with the Bank (whether or not such balance is due to the Company) in discharge of the whole or any part of the Company's Obligations.

Receivers

8.1 Any Receiver appointed by the Bank shall be a Receiver and Manager and shall (in addition to all powers conferred on him by law) have the following powers which in the case of Joint Receivers may be exercised jointly or severally:—

8.1.1 To take possession of and generally manage the Property and any business of the Company

8.1.2 To carry out on any freehold or leasehold property of the Company any new works or complete any unfinished works of building reconstruction maintenance furnishing or equipment

8.1.3 To purchase or acquire any land and purchase acquire or grant any interest in or right over land

8.1.4 To sell charge or otherwise deal with and dispose of the Property without restriction

8.1.5 To lease surrender or accept surrenders of leases of any freehold or leasehold property of the Company without restriction

8.1.6 To carry into effect and complete any transaction by executing deeds or documents in the name of or on behalf of the Company

8.1.7 To take continue or defend any proceedings and enter into any arrangement or compromise

8.1.8 To insure the Property and any works and effect indemnity insurance or other similar insurance and obtain bonds and give indemnities and security to any bondsmen

8.1.9 To call up any uncalled capital of the Company with all the powers conferred by the Articles of Association of the Company in relation to calls

8.1.10 To employ advisers consultants managers agents workmen and others

8.1.11 To purchase materials tools equipment goods or supplies

8.1.12 To borrow any money and secure the payment of any money in priority to the Company's Obligations for the purpose of the exercise of any ~f his powers

8.1.13 To do any other acts which the Receiver may consider to be incidental or conducive to any of his powers or to the realisation of the Property

8.2 A Receiver shall apply all money he receives first in repayment of all money borrowed by him and his expenses and liabilities and in payment of his fees and secondly towards the remaining matters specified in Section 109(8) of the Law of Property Act 1925

Power of Attorney

9 The Company hereby irrevocably appoints the Bank and any Receiver severally to be the Attorney of the Company (with full power of substitution and delegation) in the Company's name and on the Company's behalf and as the Company's act and deed to sign or execute all deeds instruments and documents which may be required by the Bank or any Receiver pursuant to this deed or the exercise of any of their powers

Appropriation

10.1 Subject to Clause 10.2 the Bank may appropriate all payments received for the account of the Company in reduction of any part of the Company's Obligations Interest and Expenses as the Bank decides

10.2 The Bank may open a new account or accounts upon the Bank receiving actual or constructive notice of any charge or interest affecting the Property and whether or not the Bank opens any such account no payment received by the Bank for the account of the Company after receiving such notice shall (if followed by any payment out of or debit to the Company's account) be appropriated towards or have the effect of discharging any part of the Company's Obligations outstanding at the time of receiving such notice

Information

11 The Company will send to the Bank not later than 6 months after the close of each financial year of the Company a Balance Sheet Profit and Loss Account and Trading Account showing the true position of the affairs of the Company and its subsidiaries (if any) duly signed by the Auditors of the Company and also from time to time furnish to the Bank such other information regarding the assets and liabilities of the Company and its subsidiaries (if any) as the Bank may reasonably require

Preservation of other Security and Rights and Further Assurance

12.1 This deed is in addition to all other security present or future held by the Bank for the Company's Obligations and shall not merge with or prejudice such other security or any contractual or legal rights of the Bank

12.2 The Company will at its own cost at the Bank's request execute any deed or document and take any action required by the Bank to perfect this security or further to secure on the Property the Company's Obligations

Memorandum and Articles of Association

13 The Company certifies that this deed does not contravene the Company's Memorandum and Articles of Association

Notices

14.1 Any notice or demand by the Bank may be served personally on any director or the secretary of the Company or may be sent by post or telex or delivered to the Company at the above address or the Company's address last known to the Bank

14.2   A notice or demand by the Bank by post shall be deemed served on the day after posting

14.3   A notice or demand by the Bank by telex shall be deemed served at the time of sending

Governing Law

15   This deed shall be governed by and construed in accordance with the laws of England

Interpretation

16.1   The expressions 'Company' and 'Bank' where the context admits include their respective successors in title and assigns

16.2   Interest will be calculated both before and after demand or judgment on a daily basis and compounded quarterly on such days as the Bank may select but after a demand Interest will also be calculated on the Company's Obligations together with accrued Interest as at the date of the demand

16.3   References to the Property include any part of it

16.4   Each of the provisions of this deed shall be severable and distinct from one another and if one or more of such provisions is invalid or unenforceable the remaining provisions shall not in any way be affected

In Witness whereof this deed has been duly executed

The Common Seal of the Company was
affixed in the presence of:—

Director _____

Secretary _____

The Royal Bank of Scotland plc

Debenture

Date:

Branch:

Granted by:

Certificate of the Registration of a Mortgage or Charge pursuant to Section 401(2) of the Companies Act 1985

I hereby certify that a Mortgage or Charge dated the

and created by

for securing all moneys now due or hereafter to become due or from time to time accruing due from the Company to The Royal Bank of Scotland plc on any account whatsoever was registered pursuant to Chapter I of Part XII of the Companies Act 1985 on the

Given under my hand at the Companies Registration Office Cardiff the

_____
An authorised officer

The Royal Bank of Scotland plc releases to the within named Company the undertaking and other property and assets charged by the within written Debenture

Signed Sealed and Delivered for and on behalf of The Royal Bank of Scotland plc by a duly authorised Attorney

SEAL

Date _____ 19

20320 (6/88)

NWB1057 (December 1989)

Guarantee and Indemnity subject to the Consumer Credit Act 1974

National Westminster Bank PLC

───── Branch Postal Address in full ─────

┌─ The Debtor ──
│
│
│
│
│   ── Names and Addresses of Debtor(s) in full ─┘

┌─ The Indemnifier ──────────────────────────────────────
│
│
│   ── Names and Addresses of Indemnifier(s) in full ─┘

┌─ The Agreement covered by this Guarantee and Indemnity ─────────
│
│
│

The agreement means each and every agreement described above together with any extension or renewal thereof and includes any agreement which is a modifying agreement in respect thereof or which is for the purpose of refinancing any such agreement in part or whole and any agreement described by reference to an account number shall include any current account which is a successor thereto however described.

┌─ Description of Security for obligations of the Indemnifier ─────────
│
│
│

In consideration of the Bank at your request entering into and/or giving time credit banking facilities or other accommodation under this agreement, by signing this document, you guarantee payment to the Bank on demand of all present future actual and/or contingent obligations of the debtor to the Bank whether incurred solely severally and/or jointly in connection with the agreement.

Provided that the total amount recoverable under this Guarantee and Indemnity shall not exceed

Pounds

plus interest payable (as well after as before judgment) by the Debtor in accordance with the Agreement.

The Indemnifier agrees and confirms as follows:

1   The Bank may without your consent and without affecting your liability

>   (a) renew vary or end any facility given to the debtor
>   (b) defer renew modify or release any security at any time held from the debtor or
>   any other person (including a signatory to this guarantee and indemnity) and
>   (c) relax its rights against the debtor or any such person.

This guarantee and indemnity will not be affected by anything which would not have affected it if you had been a principal debtor to the Bank.

2   This guarantee and indemnity will remain in force even if you die or incur any disability. In the case of an overdraft it may be ended by three months notice in writing from you or your agent but this will not affect your liability for the debtor's obligations outstanding at the date the notice expired (whether or not due and payable).

3   The Bank will have a lien on all your property held by the Bank for whatever purpose. The Bank may set off your liability against any credit balance on any of your accounts with the Bank whether or not due and payable.

4   If this guarantee and indemnity is ended or called in the Bank may open a new account(s) with the debtor or any other person for whose liabilities this guarantee and indemnity is security. If the Bank does not open a new account(s) it will be treated as if it had done so at the time of the guarantee and indemnity being ended or called in. All payments made to the Bank from that time will be credited or be treated as having been credited to the new account(s) and will not reduce the amount for which this guarantee and indemnity is available as security at that time.

5   This guarantee and indemnity will not be affected by any failure of or defect in any security given by or on behalf of the debtor.

6   Where repayment of any facilities cannot be enforced because the debtor is not of full age you will indemnify the Bank against any loss or damage which the Bank may thereby incur.

7   Where there are two or more debtors reference to the debtor means all or any of them. Where the debtor is a firm it will include the person(s) from time to time constituting the firm whether or not under the same style or name.

8   Where this guarantee and indemnity is made by more than one person reference to you means all or any one of them. If this guarantee and indemnity ceases to be binding on any one of them, the others will remain liable.

9   A certificate by an Officer of the Bank as to the amount at any time due will be conclusive.

10 A demand or notice will be in writing and may be served either by hand or by post addressed to you at the address or place of business last known to the Bank and will be regarded as having been received on the day after it was posted. It will take effect even if returned undelivered or in the event of your death.

11 This guarantee and indemnity is the property of the Bank.

12 This guarantee and indemnity shall be governed by and construed in accordance with the Laws of England

Dated this   day of   One thousand nine hundred and

Important — You should read this carefully

Your Rights

The Consumer Credit Act 1974 covers this guarantee and indemnity and lays down certain requirements for your protection. If they are not carried out, the Bank cannot enforce the guarantee and indemnity against you without a court order.

Until the agreement between the Bank and the debtor has been made, you can change your mind about giving the guarantee and indemnity. If you wish to withdraw, you must give **WRITTEN** notice to the Bank which must reach it **BEFORE** the main agreement is made. Once it has been made you can no longer change your mind.

Under this guarantee and indemnity **YOU MAY HAVE TO PAY INSTEAD** of the debtor and fulfil any other obligations under the guarantee and indemnity. (But you cannot be made to pay more than he could have been made to pay unless he is under 18). However, if the debtor fails to keep to his side of the agreement, the Bank must send him a default notice (and a copy to you) giving him a chance to put things right before any claim is made on you.

If you would like to know more about your rights under the Act, you should contact either your local Trading Standards Department or your nearest Citizens' Advice Bureau.

This is a guarantee and indemnity subject to the Consumer Credit Act 1974. If the debtor fails to keep to his agreement with the Bank, **YOU MAY HAVE TO PAY INSTEAD** and fulfil any other obligations under the guarantee and indemnity. Sign only if you want to be legally bound by its terms.

*Where this document is given by a Company insert 'on behalf of' where indicated

Signature(s)*

of indemnifier(s)

Signed by the above named   **Signed** by the above named

* Insert name(s) of indemnifier(s)

in the presence of: in the presence of:

Signature of
Witness _____   Signature of
Witness _____

Name in full
(in Block Letters) _____   Name in full
(in Block Letters) _____

Address _____   Address _____

_____   _____

Occupation _____   Occupation _____

I/We acknowledge receipt of a completed copy of this document

_____

_____

                                        Signature(s) of indemnifier(s)

Branch _____

Account _____

Dated _____ 19 _____

to

National Westminster Bank PLC

Guarantee and Indemnity
by person(s) or a Company
Subject to the Consumer Credit Act 1974

NWB1021 (Revised December 1989) **Legal Mortgage of Life Policy**
by person(s) or company

This Legal Mortgage is made the   day of

One thousand nine hundred and   Between

of

(the Mortgagor) of the one part and **National Westminster Bank PLC** (the Bank) of the other part.

1 If the expression 'the Mortgagor' includes more than one person it shall be construed as referring to all and/or any one or more of those persons and the obligations of the Mortgagor shall be joint and several.

2(a) The Mortgagor as beneficial owner assigns to the Bank the Policy mentioned in the Schedule hereto (the Policy) by way of mortgage and as a continuing security to the Bank for the discharge on demand of

    (i) all present and/or future indebtedness of the Mortgagor to the Bank on any current and/or other account with interest and bank charges and

    (ii) all other liabilities whatsoever of the Mortgagor to the Bank present future actual and /or contingent and

    (iii) all costs charges and expenses howsoever incurred by the Bank in relation to this Mortgage and such indebtedness and/or liabilities on a full indemnity basis

and for the payment of interest on the foregoing day by day from demand until full discharge (as well after as before judgment) at the rate payable or deemed to be payable by the Mortgagor and as calculated and compounded in such manner as the Bank may from time to time determine.

The costs and expenses referred to herein shall include (for avoidance of doubt) all amounts the Bank may from time to time require to compensate it for its internal management and administrative costs and expenses incurred in connection with the enforcement of this Mortgage and recovery of the liabilities secured by it. A certificate signed by an officer of the Bank as to the amount of such costs and expenses incurred by the Bank from time to time shall for all purposes be conclusive evidence against and binding upon the Mortgagor.

  (b) This security shall not extend or apply to any obligations under a regulated agreement except:

    (i) a regulated agreement which embodies this security as required by the Consumer Credit Act 1974 ('the Act')

    (ii) a regulated agreement to which the provisions of Part V of the Act do not apply at the date hereof including (but not by way of limitation) an agreement to overdraw on a current account within the meaning of the Act.

For the purposes of this clause 'regulated agreement' shall have the meaning given by the Act but shall also include any agreement which or of which any part would but for this clause become a regulated agreement by virtue of this security and Section 82 of the Act.

3 The Mortgagor covenants to keep up the said Policy and produce the premium receipts to the Bank and agrees that if he fails to do so the Bank may pay what is due and charge the amount against him.

4 Section 103 of the Law of Property Act 1925 shall not apply to this Mortgage and the statutory power of sale and other powers shall be exercisable at any time after demand.

5 If the Bank receives or is deemed to be affected by notice whether actual or constructive of any subsequent charge or other interest affecting the Policy and/or the proceeds of sale thereof the Bank may open a new account or accounts with any person for whose liabilities this Mortgage is available as security. If the Bank does not open a new account it shall nevertheless be treated as if it had done so at the time when it received or was deemed to have received notice and as from that time all payments made to the Bank shall be credited or be treated as having been credited to the new account and shall not operate to reduce the amount for which this Mortgage is security.

6 In case the Mortgagor shall have more than one account with the Bank it shall be lawful for the Bank at any time and without any prior notice forthwith to transfer all or any part of any balance standing to the credit of any such account to any other such account which may be in debit but the Bank shall notify the Mortgagor of the transfer having been made.

7 None of the persons included in the expression 'the Mortgagor' shall as against the Bank be entitled to any of the rights or remedies legal or equitable of a surety as regards the indebtedness or liabilities of any of the other persons included in the expression 'the Mortgagor'.

8 A demand or notice hereunder shall be in writing signed by an officer or agent of the Bank and may be served on the Mortgagor either by hand or by post. In the case of a company service by hand may be made either by delivering the same to any officer of the company at any place or leaving the same addressed to the company at its registered office or a place of business last known to the Bank. A demand or notice by post may be addressed to the Mortgagor at the registered office or address or place of business last known to the Bank and shall be deemed to have been received on the day following the day on which it was posted and shall be effective notwithstanding it be returned undelivered and notwithstanding the death of the Mortgagor.

9 This Mortgage shall be governed by and construed in accordance with the Laws of England

In Witness whereof this Deed has been executed by the Mortgagor the day and year first before written.

The Schedule

Office in which Policy effected	Number of Policy	Sum assured Add 'with profits' if applicable

Particulars of any Documents forming part of Title to the above–mentioned Policy

Date of Document	Short description

The Common Seal of *

was hereunto affixed
in the presence of

Director

Secretary

+ Executed as a Deed by the Mortgagor acting by

Signature _____ Director

Name in full
(in Block Letters) _____

Signature _____ Director/Secretary

Name in full
(in Block Letters) _____

Signed Sealed and Delivered
by the above—named

*

in the presence of:

Signature of
Witness_____

Name in full
(in Block Letters) _____

Address _____

_____

Occupation _____

Signed Sealed and Delivered
by the above—named

*

in the presence of:

Signature of
Witness _____

Name in full
(in Block Letters) _____

Address _____

_____

Occupation _____

I/We acknowledge receipt of a completed copy of this document

_____

_____

Signature(s)

National Westminster Bank PLC (the Bank) as Mortgagee reassigns the within–mentioned Policy to the within–named _____

_____

discharged from all claims by the Bank.

For and on behalf of

National Westminster Bank PLC

_____ **Branch**

_____ Manager

Date _____

NB This reassignment is not applicable when the Policy is assigned to a third party.

Debenture

Insert company's name as registered

1. _____

(hereinafter called "the Company") whose registered office is at

will on demand in writing made to the Company pay or discharge to Barclays Bank PLC (hereinafter called "the Bank") all moneys and liabilities which shall for the time being (and whether on or at any time after such demand) be due owing or incurred to the Bank by the Company whether actually or contingently and whether solely or jointly with any other person and whether as principal or surety and including interest discount commission or other lawful charges and expenses which the Bank may in the course of its business charge in respect of any of the matters aforesaid or for keeping the Company's account and so that interest shall be computed and compounded according to the usual mode of the Bank as well after as before any demand made or judgment obtained hereunder.

2. A demand for payment or any other demand or notice under this Debenture may be made or given by any manager or officer of the Bank or of any branch thereof by letter addressed to the Company and sent by post to or left at the registered office of the Company or its last known place of business and if sent by post shall be deemed to have been made or given at noon on the day following the day the letter was posted.

3. The Company as beneficial owner hereby charges with the payment or discharge of all moneys and liabilities hereby covenanted to be paid or discharged by the Company:—

 (a) by way of legal mortgage all the freehold and leasehold property of the Company the title to which is registered at H.M. Land Registry and which is described in the Schedule hereto together with all buildings fixtures (including trade fixtures) and fixed plant and machinery from time to time thereon;

 (b) by way of legal mortgage all other freehold and leasehold property of the Company now vested in it (whether or not registered at H.M. Land Registry) together with all buildings fixtures (including trade fixtures) and fixed plant and machinery from time to time thereon;

 (c) by way of first fixed charge all future freehold and leasehold property of the Company together with all buildings fixtures (including trade fixtures) and fixed plant and machinery from time to time thereon and all the goodwill and uncalled capital for the time being of the Company;

 (d) by way of first fixed charge all book debts and other debts now and from time to time due or owing to the Company;

 (e) by way of a first floating charge all other the undertaking and assets of the Company whatsoever and wheresoever both present and future but so that the Company is not to be at liberty to create any mortgage or charge upon and so that no lien shall in any case or in any manner arise on or affect any part of the said premises either in priority to or *pari passu* with the charge hereby created and further that the Company shall have no power without the consent of the Bank to part with or dispose of any part of such premises except by way of sale in the ordinary course of its business.

Any debentures mortgages or charges hereafter created by the Company (otherwise than in favour of the Bank) shall be expressed to be subject to this Debenture. The Company shall subject to the rights of any prior mortgagee deposit with the Bank and the Bank during the continuance of this security shall be entitled to hold all deeds and documents of title relating to the Company's freehold and leasehold property for the time being and the Company shall on demand in writing made to the Company by the Bank at the cost of the Company execute a valid legal mortgage of any freehold and leasehold properties acquired by it after the date hereof and the fixed plant and machinery thereon to secure the payment or discharge to the Bank of the moneys and liabilities hereby secured such legal mortgage to be in such form as the Bank may require.

4. This security shall be a continuing security to the Bank notwithstanding any settlement of account or other matter or thing whatsoever and shall be without prejudice and in addition to any other security whether by way of mortgage equitable charge or otherwise howsoever which the Bank may now or any time hereafter hold on the property of the Company or any part thereof for or in respect of the moneys hereby secured or any of them or any part thereof respectively.

5. During the continuance of this security the Company:—

(a) shall furnish to the Bank copies of the trading and profit and loss account and audited balance sheet in respect of each financial year of the Company and of every subsidiary thereof forthwith upon the same becoming available and not in any event later than the expiration of three months from the end of such financial year and also from time to time such other financial statements and information respecting the assets and liabilities of the Company as the Bank may reasonably require;

(b) shall maintain the aggregate value of the Company's book debts (excluding debts owing by any subsidiary of the Company) and cash in hand as appearing in the Company's books and of its stock according to the best estimate that can be formed without it being necessary to take stock for the purpose at a sum to be fixed by the Bank from time to time and whenever required by the Bank obtain from the Managing Director of the Company for the time being or if there shall be no Managing Director then from one of the Directors of the Company and furnish to the Bank a certificate showing the said aggregate value;

(c) shall pay into the Company's account with the Bank all moneys which it may receive in respect of the book debts and other debts hereby charged and shall not without the prior consent of the Bank in writing purport to charge or assign the same in favour of any other person and shall if called upon to do so by the Bank execute a legal assignment of such book debts and other debts to the Bank;

(d) shall insure and keep insured with an insurance office or underwriters to be approved by the Bank in writing from time to time and if so required by the Bank in the joint names of the Company and the Bank such of its property as is insurable against loss or damage by fire and such other risks as the Bank may from time to time require to the full replacement value thereof and shall maintain such other insurances as are normally maintained by prudent companies carrying on similar businesses and will duly pay all premiums and other moneys necessary for effecting and keeping up such insurances within one week of the same becoming due and will on demand produce to the Bank the policies of such insurance and the receipts for such payments and if default shall at any time be made by the Company in effecting or keeping up such insurance as aforesaid or in producing any such policy or receipt to the Bank on demand the Bank may take out or renew such insurances in any sum which the Bank may think expedient And all moneys expended by the Bank under this provision shall be deemed to be properly paid by the Bank;

(e) shall keep all buildings and all plant machinery fixtures fittings and other effects in or upon the same and every part thereof in good repair and in good working order and condition.

6. (a) At any time after the Bank shall have demanded payment of any moneys hereby secured or if a petition shall be presented to the court under section 9 of the Insolvency Act 1986 for the making of an administration order in respect of the Company or if requested by the Company the Bank may appoint by writing any person or persons (whether an officer of the Bank or not) to be a receiver and manager or receivers and managers (hereinafter called "the Receiver" which expression shall where the context so admits include the plural and any substituted receiver and manager or receivers and managers) of all or any part of the property hereby charged.

(b) The Bank may from time to time determine the remuneration of the Receiver and may remove the Receiver and appoint another in his place.

(c) The Receiver shall be the agent of the Company (which subject to the provisions of the Insolvency Act 1986 shall alone be personally liable for his acts defaults and remuneration) and shall have and be entitled to exercise all powers conferred by the Law of Property Act 1925 in the same way as if the Receiver had been duly appointed thereunder and in particular by way of addition to but without hereby limiting any general powers hereinbefore referred to (and without prejudice to the Bank's power of sale) the Receiver shall have power to do the following things namely:—

    (i) to take possession of collect and get in all or any part of the property hereby charged and for that purpose to take any proceedings in the name of the Company or otherwise as he shall think fit;

    (ii) to carry on or concur in carrying on the business of the Company and to raise money from the Bank or others on the security of any property hereby charged;

    (iii) to sell or concur in selling let or concur in letting and to terminate or to accept surrenders of leases or tenancies of any of the property hereby charged in such manner and generally on such terms and conditions as he shall think fit and to carry any such transactions into effect in the name of and on behalf of the Company;

    (iv) to make any arrangement or compromise which the Bank or he shall think fit;

    (v) to make and effect all repairs improvements and insurances;

    (vi) to appoint managers officers and agents for the aforesaid purposes at such salaries as he may determine;

    (vii) to call up all or any portion of the uncalled capital of the Company;

    (viii) to do all such other acts and things as may be considered to be incidental or conducive to any of the matters or powers aforesaid and which he lawfully may or can do.

7. The Company hereby irrevocably appoints the Bank and the Receiver jointly and also severally the Attorney and Attorneys of the Company for the Company and in its name and on its behalf and as its act and deed or otherwise to seal and deliver and otherwise perfect any deed assurance agreement instrument or act which may be required or may be deemed proper for any of the purposes aforesaid and the Company hereby declares that as and when the security hereby created shall become enforceable the Company will hold all the property hereby charged (subject to the Company's right of redemption) Upon Trust to convey assign or otherwise deal with the same in such manner and to such person as the Bank shall direct and declares that it shall be lawful for the Bank by an instrument under its Common Seal to appoint a new trustee or new trustees of the said property and in particular at any time or times to appoint a new trustee or new trustees thereof in place of the Company as if the Company desired to be discharged from the trust or in place of any trustee or trustees appointed under this power as if he or they were dead. *held on trust*

8. Any moneys received under the powers hereby conferred shall subject to the repayment of any claims having priority to this Debenture be paid or applied in the following order of priority:—

    (a) in satisfaction of all costs charges and expenses properly incurred and payments properly made by the Bank or the Receiver and of the remuneration of the Receiver;

    (b) in or towards satisfaction of the moneys outstanding and secured by this Debenture;

    (c) as to the surplus (if any) to the person or persons entitled thereto.

9. During the continuance of this security no statutory or other power of granting or agreeing to grant or of accepting or agreeing to accept surrenders of leases or tenancies of the freehold and leasehold property hereby charged or any part thereof shall be capable of being exercised by the Company without the previous consent in writing of the Bank nor shall section 93 of the Law of Property Act 1925 dealing with the consolidation of mortgages apply to this security.

10. Section 103 of the said Act shall not apply to this security but the statutory power of sale shall as between the Bank and a purchaser from the Bank arise on and be exercisable at any time after the execution of this security provided that the Bank shall not exercise the said power of

sale until payment of the moneys hereby secured has been demanded or the Receiver has been appointed but this proviso shall not affect a purchaser or put him upon inquiry whether such demand or appointment has been made.

11. All costs charges and expenses incurred hereunder by the Bank and all other moneys paid by the Bank or by the Receiver in perfecting or otherwise in connection with this security or in respect of the property hereby charged including (without prejudice to the generality of the foregoing) all moneys expended by the Bank under clause 5 hereof and all costs of the Bank or of the Receiver of all proceedings for the enforcement of the security hereby constituted or for obtaining payment of the moneys hereby secured or arising out of or in connection with the acts authorised by clause 6 hereof (and so that any taxation of the Banks costs charges and expenses shall be on the basis of solicitor and own client) shall be recoverable from the Company as a debt and may be debited to any account of the Company and shall bear interest accordingly and shall be charged on the premises comprised herein and the charge hereby conferred shall be in addition and without prejudice to any and every other remedy lien or security which the Bank may or but for the said charge would have for the moneys hereby secured or any part thereof.

12. In respect of any freehold or leasehold property hereby charged the title to which is registered at H.M. Land Registry it is hereby certified that the charge created by this Debenture does not contravene any of the provisions of the Memorandum and Articles of Association of the Company.

13. In this Debenture where the context so admits the expression "the Bank" shall include persons deriving title under the Bank and any reference herein to any statute or any section of any statute shall be deemed to include reference to any statutory modification or re-enactment thereof for the time being in force.

Given under the Common Seal of the Company this   day of
19

The Schedule above referred to

Details of registered land.

County/London Borough	Title No.	Address of Property

The Common Seal of the Company was hereunto
affixed in pursuance of a Resolution of the Board
of Directors in the presence of

_____ DIRECTOR

_____ SECRETARY

Company's Registered Number_____

The address for service of the Bank in the case of any registered land is:—

CERTIFICATE OF THE REGISTRATION
OF A MORTGAGE OR CHARGE

I hereby certify that a mortgage or charge dated the

19

and created by †

for securing all moneys now due or hereafter to become due, or from time to time accruing due from the company to Barclays Bank PLC on any account whatsoever was registered pursuant to Chapter I Part XII of the Companies Act 1985

on the   19

Given under my hand at the Companies Registration Office, Cardiff the

an authorised officer

N.B.—The above copy of the Registrar's Certificate must be completed and the certificate itself attached to this document.

† Insert company's name as registered

Debenture

RECEIPT PURSUANT TO SECTION 115 OF
THE LAW OF PROPERTY ACT 1925

BARCLAYS BANK PLC hereby acknowledges this
        day of   19   that
it has received the balance of the moneys (including interest
and costs) secured by the within written Deed the payment
having been made by*

*Insert "the
within named
Company"
or :
of   :
or as the case
may be

For and on behalf of BARCLAYS BANK PLC

A REGIONAL DIRECTOR

To be used when the Charge is given to secure the liabilities of one or more than one THIRD ᴾARTY. Any liabilities of the DEPOSITOR(S) are also secured.

This Memorandum is made the   day of   19

Insert full name(s) and address(es) of the Principal Debtor

Between (1)

(hereinafter called "the Principal Debtor")

Insert full name(s) and address(es) of the Depositor

(2)

(hereinafter called "the Depositor") and (3) BARCLAYS BANK PLC (hereinafter called "the Bank")

Whereby it is agreed and declared as follows:-

1. (A) The Principal Debtor hereby undertakes with the Bank that the Principal Debtor will on demand in writing made to the Principal Debtor pay or discharge to the Bank all moneys and liabilities which shall for the time being (and whether on or at any time after such demand) be due owing or incurred to the Bank by the Principal Debtor

   (B) The Depositor hereby undertakes with the Bank that the Depositor will on demand in writing made to the Depositor pay or discharge to the Bank all moneys and liabilities which shall for the time being (and whether on or at any time after such demand) be due owing or incurred to the Bank by the Depositor

in each case whether actually or contingently and whether solely or jointly with any other person and whether as principal or surety including interest discount commission or other lawful charges and expenses which the Bank may in the course of its business charge in respect of any of the matters aforesaid or for keeping their respective accounts and so that interest shall be computed and compounded according to the usual mode of the Bank as well after as before any demand made or judgment obtained hereunder and on such demand the Principal Debtor or (as the case may be) the Depositor will retire all bills or notes which may for the time being be under discount with the Bank and to which he is a party whether as drawer acceptor maker or indorser without any deduction whatsoever.

2. The Depositor hereby declares that the stocks shares bonds debentures or other securities deposited with or transferred to the Bank or trustees for or nominees of the Bank and specified in the schedule hereto (hereinafter called "the Securities" which expression shall include any further securities referred to in clause 4 hereof) are so deposited or transferred to secure the payment or discharge of all moneys and liabilities hereby agreed to be paid or discharged whether by the Principal Debtor or by the Depositor.

3. The Securities are warranted by the Depositor to be within the Depositor's own disposition and control and to be free from any prior charge or encumbrance of any sort whatsoever.

4. If at any time any further or other securities (whether pursuant to clause 5 or clause 9 hereof or otherwise) shall be deposited or transferred by the Depositor to the Bank or its trustees or nominees in substitution for or in addition to the securities specified in the schedule hereto such securities shall thereupon be deemed to be a part of the Securities for the purposes of this Memorandum and shall forthwith become subject to all the terms hereof and the warranties contained in clause 3 hereof shall be deemed to apply to such substituted or additional securities.

5. The Depositor hereby undertakes that any bonus stock or shares or other new securities of a similar nature which may at any time during the currency of this Memorandum be issued in respect of any of the Securities shall be deposited with or transferred to the Bank (as the Bank may require) and shall thereupon become part of the Securities and all dividends and interest and all rights moneys or property accruing or offered at any time by way of redemption bonus preference option or otherwise in respect of the Securities shall be included in the charge hereby given.

6. A demand for payment or any other demand or notice under this security may be made or given by any manager or officer of the Bank or of any branch thereof by letter addressed to the Principal Debtor or (as the case may require) the Depositor and sent by post to or left at his respective last known place of business or abode or at the option of the Bank in the case of a company its registered office and if sent by post shall be deemed to have been made at noon on the day following the day the letter was posted.

7. At any time after payment of the moneys hereby secured has been demanded or if the Principal Debtor or the Depositor (as the case may be) fails to perform any of his obligations under this Memorandum the Bank may without notice to the Depositor sell the Securities or any of them at any time and in any way which the Bank may deem expedient.

8. The Depositor shall not have any right or claim against the Bank in respect of any loss arising out of such sale howsoever such loss may have been caused and whether or not a better price could or might have been obtained on the sale of the Securities or any of them by either deferring or advancing the date of such sale or otherwise howsoever.

9. If at any time the value of the Securities shall not exceed by at least   per cent the amount of the moneys and liabilities
    (a) as referred to in clause 1 (A) hereof the Principal Debtor hereby undertakes to pay to the Bank such sum of money as shall be required to make up the required margin
    (b) as referred to in clause 1 (B) hereof the Depositor hereby undertakes on demand and at the option of the Bank either
        (i) to deposit with or transfer to the Bank or to trustees for or nominees of the Bank (as the Bank may require) additional securities approved by the Bank to make up the required margin; or
        (ii) to pay to the Bank such sum of money as shall be required to make up the required margin.

10. All costs charges and expenses incurred hereunder by the Bank and all other moneys paid by the Bank in perfecting or otherwise in connection with this security or in respect of the Securities including all costs of the Bank of all proceedings for enforcement of the security hereby constituted or for obtaining payment of the moneys hereby secured or any part thereof (and so that any taxation of the Bank's costs charges and expenses shall be on the basis of solicitor and own client) shall be recoverable so far as they relate to the liabilities of the Principal Debtor from the Principal Debtor and so far as they relate to the liabilities of the Depositor from the Depositor as a debt and may be debited to any account of the Principal Debtor or of the Depositor as the case may be and shall bear interest accordingly and shall be charged on the Securities and the charge hereby conferred shall be in addition and without prejudice to any and every other remedy lien or security which the Bank may have or but for the said charge would have for the moneys hereby secured or any part thereof.

11. The Bank shall be at liberty from time to time to give time for payment of any bills of exchange promissory notes or other securities which may have been discounted for or received on account from the Principal Debtor or the Depositor by the Bank or on which the Principal Debtor or the Depositor shall or may be liable as drawer acceptor maker or indorser or otherwise to any parties liable thereon or thereto as the Bank in its absolute discretion shall think fit without releasing the Principal Debtor or the Depositor or affecting their respective liability under this Memorandum or the security hereby created.

12. This security shall (subject to the provisions of clause 20 (b) hereof) be a continuing security to the Bank notwithstanding any settlement of account or other matter or thing whatsoever and shall not prejudice or affect any other security which the Bank may now or at any time hereafter hold in respect of the moneys hereby secured or any of them or any part thereof respectively.

13. The Depositor hereby undertakes on request by the Bank to execute and sign from time to time all transfers powers of attorney and other documents which the Bank may require for perfecting the Bank's title to the Securities or any of them or vesting the same or any of them in a purchaser or in any trustee for or nominee of the Bank or in connection with clause 5 hereof.

14. In respect of any transfers of any of the Securities which are not transferable exclusively by deed the Depositor hereby authorises the Bank at any time to date any such transfer if the same be undated and if the same shall have been theretofore in blank to fill in any blanks in favour of the Bank or any trustee for or nominee of the Bank or any purchaser.

15. The Depositor hereby undertakes to pay duly and promptly all calls which may from time to time be made in respect of any unpaid moneys under any of the Securities and any other moneys which he may lawfully be required to pay in respect of any of the Securities and in the event of default the Bank may if it thinks fit make such payments on behalf of the Depositor Any money expended by the Bank under this provision shall be deemed to be properly paid by the Bank.

[handwritten margin note: pay calls unpaid slas]

16. The Bank shall not be under any liability to the Depositor in respect of any failure to present any interest coupon or any bond or stock which may be called or drawn for repayment or redemption or for any failure to pay any call or instalment which may become payable on or to accept any offer relating to any of the Securities or for any failure to notify the Depositor of any of such matters whether or not any such failure is caused or contributed to by any negligence on the part of the Bank or of any servant or agent of the Bank.

17. The Bank or its nominees may exercise at its discretion (in the name of the Depositor or otherwise at any time whether before or after any demand for payment hereunder and without any further consent or authority on the part of the Depositor) in respect of the Securities or any of them any voting rights as if the Bank or its nominees were a sole beneficial owner thereof.

18. The Securities shall not be released by time being given to the Principal Debtor or by any arrangement in relation to other securities or by any act matter or thing whether occurring before or after demand whereby the same might have been released (except an express release executed by or on behalf of the Bank) and any moneys which may not be otherwise recoverable hereunder by reason of any legal limitation disability or incapacity on or of the Principal Debtor shall nevertheless be recoverable from the Securities as though such moneys had been advanced to the Depositor and as if the Depositor were the sole or principal debtor in respect thereof and this Memorandum had secured such indebtedness.

[handwritten margin note: No release due totno]

19. In the event of the bankruptcy or winding up or any arrangement with the creditors of the Principal Debtor:-
   (a) any moneys hereby secured shall be deemed to continue due and owing to the Bank until the same are actually paid;
   (b) the Depositor shall not until the Bank has been fully repaid be entitled to participate in any other security held by the Bank or in moneys received by the Bank on account of moneys due from the Principal Debtor;

[handwritten margin note: pend debt in full]

(c) any dividends or payments received by the Bank shall be taken and applied as payments in gross and shall not prejudice the right of the Bank to recover out of the Securities all the moneys hereby secured;

(d) the Bank shall be entitled to prove for the full amount of the claim of the Bank and to retain the whole of the dividends to the exclusion of the rights (if any) of the Depositor in competition with the Bank until the Bank has been fully repaid.

20. (a) The continuing nature of the security hereby created shall not be determined or affected by notice to the Bank of the death or mental incapacity of the Depositor.

(b) So far only as the liabilities of the Principal Debtor are concerned the continuing nature of the security hereby created may be determined at the expiration of three calendar months after the receipt by the Bank from the Depositor of notice in writing to determine it and the amount hereby secured in respect of such liabilities shall on the expiration of such notice be crystallized except as regards unascertained or contingent liabilities and additional sums for interest costs and expenses.

21. As between the Principal Debtor on the one hand and the Depositor and the Securities on the other hand the Principal Debtor shall be primarily liable for the payment of the moneys hereby undertaken to be paid by the Principal Debtor but this provision shall not affect the Bank or in any way preclude the Bank from enforcing or having recourse to all or any remedies or means for recovering payment thereof which may be available under these presents or otherwise at such times and in such order and manner as the Bank shall think fit.

22. In these presents where the context so admits the expression "the Depositor" shall include persons deriving title under the Depositor or entitled to redeem this security the expression "the Principal Debtor" shall include his personal representatives and the expression "the Bank" shall include persons deriving title under the Bank.

23. If there are two or more parties hereto of the first or second parts the expressions "the Principal Debtor" and "the Depositor" respectively shall throughout mean and include such two or more parties and each of them or (as the case may require) such two or more parties or any of them and shall so far as the context admits be construed as well in the plural as in the singular and all deposits transfers charges agreements and undertakings herein expressed or implied on the part of the Principal Debtor and the Depositor respectively shall be deemed to be joint and several deposits transfers charges agreements and undertakings by such parties And in particular this security and the undertakings in clause 1 hereof and the remaining deposits transfers charges agreements and undertakings by the Principal Debtor and the Depositor respectively herein contained shall extend and apply to any moneys owing or liabilities incurred by any of the parties comprised in such respective expressions to the Bank whether solely or jointly with each other or with any other person and references to the Principal Debtor and the Depositor in relation to the retirement of bills and in clauses 6, 7, 10, 11, 18, 19 and 20 shall mean and include any one or more of the parties comprised in such respective expressions as well as such parties jointly.

In Witness whereof the Principal Debtor and the Depositor have signed these presents or (in the case of a company) caused these presents to be duly signed the day and year first above written.

The Schedule

Nominal Amount	Details of security

Signed by the above named

_____

in the presence of

SIGNATURE OF WITNESS_____

NAME OF WITNESS _____

ADDRESS _____

_____

OCCUPATION _____   )

_____

Signed by the above named

_____

in the presence of

SIGNATURE OF WITNESS _____

NAME OF WITNESS _____

ADDRESS _____

_____

OCCUPATION _____

_____

Signed by _____

_____ on behalf of

* _____

pursuant to a Resolution of its Board of Directors
a certified copy of which is annexed hereto in the
presence of

SIGNATURE OF WITNESS _____

NAME OF WITNESS _____

ADDRESS _____

_____

OCCUPATION _____

Company's Registered Number _____

*Insert company's name as registered

**Memorandum of Deposit
of Stocks and Shares
and other Marketable
Securities**

to secure the liabilities
of one or more than one

Third Party

Any liabilities of the

Depositor(s)

are also secured.

Index